Bill Fairbairn is editor emeritus, photographer and staff writer for the community newspaper, *The Riverview Park Review,* in Ottawa, where he lives with his wife, Janina. His full-time newspaper, radio and magazine work since 1943, took in stints in Britain, Africa and Canada. He worked first as a newsboy then fulltime, at age 15, as apprentice printer and part-time rugby reporter with *The Jedburgh Gazette,* in the Scottish Borders, near where he was born. After two years of military national service came journalism, consecutively on *the Blyth News, the Derby Evening Telegraph, the Sheffield Telegraph, the Sun, the Scotsman, the Vancouver Province, the Williams Lake Tribune, the Montreal Star, Radio Canada International (CBC), the Montreal Gazette, the Ottawa Citizen (*part-time*), Legion Magazine* and *The Riverview Park Review*.

Bill Fairbairn taught journalism for two years at what was then Cariboo College in Kamloops, British Columbia, now University of the North Thompson River, and for a year at evening classes in Ottawa. He spent five years in the 1960s in Africa, working consecutively for *The Rhodesia Herald,* now located in Harare, Zimbabwe, *The Northern News* of Ndola in Northern Rhodesia (Zambia) and *The Daily Nation* in Nairobi, Kenya. From 1953-55, he was a National Service infantry corporal with the King's Own Scottish Borderers. He was the 2007 Canadian Press Club snooker champion, and in 2008 and 2016, he won the age 55 and over snooker championship at the Orange Monkey salon in Ottawa.

Bill Fairbairn

NEWSBOY

AUSTIN MACAULEY PUBLISHERS[tm]

London • Cambridge • New York • Sharjah

Ordering Information:
Quantity sales: special discounts are available on quantity purchases by corporations, associations, and others. For details, contact the publisher at the address below.

Publisher's Cataloguing-in-Publication data
Fairbairn, Bill.
Newsboy

ISBN 9781641823388 (Paperback)
ISBN 9781641823395 (Hardback)
ISBN 9781641823401 (E-Book)

The main category of the book — Biography & Autobiography / General

www.austinmacauley.com

First Published (2018)
Austin Macauley Publishers Ltd ™
40 Wall Street, 28th Floor
New York, NY 10005
USA

mail-usa@austinmacauley.com
+1 (646) 5125767

Acknowledgement

Written especially for Dylan and Kieran.
Thanks to Morgan Almeida for his cover typography.
Thank you to the late author James Hilton for inspiration in
Goodbye, Mr. Chips.

Introduction

As Emily Dickinson wrote: *"We never know how tall we are till we are called to rise. And then, if we are true to plan, our statures touch the skies."*

Good luck helped me touch skies over three continents. I found stepping stones to dance across the swirling rivers of newsboy, printer and journalist for 74 years. Now, at age 82, editor emeritus of a suburban Ottawa community newspaper, where else will fortune take me but down?

My journalism career saw me through increased civil rights, more equality, national independence from colonialism, political unrest, wars, musical genius, space exploration as well as the more relevant media transformation.

If the title editor emeritus sounds highfalutin, then consider that I also write and photograph for my *Riverview Park Review* newspaper, deliver it to doorsteps and serve on the management board. If I qualify at age 82 as a newsboy, what more could I ask, since that was my newspaper status 74 years ago in my native Scotland.

This newsboy climbed a media mountain to survive media transformation and come down to a peaceful valley below.

Prelude

When they who have striven and suffered to teach and ennoble the race
Shall march at the front of the column, each one in a God-given place
As they enter the gates of the city, with proud and victorious tread
The editor, printer and newsboy will travel not far from the head.
-Will Carleton (slightly abridged)

Chapter 1
An Apple from Canada

Time passes slowly at age 82, when one is alone at home during a Canadian winter. Snow lies outside and icicles drip-drop from above the living-room window. Frequent cups of tea, breaking television news stories and fond memory of the kiss from one's wife, Janina, before she left for work in downtown Ottawa, help pass winter.

Canadian winters only *seem* never-ending. I feel March warming as ice melts, lively red cardinals yank their tails and squirrels scramble one after the other on branches of the front-lawn linden tree. The news broadcasts are mainly on crime, tragedy and politics. Makes me want to yank my tail to relive my career of seven-plus decades, from newsboy at age eight, to newsboy at 82.

On newspaper delivery afternoons, I sit in my armchair with a cup of tea growing cold, awaiting Janina's arrival home from work, to help me get our pile of hot-off-the-press *Riverview Park Review* community newspapers out to local doorsteps. I sometimes dream of my first newspaper delivery in Scotland. That's because, while I may be the oldest newsboy in Canada, 74 years ago I was among the youngest in Scotland.

I prefer the term "newsboy" over "paperboy," since it was the *news* in the British national Sunday newspapers and two local weekly papers that I distributed door-to-door after picking up my town bundles, occasionally direct from the flat-bed printing machine with its inky odor, in my boyhood town of Hawick in the Scottish Borderland.

I was interested in good or bad news. I can never compare myself with the *newsies* of New York, whose exploits evoked a Tony Award Broadway musical of that name. These newsboys were the real McCoy, a corruption of the Scots "real leader MacKay" (first recorded in 1856 as "A drappie o' the real MacKay"). Their street shouts of "Extra! Extra!" Their strike, by one-eyed Kid Blink, against newspaper tycoons Randolph Hearst and Joseph Pulitzer for return of a few cents a day. No way do I compare!

Who could improve on the Kid's 1901 rallying call to fellow strikers? *"Friens and feller workers. Dis is a time which tries the hearts of men. Dis is de time when we've got to stick together like glue. We know what we want and we'll git it even if we is blind."*

After all, unlike for journalists and other stars, there were no Pulitzer prizes for newsboys, nor did they expect such awards.

But did Kid Blink ever fight a water rat while delivering newspapers at tenement doors for the local grocer? I recall grabbing my ankle to stop the rodent in its track, up my first worn long breeks, and squeezing it for dear life. I shouted "Rat!" Thankfully, this roused a flat dweller who came to the door, grabbed his paper, folded it three times and smacked hard the rat above my ankle. He groped for it, clutched it, chucked it down the close and asked if I was okay. I wondered if the rat was okay. My imaginary headline would have read: "Paperboy saved from rat."

Born in 1935, I remember as a toddler hearing British Prime Minister Neville Chamberlain from Westminster, on September 3, 1939, declare on the radio what came to be called *The Phoney War* after German forces invaded Poland. Can any New York or Chicago newsboy boast anything like that? In six months, *The Phoney War* became a real war. Canadians immediately, Russians and Americans eventually, became allies of a Great Britain in dire distress, while much of Europe was capitulating to Germany.

I recall the day after Chamberlain's 1939 declaration of war, stretching for a drink at a water fountain in my Scottish home town park and drawing back sharply with water running down my tiny jowls when a siren boomed out. "It's a wartime practice," my older brother David responded, as he waited behind me for a drink. At age four, I hardly knew what he meant and certainly not what the consequences would be.

The consequences were not calamitous for me or my siblings. You see my dad was a grocer. That essential service exempted him from conscription except as a reserve in the Scottish Home Guard. He continued to drive his Chevrolet grocery van around the Scottish countryside, supplying food to lonely wives and children whose husband and dads were at war. I opened and shut farm gates. Only if faced with a German invasion of Britain might the Home Guard really be at war. His rifle rested unloaded, almost throughout the duration, in a corner of our house. I remember playing with the trigger until I was found out and bawled out.

Had Britain been occupied by Germany, the local Home Guard would have resisted from a bunker in the Lindean Loch area of the Scottish Borders, stocked with silenced pistols, commando knives, plastic explosives, food and apparently expected to shoot themselves rather than be taken. Such resistance bunkers were dotted in different areas of Britain.

Because dad was a grocer, siblings Isla, David and I never went hungry as did many children under strict food rationing. My mum shared food from our shop with neighbors. We were safe in Hawick from German bombing that went on elsewhere in Scotland. We could tell by the engine noise if aircraft bombers, flying over *our* town to hit the Glasgow docks, were German. Although it seems unfair to Glaswegians, to mention our good luck compared with their bad luck, our rural town was not a target.

One day in 1941, a German pilot parachuted down in our rural area and my dad took up his rifle and set out to capture him. Rumor went around the town that the man the Hawick Home Guard captured was German Deputy Führer Rudolf Hess who, without Führer Adolf Hitler knowing, had set out on a solo flight and parachuted near Glasgow about the same time to talk peace with the Duke of Hamilton, whom he had met before the war and thought might be receptive to some sort of an agreement. Hess was captured at the same time as Hawick's more ordinary Luftwaffe parachutist. Hess was taken first to Glasgow then to London for questioning. He committed suicide after a lifetime spent in Berlin's Spandau Prison.

Saturdays were the best days for me and my two siblings. At midday dinner, provided we had eaten our once in a while minced beef and the tatties schoolboys like my older brother had dug up from the fields, one red apple all the way from Canada was our yummy treat. I had no idea that cargo ships were sailing out of the St. Lawrence Seaway and then almost over German U-boats in the Atlantic. Those that arrived safely in Glasgow or London docks with such food as apples were welcome. No such thing with bananas. *Yes, we have no bananas!* This wartime anthem was about grocers like my dad who would never say a direct no to a customer. It became a melodious chant sung with gusto in war and post-war years.

For supper, a humdrum omelet made from Canadian powdered eggs and a slice of white bread and butter sometimes were on our plates. The Canadian National Research Council in Ottawa had pioneered dried egg powder because whole eggs going *over there* cracked on board merchant ships. British eggs were stamped and rationed to keep supplies up. Only one stamped egg a week along

11

with a package of dried eggs were allowed each person. This didn't stop my dad and me rubbing the ink-stamp off the eggs, and his selling them over the shop counter as local fresh eggs.

White bread in Scotland in 1941 cost three pennies a half-loaf. I remember my mother handing me a silver sixpenny piece to take down the street to the baker's shop to buy a half-loaf. I returned with the bread and tuppence change, craftily telling my mum the price of bread had gone up. When she found out this was not true and recovered the pilfered penny, she smacked my bum. Lucky for me, she did not grass on me to my dad who could smack harder.

Mum taught me a life-long lesson from Sir Walter Scott: *Oh! What a tangled web we weave when first we practice to deceive.*

I often wonder why I easily recall those personal *little* things that only barely affected my life. It takes research to uncover details of the calamitous times of World War II, the post WW II Cold War, the Korean War, wars in Malaya, Vietnam, Aden, Kenya, Katanga, Northern Ireland, Iraq, Syria and yet another Cold War with Russia. I have no excuse for losing touch with the Irish troubles, with Mau Mau in colonial Kenya and Katanga, which I was connected with first-hand. I was a journalist in Africa long before immigrating to Canada. As a British National Service infantry corporal serving in England, I was forced to do a two-week training upgrade in Northern Ireland when the Irish Republican Army was planning another anti-British imperialism armed campaign. It was only a taste of war and the soldiers involved in it, but a bad taste remains in my old age.

I easily remember a time, that unknown to me at the time, came just before the 1940 Battle of Dunkirk. Two soldiers of the Gordon Highlanders moved into our home to make it their temporary barracks, outside the overcrowded Stobs Camp near Hawick. One of them took me to a movie starring Gene Autry. That soldier's cigarette smoking spoiled the show for me to some extent. The consolation was that Autry sang my now favorite, *South of the Border.* That was why I remember it so clearly.

The same World War II soldiers used to toss me so high in the air, that my head touched clothes drying on the line above the living-room fire. I attribute my lifelong fear of heights to them. Then both were gone! Dunkirk took Jimmy and Nobby away. Cinema newsreels depicted the British Expeditionary Force advancing through France then retreating. Finally came deliverance from German pursuers. The rescuing fleet of destroyers, fishing boats, pleasure boats and ferries, that plucked thousands of British soldiers from the Dunkirk beach may have saved Britain from defeat.

My Trinity Elementary School was disciplined by headmaster Robert Burns, an army captain in World War I. He was an institution in town, immaculately dressed with shoes polished, and above one of them, a wooden leg that pupils never saw.

> *Robbie Burns is a very good man.*
> *He goes to church on Sundays.*
> *He prays to God to give him strength.*
> *To wallop the boys on Mondays.*

For me, today sleep comes with dreams of poet Robert Burns or Burns the headmaster. I also dream of the printing shop where, at age 15, I was apprenticed to Walter Easton, owner of the *Jedburgh Gazette,* in the Scottish border town of the name, 13 miles from where I was born. My father, Wullie to all, had moved from Hawick to nearby Jedburgh for work after he went bankrupt and my mother Janet died. I lived with my Aunt Netta and Uncle Peter Douglas in Hawick, until I attained my high school leaving certificate allowing me to rejoin my family in Jedburgh.

Fate landed me my first newspaper job when my dad bumped into Walter Easton at the local pub and mentioned that his son was looking for work. Lucky for me he did! My alternative was the local rayon factory, imported into Jedburgh by an enterprising Canadian industrialist with Scottish connections. He brought baseball to the rugby town, maybe not knowing that the Scots had played *rounders* for years before it became baseball. His rayon factory became, known as the "silk mill." After three strikes, just like in baseball, it went under.

My first smart grey suit was manufactured at the silk mill. I imagined its rayon fabric indestructible after seeing Alec Guinness in the movie, *Man in the White Suit.* Women were at the mill's rayon base. Men had less chance of jobs there. When interviewed at the mill office, the boss told me that judging from my high school leaving certificate at the A-level in eight subjects, I should be going to university. My dad gave me the option of deciding what to do. That option suddenly included the *Jedburgh Gazette!*

Walter Easton was correcting proofs when I arrived for my interview dressed in my grey rayon suit and raincoat. I had waited in light rain outside the newspaper office for five minutes while plucking up courage. After hanging up my wet coat and scarf on a rack and introducing myself, Easton's first question was why I wanted to be a printer. "Well, for me, it's a whole lot better than the silk mill or university."

"You have something against universities?"

"I seek a job to help my family," I assured him. "I'm not cut out for university."

"Well, as a matter of fact, neither was I. Let's see how you do at proofreading. Although it's not a printing apprenticeship requirement, it tells a tale." He handed me a bunch of small scrap paper sheets, clipped together and numbered with his handwritten reported court story scrawled on them. "You read out the story to me and I'll correct the proofs in front of me. Take note. We're on deadline!"

The editor's ragged handwriting was not easy to read but, since I had been a book reader most of my 15 years, I managed to read the story almost perfectly to pass his test.

He looked up: "Who would you say makes most errors in the printing shop?"

"The apprentice," I replied to my advantage.

"So what experience have you of printing that brings you here for a job?"

"It's the newspaper side that interests me more than the commercial side. I delivered papers for four years serving a Hawick shop. I was regularly in and out of printing offices to pick up the papers. I liked what I saw, especially the huge printing machine, the cases of type, the smell of news."

Easton looked me in the eye, probably puzzling over my "smell of news" rather than "smell of ink" that I had meant to say, before addressing me. "Well, I'm trade union bound to say that in my printing shop, I'm allowed, by union-management rules, one apprentice to my three journeymen. A journeyman is a printer who has served his apprenticeship. My present apprentice has a deferment from army service, until his apprenticeship ends in two months and his National Service for two years starts. I'm not sure if I can take you on right now under union rules. I can call the father of the chapel in Hawick and ask him. Sit tight. I'll see if I can get hold of him at the *Hawick Express* right now."

Easton rose from his sanctum to stretch his legs I guess, but he also picked up the phone and dialed. I had no idea what father of the chapel meant. My dad had no truck with religion and neither did I. I soon realized I knew the man he was talking to. "Hello, Jimmy. It's Walter Easton from Jedburgh. I have a union rules problem."

14

"Don't we all?" I heard Jimmy reply. "Tell me about it."

"I'm losing my apprentice, Lonsdale Dawson, to the army in two months and I have beside me a young lad, a Hawick lad come to Jedburgh to live and possibly work here at the *Gazette*. The problem is that if I take him on, I will have two apprentices to three journeymen for two months."

"What's his name? I may know the family."

"Fairbairn–Billy Fairbairn. His father was a grocer in Hawick's Bourtree Place and now works for the Co-op here in Jedburgh. I met him last week. I learned that the boy's uncle is Tom Fairbairn, who worked for the Gazette some years ago as a reporter, earning a good name though little money and now working as a sub-editor on the *Glasgow Herald*."

Jimmy broke in: "Tom Fairbairn, you yourself will recall, also reported rugby for the *Express*. His nephew, Billy, by your side, delivered the paper for a few years. I ken them both. May I have a word with Billy if ye dinna mind?"

Handed the phone by an astonished Walter Easton, I was at a loss for words. "Hi, Jimmy," I came out with. "Still bringin' oot the paper without my help?"

Jimmy, I recall, laughed, saying: "So you're in the *Jedburgh Gazette* office looking for a job. That figures. I wondered where yu'd gone. You could do well with Wattie Easton. Now hand the phone back to Wattie. We'll clear up this union rules problem."

"...If it's only for two months, then there's no problem for me at my union level," Jimmy continued his discourse. "I don't report minor transgressions to the Typographical Association in Glasgow. The situation isn't new with National Service continually conscripting our youth into the forces. I recommend you hire Billy. Anything less complicated bothering you, like the way Hawick polished off the Jed team on the rugby field at Riverside Park last weekend?"

"No, that's it. You're the boss!" Easton astonished me by saying, before he replaced the phone. His mind made up, he swung round at this grinning young hopeful. "You have friends in the right places. Start Monday morning at eight. Impress foreman Ollie, who will brief you on your work, by coming in early. And have the two coke fires burning by eight sharp, at which time, I will be here in my office."

He surprised me by handily picking my coat and scarf off the rack and handing me them. I put on only the coat.

"Aren't you going to wear your scarf?"

"No, it's damp."

Walter and Jimmy had launched me on a printing and journalism career in three continents, on newspapers, radio and magazine, though at age 15, I had no idea what was in store.

Chapter 2
"With 26 soldiers of lead, I will conquer the world"

Cold in winter, was the *Jedburgh Gazette's* printing office before 8 a.m., when I got the coke stoves burning upstairs and downstairs that first morning. Hot in summer, I was to learn, because the upstairs skylight in the composing room opened only halfway. Scotland's weather is changeable, so it was just as well it did not open fully in sudden rain.

I remember before that as a boy enjoying the cinema in Scotland when, especially during wartime winter nights, my granny, with flashlight aimed down on the ground, would take my sister Isla and me to evening movies once a week. Wartime blackout meant anyone pointing a light skyward would be challenged by watchmen.

I preferred the four-penny Saturday afternoon movies with my brother, David. Screen curtains would swing open and music to a ball bouncing over printed notes and words of *Roll out the Barrel* and us singing, no, roaring, would put us in the mood sociologists had decided would relieve the bad effects of war on children. A scene from one black and white American western flick still reinforces my mind's eye at age 82! A gutsy editor stands beside the proof press wearing a green eye visor. He stands his ground against baddies, who have burst into his printing office to censor his story of their wrongdoings.

"You no good sons of guns will have to shoot me before I keep this out of the *Gazette,*" the editor risks saying. His bravado, with an ink-blackened right hand in the air and his left hand from work holding a printer's typesetting stick, still thrills me to the core. He takes a bullet for his foolhardiness and that bullet pierced *my* heart. With no apology to Randolph Scott, I ride into town to avenge the killing and set the newspaper back on its feet!

That's when I'm back in days of yore, hand-setting advertisements texts in lines of metal type or, more of a treat, headlines! Posters set in huge wooden typefaces will thrust out the news from agency shops. Apprentice compositors must first learn the lay of lower and upper-case metal letter receptacles and use the printer's setting-stick. I compose lines of moveable type-faces, set upright and upside down on lead pedestals in sizes from tiny 6-point for business cards through 36-point for headlines to 136-point for the posters.

The z-soldiers (I call the metal letters *soldiers*, since I was a soldier later) are billeted in the lower case's smallest compartment. The e-soldiers are in the largest. Other lower-case letters are arranged in different size compartments according to how often they are used. Capital letters are quartered alphabetically in same-size upper case receptacles. Metal word spaces are in various thicknesses. When the lines are set tight between thin strips of lead metal in the setting stick, I transfer them to a brass galley, tie them tight with string, ink roll them and proof them for the editor to correct.

Computers, a half-century onward, would revolutionize printing. Not even Walter Easton knew that his row by row of precious fonts of metal type in wooden compartments were destined to become obsolete and end up as scrap melted down for a pittance.

The printers' point system covered the tiny metal letters to the big wooden letters. God forgive the apprentice careless enough to spill small type and raise the foreman's wrath. Such a mess was called printer's pie. The fall pie-guy is the apprentice, and it's a devil of a job to redistribute pied letters and spaces back in their cases one at a time for reuse.

With youthful determination I set and redistribute type, season by season, year by year. The words of Benjamin Franklin, once an apprentice printer, have inspired me: "With 26 soldiers of lead, I will conquer the world."

I improve my writing and spelling from reading stories as my editor corrects the proofs. In those days, proofreaders were invaluable to save the paper from angry advertisers, finicky readers and even libel. Eighty years hence, newspaper proofreaders are almost obsolete and, due to the computer revolution, even the giant Linotype that once speeded up production is obsolete, along with the flat-bed printing machine.

One day my editor remarked: "There is a convenient belief in every print shop, that at night, or when the printer is not watching, a pesky demon inverts letters or misspells words or perhaps removes an entire word or even a complete line. Who is he, I ask you?"

He answers rhetorically as I sit mesmerized: "The printer's devil, of course!" His gaze at me indicates that I am the printer's devil incarnate. He is kidding of course. "Just remember to mind your Ps and Qs at the case," he cajoles me, turning to substitute a P for a Q with his pencil. We continue our galley proofing. "Printer's devil my ass!" I inwardly defend myself.

When the proofs are clean and typography pleasing, I ask him for weekend use of his portable Olivetti typewriter, then for his Dallmeyer press camera and, finally, I'm allowed the magic of the darkroom with its photo enlarger and chemicals. I purchase a 35mm camera and soon develop and print my own photographs taken mostly on the rugby field. This progresses to tuppence a line for a short sports column.

My printing apprenticeship is moving in mixed directions. Journeymen colleagues tease me, and I learn that tarring with black ink and feathers was at one time the dire fate of an apprentice too big for his boots. Linotype operator Dave McDonald fools me into walking into the electric utensil company shop next door, with his story that Jean, the shop assistant, might let me take her to the Jedburgh Hunt town hall ball. He knows I have a crush on Jean, because he hears me sing *Jeanie with the light brown hair* as I pick type from the cases.

"Do you have a tuxedo?" he asks.

"A tuxedo? I have the second-best thing, a smart grey suit."

What also landed me in his trap, was the fact that I printed the ball tickets on the Arab machine and could slip myself a couple. I learn later that Dave had held back laughter at my reply that I would wear a suit to the ball.

Jean is embarrassed when I tell her how honored I would be to take her dancing. But not half as much as me on being flatly turned down!

I had no idea how my colleagues knew all about my dad's affairs on Saturday nights at a private hotel in Jedburgh. To cut a long story short, widower dad had his eye on one of the maids. To the jealous female hotel owner's dismay, he made out with the maid. Next thing, she was pregnant, and I am standing next to them as a witness at their Jedburgh registry office wedding. Julie was a wonderful stepmother and, after first son Lindsay was born, she went on to bear another 11 children. Malcolm was also born in Scotland and after that another nine in Corby, England, where dad took his new family. I waved them goodbye at the bus stop, and was left renting a room with a woman of a certain age in Jedburgh and staying in Scotland to finish my apprenticeship.

Walter Easton seemed to me to be a combination of Moses and Solomon. Instead of conservatively keeping me stuck solidly to printing, he actually encouraged me to learn Pitman shorthand as the key to success in newspaper journalism. At evening classes, or at home under sister Isla's eye, I sweated blood over heavy strokes and light strokes, simple vowels and diphthongs. My shorthand for journalism book includes a French proverb, *Petit à petit, l'oiseau fait son nid.* 'Little by little, I increase my skill too'. My teacher tells me to write faster and I love her for more than that.

I'm still thinking of her when improving my shorthand a year later as an 18-year-old conscripted National Service soldier, confined to barracks and seated at a desk by the fireplace in the Quiet Room of the training depot of the King's Own Scottish Borderers at Berwick-on-Tweed.

I had confounded Walter Easton by not applying for military deferment, having learned that under union-management and government regulations, National Service at age 18 takes a year off lengthy apprenticeships, rewarding apprentices with an accelerated year's pay rise on demobilization.

Chapter 3
Soldier of the Queen

By November 1953, World War II and, to some extent, the Korean War were both over and what remained of the British Empire was becoming hard for Britain to defend without military recruits. What the British Army wanted with the likes of me, I soon found out.

Around Remembrance Day, I was transformed from a gangly 18-year-old youth working as a printer on a Scottish weekly newspaper, into a private soldier in the King's Own Scottish Borderers (KOSB). I was conscripted into the infantry for two years.

For sure, war was in the air the day I reported to the KOSB depot, a decrepit walled castle and parade ground in the debatable Scottish-English border town of Berwick-on-Tweed. The Soviets, in their sector of occupied Berlin, were exasperating French, British and American allies in their sectors. At the same time, French President General de Gaulle was busy planning a European Economic Union without Britain as a member and infuriating successive British prime ministers.

Added was the nasty British colonial war against the Mau Mau in Kenya, that was being blamed on the country's future president to be, Jomo Kenyatta. Britain was also fighting what the government said was communism in Malaya, while one of two KOSB battalions was keeping an eye on the Irish Republican Army in Northern Ireland. All the while, the war in Vietnam loomed ahead from air and on land.

I was placed in Arnhem platoon for basic training. In charge of the barracks room was Corporal Alec Irving, home from the Korean War and the fittest and smartest soldier I had ever seen. In terms of discipline, he soon had me polishing his bedroom floor, his boots, and realizing that my trespasses as a rookie on the parade ground helped make him look smart.

I wondered why it had taken him so long to discover I had never shaved. Baby hair on my chin, two weeks into training, gave the game away. He stood over me in the washroom making sure I shaved and noticing that the latrines required cleaning.

Berwick is a tourist town in summer, but in winter, it is bleak and misty with evenings of damp snow. It has a history of border warfare between Scotland and England. Human heads of Scottish fighters once hung from its castle rampart by order of English overlords, as a warning to the Scots to end their auld alliance with France.

It did not perturb me to be confined to barracks, for not just the dutiful first two weeks of army training, but as mishap punishment for the first four weeks. I had my Shorthand Book II to study and a glowing fire in the depot's Quiet Room to keep me warm.

I sat contentedly, on evenings, at a desk armed with a soft lead pencil, a notebook and a poke of Berwick cockles. These were no pigs in a poke. They were a delicious red and white mint candy. I had my own future civilian career to think of, since I had no intention of being a soldier all my life.

However, my shorthand seemed to disturb Corporal Irving, as I squiggled dots and dashes in a notebook, while my fellow recruits sloughed through snow and dark streets to Berwick's Saturday night dance halls.

What once hurt me in training more than a distaste of rifle and bayonet, was the spring of a dummy hand grenade that hit me in the eye, and even more, an officer's charge of indiscriminate firing while running under falling snow down the range. Another punishment came when on lying down on my three mattress biscuits at lights-out, my bed collapsed. I grappled with whom I thought was the culprit. The guard commander appeared and next morning the two of us were marched left-right-left-right-left, halt! The guard sergeant read the charge in front of the adjutant. "In contravention of Queen's Regulations, Pte. William Fairbairn, 22939643, was fighting in the barrack room after lights-out."

The adjutant haughtily surveyed me, uttering two words. "Explain yourself!"

"I can't," I said, arms straight down, eyes focused above him. "It was foolish horseplay over a sabotaged bed."

We were both confined to barracks for three days.

Bullet pouches were my embarrassing next blot as a soldier. I couldn't mount the pouches properly on my waist, what with the corporal roaring me on parade. Responding to last call, I catapulted down the stairs, two at time, and lined up in the back row. "What the hell are those?" the inspecting sergeant shouted, eyeing my bullet pouches before rhetorically shouting: "Brassieres?" The nickname, thank goodness, died after a time.

I nevertheless, passed rifle and Bren tests and my third place in the cross-country run had Cpl. Irving saying, "You'd have come in second if you'd kept alongside me." I recall the company major shouting "Tally Ho!" then disappearing from the race.

On the morning of the New Year's break, there arrived at the depot for me by mail, a cardboard box, and inside, a big iced cake baked by my Aunt Aggie. Her husband, my Uncle Jim Douglas, had a strong link to the KOSB depot in Berwick. He had enlisted in the army in 1916 and, having 10 years of driving experience, chose the Royal Army Service Corps. On October 28 of that year, he set sail for Mesopotamia via Cape Town, Durban, Dar es Salaam, Bombay, eventually arriving at Basra on the Persian Gulf on December 31. There he was attached as driver to a small party of British Secret Service agents. Their mission was to rescue allied consuls stranded in Armenia.

The party was captured and imprisoned in a farm building. Each morning, one of them was taken out and shot, until James Douglas was the sole survivor but, he reckoned, likely to be shot the next day. However, he found that the barn door had not been locked, so he made a break.

After wandering about the steppes without much idea where he was going, he was confronted by a Cossack charging on him, whirling a sword above his head. Expecting instant decapitation, James was surprised when the Cossack asked him in English who he was and where he was going. It transpired that the Cossack had lived in Canada for some years but had returned to fight in the Russian Revolution. The Cossack directed him to carry on in the same direction and James would find a train that would take him near his own lines.

He found the train and boarded it. The train was carrying sacks of grain and each time it stopped and was searched, he moved the sacks around or read a Russian paper to indicate he belonged there, although he could neither read nor speak Russian.

James Douglas was eventually recaptured and taken to Moscow, where he was imprisoned for more than a year.

A dire recollection, he stressed, when I lived in his home as a boy when my mother was ill, was the food. He described it as "fish heads floating in dirty water with lumps of black bread."

In 1919, he and another seven prisoners were exchanged for a Russian admiral. They were taken to St. Petersburg, and from there, they sailed down the Baltic Sea and he soon came home to Scotland.

The upshot was that in 1921, James Douglas drove from his cottage at Abbotsford, where he was chauffeur/handyman at the historic former home of Sir Walter Scott, to the KOSB depot at Berwick-on-Tweed. There he was presented with the Distinguished Conduct Medal, the Military Medal and the Russian Medal for Gallantry, awarded him by the Czar of Russia, before the Czar and his family were executed by the communists.

I, William Douglas Fairbairn, shared my Aunt Aggie's cake with fellow soldiers at Berwick, two hours before traveling by train home on leave. Corporal Irving enjoyed my story and his slice of cake. He smiled at me in a way that warmed my heart and handed me a book on cross-country running.

I marched around my hometown like a war hero for five days, tried to find a girl at the Palais de Dance in Hawick and sang *Auld Lang Syne* off-key. I wondered if I would soon be eating mangos in the Malayan jungle, where a KOSB battalion was serving, or, as human compost feeding mango bushes. "Kill the enemy," was the message rattling my mind when, back in training, I took a mouthful of army invective for timidly bayonet-charging sacks filled with straw. If posted to Malaya, I knew that I would be the enemy.

Just two of us from my company were not sent to Malaya after our passing-out parade. We two were sent on a course to the Infantry Clerks Training Centre (ICTC) in Chichester, Sussex, to study routine orderly room work along with two soldiers from almost every infantry regiment in the British Army. We, of Leslie tartan trews, Scottish thistle and Glengarry bonnet, met soldiers wearing the English rose, the Welsh leek and the Irish shamrock. Some marched faster than others. Durham Light Infantry and Highland Light Infantry soldiers were quicker on the step. We spoke different dialects of English, some I could hardly understand.

The ICTC location comprised six low-slung wooden barracks and a parade ground attached, over a wall, to the depot of the Royal Sussex Regiment. The barracks formerly had been used by World War II Canadian soldiers. One of the bleak buildings was the Orderly Room, the rest used for accommodation, lectures and typewriting practice. Students took notes for six weeks on, not just orderly room, but war office procedures. Our bible was *Queen's Regulations*. We touch-typed our fingers off. My KOSB comrade came out first in final examinations. I came second.

I later learned that with a vacancy existing in the ICTC Orderly Room itself, the commanding officer, Major Munro, had asked that my top-of-the-class comrade be transferred from prospective duties at his KOSB depot in Berwick, and posted to the ICTC instead. "No, no!" the adjutant responded from Scotland. "We want this soldier for *our* orderly room." That left the ICTC choosing me. The adjutant in Berwick probably welcomed the result. I did too.

I spent two of the best years of my life in Chichester, on an ICTC permanent staff of 12 soldiers that comprised two cooks, three sergeant instructors, a corporal clerk, a lance corporal, three privates, a company sergeant major and the major in command. One reason to celebrate, was the fact that the Royal Sussex Regiment could not collar me for overnight guard commander duties at its depot, though their jealous orderly room corporal tried it on.

Advised by instructor Sergeant Taylor, I pointed out to the Royal Sussex corporal that *Queen's Regulations* did not allow a soldier of one British Army insignia, to do guard duty for a regiment of another insignia. I had been promoted corporal in the KOSB, not the Royal Sussex. The Royal Sussex order was reversed the next day.

Success in further army clerical tests eventually gave me five stars with more pay. Knowing regulations for national servicemen allowed me to arrange three rail travel warrants a week, to take typographical evening classes at Brighton College of Arts and Crafts and consequently enjoy late evening dances in that grand English south coast holiday resort.

A secretarial science book I borrowed from the Chichester public library, helped student soldiers who were failing to type the required 15 words a minute with fewer than three errors. Brawny guardsmen, perhaps with oversized hands, were among those unable to reach the required speed and accuracy. When I showed Major Munro the library book, he arranged evening access to typewriters and I supervised them once a week. Day-time typing classes were reorganized so students faced surrounding classroom walls, each with a typewriter keyboard map before their eyes on the wall and with covers over the keys to encourage touch-typing. The changes must have increased pass statistics by 10 per cent. Entering Major Munro's office with the mail one morning, I saw him clicking away with fingers under a cover over his typewriter keys.

My civilian newspaper career ever in mind, I corresponded with Canadian Lord Beaverbrook's *Daily Express* in London's Fleet Street and, with an introductory letter from Walter Easton, toured the Express offices, then under legendary editor Arthur Christianson. I never imagined I would one day be a desk editor, then foreign news taster, not on the *Express* in London, but on its future upstart opposition, the *Sun.*

I twice broke an army rule by writing articles on army life for *The Scotsman* newspaper and on army food for the Edinburgh *Evening News.* The *News* illustrated my story with a spud falling off the table and exploding like a mine. For a month I feared being found to have broken the Official Secrets Act. I had my real brush with military law on a later occasion.

The major was dutifully signing me the three rail passes a week to travel to Brighton for evening classes. Returning to Chichester railway station near midnight one very cold winter's night, with greatcoat buttoned up and collar wrapped around my ears, I only just heard the words, "Leave pass, soldier!" and turned to face a military policeman in white gaiters, white belt and red-topped cap.

"Pass?" I repeated stunned, because I *had* no pass. I searched in vain for my Army Book 64, Soldier's Record and Pay Book. Frustrated, I thrust my military rail warrant with the major's signature at the redcap, pointing out I was on my way back to my barracks at the Infantry Clerks Training Centre, attached to the Royal Sussex regimental depot, after evening classes in Brighton. I did not mention that the dance after the class ended had made me late.

"That ain't no military pass, soldier! You're stationed at the Infantry Clerks Training Centre, you say, soldier…"

"Wait a minute! I have a receipt from the Royal Sussex NAFFI in my wallet as evidence."

The Red Cap smirked, confused by knowing nothing about any such outfit as the Infantry Clerks Training Centre and, under the lamplight, unable to read my NAFFI receipt for a pair of gloves I had purchased.

"Aye, I'm a clerk in the ICTC Orderly Room. I'm wearing the new gloves I bought at the depot just seven hours ago."

"From the ICTC orde-r-r-ly room, with no pass past midnight and improper-r-r-ly dressed. How do you intend to get into your bar-r-racks at midnight without a pass to show the guard?" he callously asked, making me wonder for a moment if he was himself Scottish.

"We have a back entrance with no guard," I whimpered.

This reply stunned the policeman into a moment of silence, broken when his military sidekick intervened. "Come on, mate. I'm freezing my balls off standing here. Let him go on his way or we'll

26

be discussing this all night. We can catch up with him through administrative channels. He's committed no grave crime by being out late without a pass. We're out late too!"

"If what he tells us is true!" the interrogating policeman responded like Sherlock Holmes to Dr. Watson.

Not without reason, both were confused by a soldier wearing the KOSB insignia, speaking in a broad Scottish accent, referring to ICTC and identifying himself as a soldier stationed at the Royal Sussex Depot. All three of us were shivering and maybe, I ventured to think later that, he wondered if I was in secret service or intelligence. To my relief, the red cap gave way. "Well, Jock," he grunted reluctantly, "we'll send a report to your commanding officer through the Royal Sussex. Give us more details for the record and we'll let you go on your way."

Two weeks later their report found its way to the ICTC orderly room. One of my office duties was to open the mail and at first sight, I thought about throwing it in the garbage can since I was marking my calendar down to demobilization day. I was more cautionary in showing the report to Major Munro and giving him my side of the story. He smiled saying: "From what you say, the military policeman addressed you several times as 'soldier' and put on a Scottish accent. Did he not know you were a corporal with the same rank as himself?"

"He mocked my Scottish accent, addressed me first as soldier, then as Jock, and refused to believe I was stationed here at the Infantry Clerks Training Centre. He didn't take note of my rank. He suspected something worse than my being out late with an upturned collar and sore throat on a very cold night."

"I see," Major Munro said. "By Jove, I'll challenge the military police to explain why you were not treated politely. Type out a letter defending this soldier's position. Say this soldier missed his earlier train from Brighton and was returning peacefully to his barracks, albeit with upturned collar to ward off a sore throat. I doubt they'll pursue the matter. You know the routine. I'll sign the letter. But don't let anything like this happen again. Whiten those stripes!"

Before my two years of army service ended, Major Munro urged me to sign on for five years as a corporal soon to be sergeant. The trouble is, as my Canadian wife says today, I was more a Corporal Radar of the popular television program *M*A*S*H* than a soldier of the Queen. So I declined. Major Munro testified in my Army Book III discharge certificate that my military conduct was very good, and described me as honest, sober and reliable.

Chapter 4
"Charged the foe with native valor"

I returned to Jedburgh to serve out the remaining years of my apprenticeship at the *Gazette*. Thanks to the Brighton School of Arts and Crafts, I had a City and Guilds Certificate in Typography. I hoped this would help end the days of my taking the rap as the printer's devil.

Lonsdale Dawson had moved on to journeyman status and truth to tell, I was envious because unionized pay was high for qualified printers. British newspaper owners were finding out that, whenever they tried to mess with staff pay and work conditions, the printers' union was the strongest in the country. Printers had their fingers on the buttons that set rolling the rotary presses that printed the national papers, and they used that strength to their advantage against tycoons such as Cecil King of the *Daily Mirror* and the Canadian Lord Beaverbrook of the *Daily Express*.

Jedburgh had not changed in the two years I had been in the army. The town was still semi-depressed, unlike prosperous Hawick with its hosiery mills, cattle and sheep markets, and a spirit that had endowed itself Queen o' the Borders. Its partisan outlook went back centuries. In 1514, Hawick's youth had avenged the town's loss of men at the Battle of Flodden, when even the Scottish king was killed in combat with the English. Hawick youth, too young to fight at Flodden, had attacked a company of English raiders when they were asleep near the town. Hawick records show they "drew their swords like veteran heroes, charged the foe with native valor, routed them and took their pennant."

The victorious English army at Flodden, under the Earl of Surrey, had divided for plunder. A detachment under Lord Dacre was encamped near Hawick, intending to burn the town to the ground as they had other border towns. Hawick's young men forced Lord Dacre to think again!

This was maybe the only bright spot in the Scottish defeat at Flodden, that had not only taken the life of King James VI but 10,000 other Scotsmen including many of Hawick's men, leaving their women and children grieving. The Scottish lament over Flodden is worth repeating:

Flowers of the Forest
We'll nae mair lilting at the yowe milking
Women and bairns are dowie and wae
Sighing and moaning on ilka green loaning
The flowers of the forest are a wede away

The Gazette's Lonsdale Dawson was an underestimated 100-metre sprinter, until he made headlines by winning the prized professional Powderhall sprint in Edinburgh, under the running name of John Franklin. Before the race, he had been spirited away for two weeks of intense training by local coaches. He was also a fast rugby player when he caught the ball. Walter Easton was delighted that Dawson's success helped fill the paper.

For my own part, I ran a fair half mile as an amateur, but I was never a money winner in the professional Border races. However, from my boyhood in Hawick, I had played billiards well enough to be chosen at age 15, to represent Scotland in the 1950 British Boys Billiards Championship at Burroughs and Watts salon in Soho Square, London. I reached the second round before being narrowly knocked out by a Londoner.

I was shocked to see prostitutes and their pimps out in force on London streets. In our chosen hotel, I had my first Coca-Cola! "Blimey! You've never had a coke," our guide reflected, when I asked him what a coke was.

So, while Dawson made headlines as a winner, I was given two paragraphs as a second-round loser. But the experience of being in London made up for it. I saw everything from the Windmill Theatre to Hyde Park. On the tube, I discovered my eyesight was faulty, when unlike my compatriots, I couldn't read underground station names on maps on the opposite side of the carriages. I was soon to wear spectacles. This increased my shyness with women.

Dressed in a Glengarry bonnet and Leslie tartan trews of the King's Own Scottish Borderers infantry regiment, Pte. Bill Fairbairn prepares to throw up the first ball in the 1953 Jedburgh ba' game, an annual tussle between town Uppies and Downies.
PHOTO: WALTER EASTON

I fancied one of my editor's twin daughters. I imagined I might one day marry her and inherit her father's newspaper. Each time I delivered galley proofs to his home, where he burned the midnight oil after leaving the office early, was the hope of a glimpse of Mary at her father's door. One night it happened! After handing over the proofs, I picked up courage and asked: "Wad ye gang tae the pictures wi me on a Saturday night?" She was shyly shaking her head, then to my mind almost nodding, before her more forward twin, out of sight behind her, giggled. I laid low when the story went abroad.

I graduated from the type case to the linotype. Its keyboard layout was similar to that of a typewriter. There the similarity ended. The dragon in front of my stool at work petrified me. Metal ingots fed the dragon. They hung by a chain dipping into its hot pot and melting for its use. I was thunderstruck by a maze of iron wands that clanked and thrashed, and that, I read, had been created by some German-American sorcerer.

To set up lines of newspaper text in metal, I tapped keys that dropped letter-indented brass matrices and space bands into an assembly carriage. There the keys stood one beside the other, a column wide, above the keyboard. A handle on the right pressed the assembled keys down on molten metal, and amid a spattering of slivers of an alloy of lead, antimony and tin, appeared a solid line of metal type pushed up against other lines of type. These silver slugs were the week's news. They next had to be assembled column by column, separated by rules with headlines on top, and page by page, pressed together by coin keys in heavy chases, for the flat-bed printing machine.

Once every two weeks, I had to melt the slugs of metal type in a hot pot and turn them into silver ingots for reuse. The Linotype returned matrices and space bands to their compartments so the monster could reuse them. My editor once recited a Robbie Burns-style poem he had written on its occasional malfunction:

Oh disser damned thou weird contraption.
I've jigged thee many a weary fraction.
Thou'll drive a printer to distraction.
Or to the beer.
Or else he'll hae a wild reaction
And curse and swear.

A huge flatbed machine on the lower stone floor below the composing room printed the newspaper. It moved back and forward, its inked rubber rollers whirling over metal type locked in chases. It resembled a disarranged locomotive shunting up and down rails, and it scared me as its operator. Each huge sheet of newsprint, fed by hand at about 500 an hour, faced off with the inked metal type below the rollers. Printed broadsheets would emerge on deft flyers that flopped them on a growing pile. That was the theory. Badly fed sheets of paper printed every which way or wrapped around the ink rollers. With kerosene and elbow grease. the printer's devil cleaned the rollers.

If setting up type and printing newspapers were acceptable, hand folding the papers and counting them challenged the imagination. I usually sang to myself to get through publication days. Then came delivery to the newsagents. With billboard and bravado, I'd get the *Jack the Ripper* story to the public. Imagination helped overcome youthful lack of confidence at age 15. Sixty-five years later, it helps me write this book. As film star, Betty Davis once said: "Getting old is not for sissies!"

In this modern age in the year 2018, I often compare newspaper production with that of the past. Articles and advertisements in my *Riverview Park Review* are assembled by an operator using a computer layout program entitled *In Design.* The design is typographically boring. The efficient part is that when the final front page has been checked on the screen for errors (or *typos* as printers call them), we three layout staffers shout out, "*That's it!*" The touch of a keyboard button sends the pages almost to the rotary press. The printed newspapers are delivered two days later. And I'm back as a newsboy with my wife, delivering them street by street on doorsteps.

Chapter 5

"Are you the Moors murderer?"

From about my first delivery as a newsboy at age nine, I was determined to become a journalist like my Uncle Tom. So when my printing apprenticeship finally did end, I jumped from printing in Scotland to journalism in England. But not before consulting Tom about the option that Glasgow and Blyth newspapers presented me with. He ruled out Glasgow as being a less solid offer. So, I was interviewed and I accepted a reporter's job in the North Sea coastal port and pit town of Blyth, in northeast England.

The Blyth News, a twice-weekly, called on its reporters to find stories often from port and coalmine, and fill the paper without the aid of news agency copy. I trudged my beat like an English yeoman from Scotland helping to fill the *Port, Pit and People* column twice a week. I learned my craft from able colleagues and another great editor in Bill Hogg, who either never knew of or questioned my printing and newsboy background. However, the weekend I arrived in Blyth, the future took a foreboding turn.

Having moved into my digs that Saturday, I went to the local dance in the evening. I enjoyed myself without walking home a girl, and being a keen runner, jogged to my lodgings. I was only vaguely aware of passing the town police station on the trot, when a figure on a bicycle came pedaling after me shouting "Stop!" Glancing around I saw a policeman. He came abreast and requested I return to the station with him.

An inspector first asked my name and address and why I had been running away. "I enjoy running," was my answer. "I was jogging home to my digs. Is that a crime in Blyth? I'm from Scotland, here to work on the *Blyth News.*"

Not buying this, he went on to interrogate me for an hour, apparently believing I would admit to being the sadistic moors murderer who was in the news. Scotsman Ian Brady and his girlfriend Myra Hindley were on the run from police, on suspicion of having murdered five children and sexually assaulted four of them. The inspector finally, at about 1 a.m., decided to phone the editor of the Blyth News to confirm what I had told him, Bill Hogg, no doubt in his pajamas, corroborated my story. The inspector had no option but to let me go, and from then on, I was in an excellent relationship with the Blyth police and the station that I was bound to visit each other day for crime story ideas.

On the Monday morning, Hogg related the story of the previous police contretemps with a laugh to my Blyth newspaper reporter colleagues and, rather than given a black mark, I was deemed an audacious reporter.

After taking over the news beat of a nearby village from reporter John Ritson, my first story was about ruffians creating havoc at the local cinema. John and I twice went to a movie and witnessed the fun for a few and disturbance for others. Movies for work was right up my street!

When Ritson reported for National Service, I inherited his *Youth Notes by Kim* column. I soon learned that he had covered mainly male activities and that this was resented by the young women of the local ballet club. They made their view public in a letter to the editor. As a result, I gingerly approached their rehearsal hall and entered. Mirrors reflected about 15 slim athletic women working wall bars and their female instructor in front. One young male dancer stood out. I watched all of them perform, then I interviewed *him*.

That one male dancer headlined my story and the female ballet dancers again complained that male bias was indigenous to Kim's column. To me this miner's son was a star before Billy Elliot in the great British musical stage performance that went all over the world.

I reached Blyth's under-sea coalface for a story covering a social visit by 16 London boys. In their tour was a 50-yard crawl along a tunnel that stretched a mile out. I was with the party when a cage took us down 750 feet to double shaft sidings and a waiting diesel locomotive and its driver. I behaved like a man, even though I was scared. I knew that years ago, a winding cable had snapped at the pit and killed eight men. "It's like the underground in Piccadilly," said one encouraging London boy.

A cooling wind blowing along the wide, illuminated main haulage way was deceptive of tough working conditions farther out. After leaving the train to make its return journey and during a steady march, the air grew mustier with a taste of coal dust, and underfoot wet and muddy.

"Anyone with surplus clothes, off with them here or you'll soon feel the heat," shouted Walter Eadington, a material economy officer who had worked in the pits for 46 years. Nearing the coalface, the tunnel's height was less than three feet, width little more than three feet and ventilation poor. A coal-transporting belt took up much room and crawling along a heading to near where the coal was proved nightmarish for me. I knew that for safety reasons, the wooden pit props supporting the tunnel from the North Sea above were being replaced by more efficient metal props that I had written about.

We visited the pony stalls and some of the boys were surprised to hear of the long pit service given by ponies. "Why can't they be replaced more frequently?" asked 14-year-old Christopher Clowes. "It's the training aspect," replied Eadington. "It takes two to three years to train a pit pony into a valuable animal."

Four men were waiting to enter the cage and ascend with us to the earth surface. Each man carried a leather equipment case. We were told they were firemen, who each morning, tested the mine for gas. If the concentration of methane was unacceptably high, they ordered the miners not to work until ventilation fans cleared the gas.

I learned the value of pit ponies when covering another story. Miners sympathetic to an old pony that had toiled for years underground, went on strike when the mine owners refused their demand that it be retired to green pastures. The pony had slowed up and I realized how good a story it was when I discovered its name was Jet!

I told my news editor about it and he immediately sought a photograph of Jet to go with my story. Our photographer was brushed aside when he went to the mine. "I can't get a photo of Jet," he told the editor. "Okay, just photograph any pit pony. Any pony will do the trick." And so it did! The strike ended when Jet was put out to pasture.

I covered industrial news at Cambois, a village separated from Blyth by a river, where a mammoth Central Electricity Generating Board power station was being built. Then there were the villagers fighting for toll-free ferries. Next came a mud-flats menace endangering children's health. After that, an account of a wait for decades by miners to see their aged homes improved. "Will we live to see it?" one pensioner, coughing up coal dust, asked me, and his question gave my newspaper a striking headline.

A robin's nest with eggs between harbor train rails, convinced the Harbor Master to put the rail track out of action for a month.

Then came the shipyard strike, and fast on its heels, the Conservative election contender who accused me of libel, because the day before the general election, I had disclosed a photograph in his publicity material of him shaking hands with a miner. The miner said it had been taken and distributed without his consent. I didn't consider it my fault that the Conservative MP lost the election to Labour by about 17,000 votes.

After work, we Blyth News journalists would go to the Alexandra Hall for a game of snooker. All but one of my colleagues were soon losing. I did not tell them of my British billiards championship experience. The sad thing was that news editor, Ronnie Cross, and I played our last game there. A hall rent increase and competition from bingo lost Blyth its last public billiards salon, just like cinemas were disappearing for the same reasons. My story of the closure related how Alexandra Hall's 15 billiards tables were dismantled and sold practically for the value of their slate beds at fifty shillings each.

When the *Blyth News* consolidated to come out weekly rather than twice weekly, newspaper management transferred me to Morpeth to write for both the *Blyth News* and the *Northumberland Gazette,* the latter headquartered in Alnwick. The snag was that the newspapers had no branch office in Morpeth. Also difficult for me to handle was the *Morpeth Herald*, having a main street office with a smart opposition reporter nicknamed Scoop.

I solved the office problem by taking up residence in a corner of the open and empty Corn Market Hall, and there conducted interviews with my portable typewriter and camera beside me on a long wooden bench. My lodgings overlooked the town library, so books and files of newspapers there helped me cover police courts and county fairs. I was gulled into doing a story about so-called starving ducks in the local Wansbeck River. Scoop became a friend and he helped me keep abreast of routine and extraordinary meetings of Morpeth town council, although he kept his scoops to himself as did I.

One human story took me back to my newsboy delivery days, when a water rat ran up my trousers. The same thing happened to a farmer walking by the side of the Wansbeck in Morpeth. This time, it was no imaginary headline that appeared in the *Northumberland Gazette!*

On Thursdays, it was routine for me to journey to head office in Alnwick to pick up my wages, all the while pestering management to set up a *Gazette* office in Morpeth and take me out of the Corn

Market Hall. Head to head, something had to give. What gave was my being on the train south to Derby, to be interviewed for a reporter's job on the *Derby Evening Telegraph*.

Chapter 6

"Bewitched, bothered and bewildered"

I stood across the street from the *Derby Evening Telegraph* office, in the center of the city, wondering if a newsroom actually lay within the imposing dome before my eyes. As a former newsboy, it looked too formidable for *me* to work there as a journalist. I was in Derby for an interview that I thought I would likely botch. I wondered what would become of me back in Morpeth if rejected.

Chief sub-editor Bob Randall, in the absence of the editor emeritus, showed me into his office and immediately asked my experience as a journalist. "I was a sports reporter for the *Jedburgh Gazette,* and general news reporter for the *Blyth News* and the *Northumberland Gazette,"* I told him, adding that I wrote a column– I didn't say youth column–in Blyth and, using shorthand, covered city hall. "I wrote features on everything from a power station being built in Cambois, to the only boy taking ballet lessons among a score of girls. I have newspaper cuttings with me."

My account apparently impressed him since he did not ask to see my cuttings. He did ask if I enjoyed my work.

"Immensely! I was realizing my dream of being a reporter like an uncle of mine who subs for the *Glasgow Herald."*

He asked what type of assignments I enjoyed most. "All of them!" I replied without hesitation. He smiled at that and asked if I had completed my National Service. "I was a corporal in the King's Own Scottish Borderers for two years. Served in England and briefly in Northern Ireland. I can't say I was the perfect Queen's soldier, but I have a reference in my briefcase from Major Munro, my commanding officer at the Infantry Clerks Training Centre in Chichester. May I show you it?"

I believe it was Munro's "honest, sober and reliable" line that made up Bob's mind. Or else, I was keeping him from his work putting the final afternoon edition of his newspaper to bed and he wanted free of me. "You must have impressed the military to be promoted corporal and you sure did impress Major Munro," he complimented me.

"It was lock-step promotion in the orderly room in Chichester, where I was stationed for 18 months," I modestly replied.

"What production line is that of Rolls-Royce?" he suddenly threw at me.

"Particularly the aero engine. Helped win the war. Then there's the motor car that big shots drive," I replied without hesitation. "Derby firm too."

"So when can you start?"

"A week, Monday morning, at whatever time work starts."

"Your hours are from 8 a.m. to 5 p.m. with an hour's break. There will be evening assignments and football to cover on alternative Saturday afternoons." He handed me a booklet on the history of the *Derby Evening Telegraph,* and a smaller one on the salary range and working conditions agreed with the National Union of Journalists. "Of course, coming from Blyth, you must already be an NUJ member."

"Blyth was once the parliamentary seat of Alf Robens, now chairman of the British Coal Board. He could count on 20,000 Labour majorities through strong support from unions. Miners and shipbuilders have voted that way since the war. Closed union shop in Blyth for printers and journalists," I assured him.

I wondered if I had been too partisan in supporting what one would call the left wing since Bob was on management, but he said support for Labour MPs in working class Derby was strong too.

In the newsroom he introduced me to Max, one of two news editors who ran city reporters as apart from rural reporters, and whom I immediately liked when he suggested ideas for accommodation. Max introduced me to each of eight or so male reporters and one female, and briefly described the lay of the building. When his phone rang, I dissuaded him from showing me out, saying his time would be wasted since I already knew my way around. I left him with a handshake and, with a curt wave to the staff, headed for the cafeteria I had spotted on coming in from the street. I was yearning for a bacon roll, a cup of tea and any chance to reflect on my success if only to myself.

That chance came when I peered through this hole-in-the-wall hatch at the prettiest of women. "Do you like your bacon crispy as I do?" she asked.

"How did you know?" I noted at once her brown eyes, glossy dark hair, lipstick-free lips and white apron framing an elegant neck.

Her smile seemed to me like that of Mona Lisa tempting a lover. She said she would tend me at my table and moved to the kitchen range. Five minutes later, she came out through a side door and did just that. "Do you work here permanently?" I asked her.

"Oh, no. It's a summer job from teacher training. I'm filling in for my mum. She's taking a break. I haven't seen you before. Are you a reporter?"

"Half an hour ago I was interviewed for a reporter's job–and I got it!"

"Good for you! Then enjoy your crispy bacon roll. I may see more of you, but for only a short time because my college restarts soon. Your accent tells me you're Scottish."

"My name is Bill and, yes, I'm Scottish."

"I'm Andrea. So, when do you start reporting?"

"In 10 days. I have to… "

Our conversation was interrupted when a tall, blond fellow entered the cafeteria and made his way to the service hatch. I looked around to see that 15 seconds later, he was being served by Andrea whom, I noticed, had blushed while running over my toes to get through the side door to serve him. After an exchange of words, he approached my table carrying a cup of coffee asking if he might join me.

"Aye, of course."

"You're from Scotland," he said, hardly surprising me. "I'm Mike Charles. Don't you remember shaking my hand in the newsroom? No. Well, I guess you had a lot of hands to shake. You must have met Andrea. What a doll! I take her out on Saturday nights. Her mother doesn't allow me much time with her because she has her teacher college studies to contend with. It doesn't help that her father, a police constable, has her on curfew. I guess that's because at age 18 she's a good bit younger than me. Now, on break from her college, I see more of her. I'd love to take her up to Scotland for a romantic adventure." Lowering his voice, he added. "I'd like to get inside that apron and kiss her precious tits. How do I address you by the way?"

His rude intention incensed me but I tried not to show it. "My name is Bill Fairbairn."

"Your interview with Bob must have gone well. You're lucky the editor emeritus is sick. He usually does the interviewing. Bob is easier to get on with and he's a damn good chief sub-editor. He runs the newspaper from the subs room. He'll be editor one day. Mark my words."

"He gave me the job after five or so questions."

"He had things to do downstairs with the printers."

"Really? You mean put the paper to bed?"

"No offence meant. He takes his job seriously, especially with the editor emeritus off ill and us needing a new editor period. What part of Scotland are you from?"

"The Scottish Borders. My home town of Jedburgh is the first you arrive in after crossing from England. Have you visited Scotland?"

"Edinburgh. In and out. I have relatives there. I told Andrea that I'll take her to Scotland whether her parents like it or not–when she falls in love with me. She said that might not happen. Do you have a clan?"

"With two different kilts. The Fairbairns are a sept of the Armstrong clan. Historically we were a bunch of border reivers, or plunderers, stealing cattle in England. Steel Bonnets you English called us three centuries ago, when Bonnie Prince Charlie raided England as far south as here in Derby and put London in a panic. On the other hand, you English used to cross the border to steal our women and I know for a fact that you still do so!"

Mike was nonplussed for a moment, saying he was not responsible for his birthplace and never needed to steal a woman. "They come to me," he boasted. "If you're not exaggerating, you may have a stirring historical feature story for the *Telegraph.*" Then he changed the subject. "I'll introduce you to Andrea."

I did not wish it so but before I could stop him, he had called her through from the kitchen. She had discarded the apron that had hid an orange and yellow dress that now revealed a perfect figure. "Andrea, say hello to Bill Fairbairn down from Scotland to report for the paper. But maybe you have already met."

I raised my eyes over her head. I was still seething inwardly over Mike's remark about planning to seduce her. I was lost for words other than to repeat softer than her soft hello, so I quickly bid Mike and her goodbye. I bowed out of the cafeteria bewitched, bothered and bewildered.

Chapter 7
Mickleover and Littleover

My landlady in Morpeth had accepted a week's notice as did my *Northumberland Gazette* newspaper, though management had tried to hold me to two weeks. Through a *Derby Evening Telegraph* small ad, I phoned a woman renting out a room in the Derby municipality of Mickleover. I booked it for two weeks hence, with likely renewal. So, I was soon heading back south on the train. My possessions included a brand new 35mm camera and a new suit to replace my rayon attire.

A bus from the Derby railway station took me to Mickleover, neighbor to the municipality of Littleover. Landlady Madeline Malone welcomed me at her door and despite my protest, carried my case upstairs before showing me my room. "I'll have dinner ready in an hour," she said. "You must be hungry having come all the way from Scotland."

"I came from Morpeth in England," I corrected her.

I found the dining room homey and she served chicken and rice followed by custard and apples. A fire glowed in the hearth, we sat around with cups of tea listening on the radio to dance music and a contest called *Write a Tune for a Hundred Pounds* from London's Hammersmith Palais. I told her I had the weekend off before starting work Monday on the newspaper.

This prompted her to pass me the Friday afternoon edition of the *Telegraph*. The front-page headline shook me: *"Martin Luther King stabbed in the chest signing book."* I must have closed my eyes because she asked me if there was something wrong. "Well, the news," I said, turning the front page so she could see it. "Oh, you need not worry. America is a long way off. Nobody gets stabbed here. They're always stabbing and shooting over there."

"But it was Martin Luther King!"

"Is he the one who makes trouble for the American government?"

I did not know what to say. I had profound empathy for King. I guardedly blurted out: "Yes, that's the man."

The story was from the Reuter-AP news agencies and indicated clearly that the *Telegraph,* owned by Lord Northcliffe, had British news agency as well as international agency stories at its disposal, unlike the *Blyth News* that depended on its own reporters and freelance contributors.

"It's getting late," my landlady eventually said, putting down her knitting after the radio program ended. "Let's sleep on a perfect evening. What time do you take breakfast?"

"Would a lie-in tomorrow until 8:30 be okay? On work weekdays I'll be starting work at 8 and finishing at 5. My timetable has been roughly worked out. I'll catch the bus before 7:30 each morning and, if I have an evening assignment, skip dinner. Alternative Saturdays will be different with football match reporting."

"Very confusing," she said. "I'll call you in the morning and knock on your door if you don't answer. You have an extra blanket on your bed because it's still cold."

I fell asleep almost as soon as my head hit the pillow and woke only to the knock my landlady had promised. "Time to rise and shine," she alerted me. "Breakfast ready. Come and get it!"

We enjoyed bacon and eggs, and she told me where to catch the bus and how much to pay. It worked out. In 30 minutes, I was again in Derby town center. My bus trip, however, had convinced me to find a downtown flat rather than lodge in a suburb and risk missing buses. Derby, at first sight, appeared nondescript, with little to photograph except the *Evening Telegraph* office dome, to the extent I was tempted to pop into a cinema to see Peter Sellers play an Indian doctor opposite Sophia Loren as his patient. I picked up the weekly *Advertiser* newspaper and over coffee in a café, scanned the small ads. There was room with kitchen for rent at 436 Uttoxeter Road and, according to my map, well within walking distance of work. Max had mentioned it was a good street to find a flat.

I found Uttoxeter Road fairly busy with cars and trucks plying its two traffic lanes. On the plus side, a 440-yard running track lay like a green oasis opposite my targeted flat. A small sign said the track was private property, used by students of Derby Teacher Training College and the University of Derby. That immediately brought Andrea to mind. Might she be one that used the running track? Clearly her college was located nearby. A passer-by indicated it was further up Uttoxeter Road on the right-hand side. I had little else to do, so I walked up the road to find a big grey college building, surrounded by a grey wall with a teacher training college sign at the entrance.

So, this was the college Andrea attended. Maybe she boarded in a college dorm. I rejected that on remembering what Mike had told me. I thought that if I were to take the flat down the road, I might see or meet her on the sidewalk. And, if I could knock Mike's eye out, I'd be there for her. There would also be lots of other female student teachers for me to study. I could easily pass as a Derby University student when using the running track. With those promising thoughts flashing through my mind, I retraced my steps and rang the doorbell of the house with the room to rent.

A bespectacled young woman came to the door. "Yes?" she asked.

"I've come about the room and kitchen you advertise in the newspaper."

"Dad!" she turned inward. "Someone about the upstairs room."

Her father was burly and grey haired, with an accent that my ears and mind had no difficulty placing. "Come on in," he said. "I'll show you the room. There's a nice kitchen if you don't mind sharing with another lodger. The two of you determine the reasonable rent we charge."

The room looked out over a back garden bordered with flowers, overlooked by a tall linden tree. I thought how quiet and cozy the room was compared with the noise and cold on the road outside. The small kitchen had a fridge, stove, kettle, cupboards, other utensils and a side view of the garden. "This will suit me," I assured him without ado. "I'm here in Derby to work for the *Telegraph*."

"My name is Joe Bowers," he said. "You met my daughter Grace. You are…?"

"Bill Fairbairn. Just moved to Derby from the northeast. I like the flat, but I can't move in for a week, since I must give notice at my temporary Mickleover lodgings that I find too far from my work. I can put down a deposit."

"That won't be necessary. We'll talk about rent when you move in. My wife knows how much, but I can't remember. We'll discuss it when you arrive. I'll give you our telephone number, which is in the directory under J. W. Bowers. You'll be glad to know you can easily walk to the *Telegraph* office from here. What job do you have at the newspaper?"

"I start on Monday as a reporter."

"Blimey! I might be reading your articles. We get the newspaper. Just let me tell you, there is no room for a parked car here and we appreciate as much silence as possible. You won't be clattering away at night on a typewriter, will you? We have enough noise from the traffic."

I know not what got into me but, off the top of my head to break a silence, I asked him: "What do you think of the stabbing of Martin Luther King?"

He took time to reply: "Strange you ask me that. I think King is about the only sane man in America. Well, blimey, he nearly died being stabbed while only signing his book."

"You use the word blimey like a Londoner."

"I'm a Cockney! I detect a Scottish accent in you. I came to Derby from London 10 years ago to work as an engineer at Rolls-Royce. I'm retired now. My wife is a Londoner too. Stay for lunch and meet her and my daughter. My missus was about to serve when you rang the bell. There's room for you at the table."

"Well, I already ate and you must be anxious to get to the table before the food is cold."

"Okay. Hold on. Here's my old business card so we can stay in touch."

Chapter 8

First Assignment

Madeline Malone was not at all put out, when I told her next morning that I had decided to lodge nearer my work.

"I understand," she said. "In fact, use my phone and make certain of the flat. Your convoluted work hours as a reporter are too complicated anyway."

"If you're sure, then I'll give you a week's rent in lieu of not living up to what we both had agreed."

"No, no, no! Just make your new arrangements final and pay me for the weekend. You can't wait a moment longer. You start work tomorrow."

Joe Bowers was not surprised when I phoned. "You're coming tonight and you start work tomorrow. Your room is ready. Food is your concern. I'll ask my wife to look after your supper tonight, since you can't fill the larder on a Sunday. Your fellow lodger is visiting his folk at Melton Mobray and may be back tomorrow. He shares the kitchen at the same three pounds a week."

Before darkness I had moved in. After warming up with a cup of tea and enjoying a steak pie left in the kitchen, I enjoyed a full night's sleep. Was I ready to take on the *Derby Evening Telegraph* in the morning? It felt like I was trying to climb that dome down town.

The *Telegraph* was ready for me that morning! I walked into the newsroom as Max was putting down the phone. I also walked direct into my first assignment. My chair was at a long desk with several typewriters on it. Max marched straight over saying I was first to arrive except for himself, and that a photographer was waiting with a car in the garage downstairs to drive me to cover a suburban house fire. "I know it's your first day. Grab a notebook and pencil from the cupboard. Talk to the photographer about what he knows of the fire. Phone in the story to catch the first edition at noon. Here's the number in case you don't have it. We need story and photos for the afternoon paper. So, go. Now!"

Photographer Alan Black drove too fast for my liking, but he knew the city well. Firemen were hosing water downward from a hole in the roof of the house, sending smoke up when we arrived. Two police cars were lined up beside the fire engine.

Black snapped pictures of the firemen above the roof. I identified myself to a fireman far too involved to do anything for me, except point out his fire chief sitting in one of two fire trucks by then lined up. I took in the scene and with notebook in hand, stepped over fire hoses, and identifying myself, asked the fire chief to tell me the story behind the fire.

"What happened?" you ask. "Well, an elderly couple came home from a holiday late last night, and the husband plugged a block heater into his car beside the house. We believe that gadget caused the fire that ruined car, kitchen and roof, since the firemen had to go through the roof to get to the seat of the fire. Those block heaters are new on the market you know. The occupants were lucky. A fellow whose first name is Dave, cycling to his work at the Derby Athletic Club, noticed smoke. He banged on the door and roused an elderly lady. She had been half asleep upstairs and apparently could hardly hold the phone never mind make a fire call. She managed to rouse her husband upstairs. With great presence of mind, Dave rushed the two out of the house in their robes and phoned the fire brigade."

"I tell you," the fire chief stressed. "They could have been smoked out of existence."

Pointing to the other side of the street, he added: "The couple are standing over there with neighbors who gave them clothes. I guess the hero for your story cycled off to work before you and I got here. "

The fire victims were hardly able to tell me a thing. Their neighbors motioned me away as if I was about to give them heart attacks. They gave me the couple's names and that did help. I crossed the street to my photographer and suggested he take a picture of the bedraggled pair. "After that, how much longer do you think I need to be here?" he asked.

Alan Black said that with the paper's deadline approaching, he was happy with the photographs he had taken. I asked him if he knew where the Derby Athletic Club was located. "I once used it," he replied. "What's the interest there?"

"The man who raised the alarm and saved the lives of that couple you just photographed works there. The fire chief called him a hero. We should drive to the club and photograph him. But, wait, I forgot to get the chief's name and station. I'll be back in a minute."

The commotion had left me nervous. I again hopped over hoses and dodged firemen to find the chief still in his truck. He gave me his name and phone number. "I'm 90 per cent sure the block heater started a fire in the car's engine that spread to the house. It's rare. We're on top of it now though. You can quote me saying we were on top of it in an hour. Half an hour late and that house would have been lost, and the couple in bed, dead. I have Dave's full name now. It's Dave Bradley of the Derby Athletic Club."

Alan and I were outside the club's entrance in 20 minutes after I told him what the chief said. We approached the main desk inside asking for Bradley. He turned out to be the membership manager sitting in a corner office opposite the member entry desk. I introduced the two of us explaining we were from the *Telegraph* covering the fire at Overbrook Crescent. "You raised the alarm. How come?"

"I saw smoke as I passed on my bicycle at 7:30. I banged on the door, rousing an elderly woman dazed by smoke and hardly knowing what was going on. She said her husband was upstairs in bed asleep, so I went up, pulled him out and down the stairs, before I filed them both pretty groggy, outside into the fresh air. I then phoned the fire brigade from a number I could hardly see on the fridge. Are they okay?"

"You probably saved their lives. Your name is Dave Bradley and you're membership manager here. Right? What else can you tell us?"

"Only that two fire engines arrived and neighbors came out with clothes and coffee to look after the couple. I had to get to work. There was no need for me to stick around. Fire crews were already hosing down the house when I left, leaving my name and place of work, that a fireman confirmed on the phone here just a half hour ago."

"Dave, we need a quick photo of you," Alan appealed. "I'll take it out in the gym in front of the fitness machines."

"Sure."

After a short experiment with light and subject, Alan shot it. We thanked Dave and returned to his office.

Alan curiously asked: "Are you by any chance the Dave Bradley who played football for Derby County about five years ago?"

"You have a good memory," Dave replied. "I had a short season in professional football. I scored a couple of goals for Derby. I played on the right wing for half a season, before a knee injury took me out of the game."

Alan, whose news judgment was impressing me more and more, turned to me: "I should get back to the office fast now, to develop and print my photos. Are you coming or phoning your story from here? I can pick you up later if you wish." I elected to stay, since proximity to the hero of the story would allow me to record further of his quotes. I said to Dave that I had a deadline and he responded saying I could use his phone, desk and typewriter. I thanked him, revealed it was my first day of work for the *Telegraph*, and sat down at his desk asking what more he could tell me about his personal lifestyle.

He disclosed that his injured knee was much better, and that he was refereeing junior league football hoping he might rise in rank with the help of his daily training schedule at the club and a football association test. With that and more in my notebook, I typed up and phoned in my story.

The front-page headline that afternoon, along with his picture, was *Former Derby County winger a fire hero.* What a start for me on the *Telegraph!* How much more experience as a reporter would come my way? This wasn't just newsboy stuff. It was a lot bigger than the trivial rat-up-a-farmer's-trousers story I had filed in Morpeth. It was front page. The real McCoy!

I covered a fire every three or so weeks as time passed in Derby, and there were regular Belper Town Football Club match reports to phone into the office, at half and full-times, on alternative Saturday afternoons.

My news editor favored me with guest tickets to the Locarno Dance Hall, to cover the fun there. This prompted me to write a story about Derby's lovely young women. One, in particular, I danced with and afterwards walked home. She told me of some great places to hike in the Peak District of Derbyshire. When that story was published, it had my *Derby Advertiser* rival telling me, he and his mates had used my story's photograph as a target for a game of darts. But that didn't rile this newsboy!

Band leader Ray McVay brought a Glenn Miller type orchestra to the Locarno. I loved the guy's music, until one night he turned the spotlight on me: "Jock, the reporter, covering the dance." The shy Scots-born lass I was dancing with was turned off. I tried to explain it was not my doing. Some silly things always came between me and my female choices.

Ray was closely linked to a tragedy that gained me a headline in the *Telegraph*. His life was saved by a last-minute decision to swap transport with American rock 'n roller Eddie Cochran. Ray was to have been in the taxi that crashed, killing the 21-year-old Cochran. He had swapped his taxi for a car.

Then, into the Derby area in late 1958, came pop singer 19-year-old Cliff Richard. I interviewed the up-and-coming star who, with a mix of religion and rock 'n roll, was giving English parents mixed warnings to look after their daughters. I learned that he was about to travel to do a concert in South Africa, so I asked him if he would sing to segregated audiences. He didn't know what to say, so his producer, Harry Welch, answering for him, said he would do so. The result was a question and answer cover story, prophetically headed: *Roses all the way for Cliff Richard.*

My newspaper editor zeroed in on a possible feature series, *Gossip from the Estates*, and I was assigned as its columnist. Every story was a family affair, since there were lots of young wives and even children to interview once a week while their husbands were working. I covered every housing estate in suburban Derby for the six-week series.

When reporting a Belper Town football match, heavy rain came down and the match cancelled. I phoned Max saying I was free to cover the Women's Rural Institute garden fete in Belper that afternoon that had not been put off by the rain. Doing so would save from the rain Elizabeth, a sprightly reporter whom I could hardly keep my eye off in the office. I made progress when she told me the news editor had let her off work early that rainy Saturday, thanks to me. When she complimented me on my Cliff Richard story, I mentioned that in becoming a reporter she had beat the gender odds.

Elizabeth played along with my ploy that when the office was not too busy, some mornings I would rise from my desk, stretch my arms, and exit the newsroom. Elizabeth would follow and together we would go for a quick coffee and a romantic chat. We had to end this innocent affair when the penny dropped on the news editor and it did not do me or her any good. I squandered chances of a closer relationship with Elizabeth. Keeping a girlfriend was hard to accomplish.

What convinced me that *Gender times they were a Changin'*, came when Andrea's mother's replacement in the cafeteria was a young man! A man had come into the *Telegraph's* café and there were two women in the newsroom.

Surprise, surprise! Mike Charles approaches me in the corridor with a proposition. He is taking Andrea to the cinema the following weekend and she has a young woman friend from her college staying the weekend with her. Would I like to make up a foursome? If so he would pick me up in his car at my digs.

So there we were, Mike with Andrea, me with physical training student teacher Marian, off to see the movie *Hans Christian Anderson* starring Danny Kaye. Marian wasn't tall and slim like Andrea, but stocky, befitting a gym teacher. The film was perfect for holding hands. I actually closed on her lips in the sultry darkness, but her responses were so-so. As were mine.

On the car ride back to Andrea's home, we sat well apart in the back seat, although at one turn my hand went down on hers and our eyes met momentarily in the dim light. Mike parked his car some distance from Andrea's home, so we walked through a small park then stopped under a chestnut tree in the moonlight.

In a flash, Andrea was in Mike's arms. They sucked each other's mouth like, I thought, thirsty donkeys. I already considered him a sex fiend, and jealously saw she was enjoying his advances. I noticed that Marian had her eyes stuck on Mike. The kissing went on for five minutes within our sight under the moon.

When their lips finally parted, his right hand went further down to her bum and I imagined he pulled her to his penis, thankfully, in my opinion, inside his pants. It was a warm evening and she, in a thin dress, stood there wiggling her hips right before my very eyes.

Marian and I stood gaping. I was wishing I had Andrea in my arms, and obviously both Marian and Andrea were dazzled by Mike. From my years gaining experience as newsboy, printer, soldier, columnist and reporter, I had missed out on women. And maybe Marian had missed out on men while training to be a teacher at a college for young women.

Chapter 9
"Best provincial newspaper in England"

After four years in Derby I applied for a sub-editor's (desk editor as they say in America) job on the *Sheffield Telegraph*. The editor was a gruff old fellow who, I think somewhat against his better judgment, offered me the position that meant I was earning more than one thousand pounds a year. What a change from my five shillings a week delivering newspapers! Derby news editor Max congratulated me on a good move. I celebrated with a going-away party for my colleagues at a local pub, before next day catching the northbound train to the steel city.

A place to lodge was again first priority. Residing in downtown Sheffield was out of the question because of pollution. Instead, I found lodgings out of the city near the Upper Derwent Valley area of the Peak District and commuted to work by bus in the late afternoon and walked or ran back home in the early hours.

The craft of editing, headline writing and layout was what I hoped to master. I messed up shortly after starting. The story I had to edit and headline was about the invention of a dog lead that allowed a long extension. My mistake was to catchword the story "lead." The catchword system of that day and age in journalism, identified numbered pages of a typed story as they proceeded, separated for speed, through different linotype operators to proof readers and almost to the printed page. Use of the catchword "lead" misled the printers into assuming the story was the main lead story for the front page. And it nearly landed there! The editor helping the printers on the stone was mad as a March hare. Was I ever embarrassed!

Troublesome were two colleagues sitting smoking pipes on either side of me. This inflicted on me eye sties–inflamed swelling on an eyelid–and handicapped my work. Not only did they smoke, but they relished their pipes, suggesting I should smoke too. I never complained. Smoking in newsrooms was part of the job in movies. But it was affecting my eyes and career.

Troubling, too, were two fellow Irish boarders who rather picked on me, I believe, because I worked on the *Telegraph*, which never missed a chance to editorially condemn the Irish Troubles, as they were termed in relation to Britain's governance of Northern Ireland. The Irish pair pinned this anti-Irish attitude on me.

The Sheffield Telegraph was voted Best English Provincial Morning Newspaper of 1960, the year I was on the desk. Part of the reason was a series of front page stories it fearlessly ran on police brutality. I was proud of the award since I had written some of the headlines. Finally, after nine months of eye sties I confronted my editor. My news shocked him. I had been offered a desk editor's job on *The Rhodesia Herald* in the British colony of Southern Rhodesia and would be leaving the *Telegraph* in a month.

"To Africa?" He was taken aback, to the extent that he told me I still had a lot to learn about journalism and asking me critically if I thought Africa a good place to learn. He said Southern Rhodesia was at least a better choice than Northern Rhodesia, where he said black revolution was in the air and whites being harassed by blacks in the name of fighting for independence from Britain.

When the editor urged me to procrastinate on Africa, I told him in similar high tone that the dye was cast and I had crossed the Rubicon. I said that the credence of his view, of the peaceful south and dangerous north in the two federated African countries, was shaky to me, but I admitted his words of warning made me wonder what faced me in, what he had termed, darkest Africa.

Before flying to Africa, I visited London's West Finchley, where my grandfather's brother, impresario T.C. Fairbairn, lived with his two sons. I enjoyed *Oh, what a lovely war* at a London cinema. Next day I walked miles in the heat to find Karl Marx's grave in Highgate Cemetery. I sailed up the Thames to Kew Gardens and Richmond. Lines written on a board in Richmond Park, commemorating the poet James Thomson (1700-1748) who was born near my home town of Jedburgh, inspired me:

Ye who from London's smoke and turmoil fly,
To seek a purer air and brighter sky
Think of the Bard who dwelt in yonder dell
Who sang so sweetly what he loved so well
Think, as ye gaze on these luxuriant bowers

Here Thompson loved the sunshine and the flowers.

I thought to myself that his first line on fleeing from smoke was exactly what I was about to do.

I had only the scantiest understanding of Africa from Trevor Huddleston's *Naught for Your Comfort*, so I had to learn fast. And where better than at the open-door London School of Oriental and African Studies, if for only two weeks.

Chapter 10
Part II
Africa at First Sight

The elderly *Rhodesia Herald* editor introduced himself as William, my namesake, when I found my way to his office before starting work. He called me over to his window overlooking the main street in Salisbury. People of all skin colors were walking by and he wondered what I thought of that.

"Diverse in the extreme to eyes direct from white Scotland," I responded not knowing what else to say.

"Soon, near all of us will have grades of color in our skins here," he said. "It's inevitable. Does that bother you?"

"Not a bit, since it will likely happen after I'm dead."

"Really? Don't you know that there are six million black people here in Rhodesia and about 166,000 whites who virtually rule them? Does that not convince you of imminent change?"

"It tells me that white rule cannot go on forever."

With that he shook hands with me and curtailed our talk. I went off to start work at the editing desk. I was impressed by my editor, but soon realized that his *Rhodesia Herald* was not staffed to produce a really good newspaper or improve my skill as a journalist, as my Sheffield editor had warned me.

Shouts for tea directed at African canteen boys, almost every half hour from the desk, distracted from good editing. Desk editors also filled the room with tobacco smoke, partly because the colony's white farmers grew and exported tobacco leaves that made them rich through cheap African farm labor. The smoking inside and the invigorating clean air outside soon had me agitating for a reporter's job. I figured I wouldn't learn much about the country stuck inside on the desk. Tobacco smoke seemed to have followed me from Sheffield to Africa.

On the other hand, when outside, the sweet scent of jacaranda and hibiscus filled up my senses when walking to work these first evenings. I habitually stopped to view a statue of Cecil John Rhodes at the head of Jameson Avenue. My studies in London had made me disapprove of self-serving colonial power seekers like English hero Rhodes and Scotsman Jameson. I had read, at the London School of Oriental and African Studies, a minority view that they had been imperialists to the core, and from a long-term standpoint, had done little real good for the majority of African people.

I purchased early the necessary bush hat and sunglasses. Sleeping with only a cotton sheet covering me on warm nights, enticed me into dreaming, with a pillow in my arms, that I had rented a flat and hired a black servant. I had chatted with a hotel contender before withering looks from white fellow residents, and a warning from the manager alerted me to avoid any black-white romantic relationship in narrow-minded Southern Rhodesia.

The *Rhodesia Herald*, with stories I had headlined, arrived regularly at my hotel room in the early hours, delivered by a black-skinned newsboy as I had once been with a white skin. On ending work after the midnight deadline, I had to climb over black Africans dozing or fast asleep on the staircase, waiting to deliver the printed papers. Had I been one of them, I likely would have been a newsboy until I died.

My newspaper management had allowed me two first weeks of residence in the unbelievably well-named White's Hotel. The bedroom maids and cleaning staff were those I had been warned not to get too friendly with. *Never the twain shall truly meet* had resounded in my mind, as white residents after dinner were served drinks by black waiters, while playing or watching carpet bowling on a squared off hallway floor near the hotel entrance lobby.

I watched this throwback to indoor games played privately by rich people in Britain, before television and before bingo for the less well-off became widespread public leisure pursuits. Neither bingo nor television had yet arrived in Africa. I contrasted the segregation in Rhodesia to the increasingly multi-cultural world overseas. Where, after dark I asked myself, were the country's vast majority of black people that the editor had referred to? Certainly not in my hotel, nightclubs or on quiet city streets after 6 p.m. Not on the *Rhodesia Herald* editing desk or in its newsroom. A few served tea and coffee in the canteen, swept the floors, and at least a score delivered the newspaper throughout the city after midnight.

I increasingly found that the undeniable architectural beauty of the city and its parks were skin deep. I realized that cinemas and restaurants were racially segregated, municipal swimming pools for whites only, and separate facilities served people at government post offices and in most other public places. In hospitals, white nurses were superior to colored or black assistants. Schools and pupils were almost all segregated.

Those threatening the predominantly white government's racial laws, were kept firmly in place. It seemed as though the colony's few black African members of the legislature, were government threatening monsters rather than timid academics. It took only a week in Salisbury for me to know that Africans working in the city by day, hustled off to their homes in black townships of Harare and Highfield before sunset.

As the weeks passed, I realized that staying in power was the objective of white rulers. This through power, control of labor, land and mineral resources. The rub for the whites was that though white emigration to Africa was rising, so, too, was African nationalism. Some black Africans had served Britain in World War II, just as had white Rhodesians and South Africans fought for Britain and had now found this paradise overseas for themselves to virtually rule. The black veteran, home to Africa after the war, sought a fairer deal from Britain. This former newsboy secretly pledged within to do what he could to help them. It broke my heart knowing that had I been born black in Rhodesia, I likely would never have been more than a newsboy. The challenge was to peacefully transgress white colonial rule when safe to do so. I first had to escape editing the news and be transferred to the less well-paid job of reporting the news.

The front-page *Rhodesia Herald* story that did most to secretly turn me native, was mind-shocking racism that had occurred before I had landed in the colony. An African had tried to win an order in court, allowing people of all races to use the Salisbury public swimming pool. He took the city to court and won his case. But he did not succeed in gaining the right for native Africans to swim in the public pool. The city closed down the pool until authorities could pass another law keeping it for whites only.

Terence Ranger, a professor at the University of Rhodesia and Nyasaland, protested on the edge of the pool. He was thrown in, clad in his suit, after telling white Rhodesian rugby players that blacks should be allowed in the pool they were using.

A newspaper clipping of a photo I came across in the *Rhodesia Herald's* library had the heading:

Well dressed and dripping

I wondered if any headline writer had been reprimanded for such cruel words about a brave protester against racism. It occurred to me that the photograph might have been set up, but I dared not breathe a word of it. I rightly predicted that Ranger was setting himself up for deportation, when next he led an African freedom march through the city center. As a journalist, I stayed out of the fray while convincing my editor that I would be more valuable as a day-time reporter. The switch was made!

Suspicion that I was soft on black Africans, was soon revealed by the tough newsroom editor who controlled the assignment diary. His suspicion of my black partisanship actually worked in my favor. I was assigned northward to Lusaka to cover prospective legislative elections in Northern Rhodesia, and to freelance on other stories particularly around a certain upstart, Kenneth Kaunda, who was making ground fast as a black agitator for majority rule.

My newspaper's editor briefed me that it was a roving assignment for the length of the election campaign, but longer if I covered well what stories I could find. To do so, I would have access to my salary and expenses at the Standard Bank in Lusaka.

Studying the northern situation by chance, I came across the tiniest of filler reports telling me that in Salisbury, two years previous, a young Northern Rhodesian African by the name of Yotham Muleya, had won a three-mile race in a time of 14 minutes and 30 seconds against top distance British runner Gordon Pirie. It wasn't the best of times, but it was a Rhodesian record. Being a half-assed athlete myself, I sensed a good story that in Britain I had missed and wondered why it had not come to my awareness. I knew the three-mile world record was 13:10:08 so his time was not fast. But he had outran a champion of mine.

I was as curious as any journalist trained in Britain could be. I went on to learn that black athletes were, on the whole, banned from membership of sporting clubs that were confined to whites in Rhodesia. Such rote rules denied them selection for the Olympic Games, no matter their ability.

I detected a kink in the armor of segregation, when on the BBC radio, another international British distance record holder voiced plans to run in African destinations including Southern Rhodesia.

Surely, he would want to compete against the best black or white runners.

How could I exploit this situation? The Northern Rhodesian black runner who had outrun Gordon Pirie intrigued me. I packed a bag and purchased a small upright Ford to drive early to Northern Rhodesia. I planned to visit the Mudukulu village, where I understood Yotham Muleya lived. My mind even grappled with a book, featuring a black runner who had broken the color barrier in track and field in southern Africa.

Chapter 11
Peace at a High Price

Few people but the villagers knew much about the Mudukulu I was heading for. The village would be unknown to even motorists who passed within 20 kilometers in their cars, on way to the spectacular tourist destination of Livingstone, where the Zambezi splashes furiously over the Victoria Falls. They would rarely even see the main road turnoff I, myself, nearly missed, while distractedly pondering over what history of Africa I had learned, during my so far short time in Southern Rhodesia and from research at the School of Oriental and African Studies in London.

Road, rail and river lines, in the area of what was the British Protectorate of Northern Rhodesia, converge at the Victoria Falls. A statue of the town's namesake, 19th century Scottish explorer and missionary David Livingstone, symbolically watches the torrent splash down. Books had told me, Livingstone had seen more of Africa in one day than millions of British people in their whole lives.

Tar-strip automobile travelers like me, caught near or distant picture postcard glimpses of African villages while crossing into Northern Rhodesia. Adventurers were usually bound north on safari or returning south, to what they regarded as the civilized white Rhodesian bulwark of a Central African Federation, that under minority white leadership was destined, by default, to revert to three separate countries.

I regretted what little history I knew of French, Portuguese, British, German, Spanish, Italian and Belgian sovereignty over different African mainland or island. I knew that some land takeovers went back a century, to when soldiers and pioneers moved in at the native African human expense. The scramble for riches rendered millions of Africans second-class in their homeland. Life was sweet in Rhodesia for British and other expatriates like me. I reflected that it was even sweeter for the long-time settled white Rhodesians, who went out of their way to teach newcomers like myself, the ropes in dealing with a growing number of black agitators for self-progress and even liberation.

As I said, the rub for the settlers was that though white immigration into Africa had risen after World War II, so too had African nationalism. *"Uhuru!"* in Kenya, echoed the shout of *"Kwacha!"* in Northern Rhodesia. The shouts grew louder as contemporary lions of African independence Jomo Kenyatta, Julius Nyerere, Hastings Banda and Kenneth Kaunda came to the fore in Kenya, Tanganyika, Nyasaland and Northern Rhodesia respectively. While in Southern Rhodesia, Joshua Nkoma, soon Robert Mugabe, and in South Africa, Nelson Mandela, would also fight white minority rule.

World War II had taken black African soldiers to British Somaliland, Ethiopia, Burma and a few to Britain itself. Some had returned post-war to their homeland, seeking a freedom they saw as just reward. Their frontline foe in Southern Rhodesia, were the Rhodesian colonists who had taken over the country the Africans sought to call Zimbabwe.

As I travelled the long African road, my mind was fixed on colonialism's devastating effect on native people. Veering off the main road and nearly toppling my car, I steered along a steep, dusty, narrow track, climbing as instructed, past a Sikalongo Mission sign and glimpsing the Zambezi Valley below. After a long haul and a few turns, I found myself descending what seemed to be the same track and wondering if I was altogether on the wrong hillside.

My upright Ford, purchased from a school headmistress in Salisbury, creaked tortuously, its tires grinding the stony sand surface and raising a cloud of dust. I dreaded being stranded with a puncture in the African bush. The Muchinga mountain range is one great hill after great hill, forming a short side of the Great Rift Valley running down through half of Africa. I knew of high points further north that topped 4,000 meters and I imagined I might be driving on one of them.

I grounded the brake pedal on seeing a native working alone in a field. I thought that maybe he was finding my Scottish accent disconcerting when, from the car, I shouted for directions. Alighting to ask closer and more politely was an act of faith. Machetes and knives scare me. I prayed that the panga he carried was a tool, before asking: "Please, where do I find Mudukulu?"

I slowly asked a third time. He stared at me as if I were the ghost of Gregory Peck come down from Kilimanjaro. After a poignant pause, he directed me to what turned out to be maybe a 1,200-foot high plateau. I backed away when, with upraised panga, he pointed out my direction.

I should have been grateful, because soon I could see mud huts and on passing them, Africans staring at me. Perspiration and apprehension almost overcame me before I was guided to the Muleya home by a friendly black man.

Yotham's father, Emmanuel, and his uncle Benjamin, awaited me by virtue of a message I imagined had been delivered in a cleft stick from Lusaka. They welcomed me with handshakes and cups of tea, but after I had explained the reason for my visit, both shook their heads. With drawn faces they led me to a large plaque on a nearby hillside. To my dismay, it commemorated the death, in America, of Yotham Muleya.

The runner I had envisioned making multi-racial sports history through me, his would-be chronicler, was no longer with us. Nothing I had found in my newspaper's library had recorded his death.

"We'll tell you what happened," Benjamin said after a moment's silence.

"First tell me about yourselves," I insisted, hoping to still find a story *somewhere.*

Both men are tall, greyish haired and transparently intelligent, though Emmanuel is slower to talk. The fact that the two were boys, when white men first appeared in numbers in Northern Rhodesia, interested me. I knew white settlers had reluctantly supported Britain legislating Northern Rhodesia, a protectorate rather than a British colony like Southern Rhodesia. I soon learned Emmanuel had read articles and seen maps as he convalesced in Britain, from injury suffered in Burma with the 1st Battalion Northern Rhodesian Regiment attached to the British Army. His first duties had been as server in the officers' mess, before going forward behind enemy lines in a fighting platoon. His convalescence in Britain from injury, had gained him knowledge of Africa's place in a British Empire, where it was said the sun never set.

Benjamin, on the other hand, had worldly exposure from an Episcopalian Church ministerial exchange in Boston, America.

From a bad start, I had hit pay dirt and decided to find out as much as I could while the going was good. I might never return to Mudukulu. I had risked driving there in a second-hand car with worn tires. I had faced an upright panga from two yards. The truth of Yotham's death had dealt me a blow. This was not small-town Scotland, even if Scotland could boast of native son David

Livingstone's Africa adventures and the good he had done. The two men I was interviewing were Africans of singular experience.

Emmanuel had once been the taller and stronger. He recalled years of work, helped by his wife and Benjamin, in clothing and feeding the family on crops grown and stored in the village granary or sold to the trader. This had sapped strength left from Emmanuel's war duties as a private soldier on call as mess server, trench digger, emergency regimental dispatch carrier, corporal and casualty.

I recognized that the World War I duty of company runner had spilled over to World War II in Burma, where unorthodox British strategy in fighting the Japanese, set Emmanuel on a voluntary dash through monsoon rain and rifle fire, to save soldiers cut off from base supplies and transport, and rewarded him with promotion to corporal.

His younger son, Yotham, was born in the 1945 summer of victory for the British Empire and its American and Russian allies, over Germany and Italy and the autumn defeat of Japan. The year 1945 was for some countries the best of bad years, and for others, the worst. Germany and Japan may have been defeated, but it took Britain a decade to pay back war loans from America, and its people to profit from victory.

I learned that when Emmanuel was a boy, formal education was unknown in Mudukulu and later reasoned that his sons had inherited ability from a father's unschooled insights and an old soldier's guile. Added to their education were lessons from Benjamin, whose study of theology in America had taught him harsh white power stretching from Washington, even into the world of sport. Benjamin noted in conversation that in 1830 there were more than two million black slaves and 320,000 free blacks in America.

I turned to Yotham's mother Nandi, a short woman with strong legs that, I conjectured, she had passed on to her children. During wartime, Nandi had regularly walked the 15 miles to Mukabwa trading station for food, matches, pots and pans, soap and lamp wicks, and she still did. The trading station sold luxuries beyond the staples villagers grew in Mudukulu fields.

"You must have trekked how many miles?"

"I can't count how many, but I managed crops and hens when my husband was at war."

I boldly asked *her* what had had happened to Yotham.

"He was killed in a car crash," she said. "He was in America on a university sports scholarship. Two were killed on way to compete in a race. The other was a Rhodesian policeman and runner. They were in a car. My husband can tell you more of how we found out. Or Benjamin, who was never keen on Yotham going to America in the first place."

Darkness was falling and as I rose to shake hands with family members, Nandi disappeared for a moment, returning with a brown bag and in it, six eggs. "Please take this gift," she said.

I bade farewell to all the unseen generous people like Nandi, living hidden in the hills of Northern Rhodesia, and drove off in the quickly descending darkness.

As far as writing a book was concerned, I had so far wasted my time. Yet, I had absorbed a great deal of knowledge to help a journalist so new to Africa.

Chapter 12
Power Brokers

I had five more days before my election-campaign assignment was due to start.

I used some of the time to confirm that the Muleyas were indeed of the Tonga tribe, and that their people were at home in the hills above the Zambezi and in the valley when Livingstone explored the area in 1855. Some of their ancestors had trekked north from South Africa in the early 19th century to escape Shaka's warlike Zulu empire. The peaceful Tonga people had lost traditions of earlier homelands, but stories of their movement north and also from the east had survived.

Under imperialist Cecil Rhodes's British South Africa Company (BSAC), to which the British government in 1889 handed over administration of African lands beyond the southern Limpopo River, native Africans lost more freedom. Nevertheless, Britain made Southern Rhodesia a BSAC chartered territory. Its native inhabitants had peace at a price and white settlers continued to take the best land, seek out minerals and curtail their liberty. I also learned the wider history of Britain seeking to prevent Portuguese expansion in the southeast by taking back administration of Southern Rhodesia in 1923, proclaiming Northern Rhodesia a protectorate in which African interests would be paramount. At the same time, Britain legislated Southern Rhodesia a self-governing colony with native affairs under British surveillance and its white colonial prime minister accepted at imperial summits.

British and South African settlers became so powerful in the Northern Rhodesian protectorate and the Southern Rhodesian colony, that effectively they ruled the south and sought to rule the north through federation. As the years passed, the legislated idea that Africans would eventually rule their country of Northern Rhodesia was opposed by the sons and grandsons of the white pioneers. Many were by then farmers, shop owners, mine overseers, politicians and bankers, right up to prime ministers living comfortably with black servants at the heart of their own economy. A few became powerful publishers of newspapers like mine, often with head offices in South Africa, and whose expatriate staff of journalists influenced the world in their own way.

As a journalist, I had met some of the power brokers after flying into Salisbury. They were not to be trifled with from land ownership, mineral and tobacco production, and exports, to their opposition against majority rule in their God-given land of Rhodesia.

What a contrast Mudukulu! Fertile land below the village had been legislated to white ownership. The land high in the hills was unproductive. This meant that frustrated black men were leaving villages to dig for copper under white supervision and benefits. They worked near the Copperbelt towns of Kitwe and Ndola, hardly aware that those towns bordered war-torn Katanga, a mineral-rich Congo province, effectively ruled by breakaway Premier Moise Tshombe and Belgian settlers when I was there. Tshombe was the man who threw democratically elected Congolese Prime Minister Patrice Lumumba's remains into the scrap heap of history.

Before his sorry end, Lumumba had led a left-wing government that had angered not only Katanga's breakaway ruler Tshombe in Elizabethville but also governments in Brussels and Washington.

I was aware that modern methods of exploiting mineral deposits had attracted European overseers to Katanga and Northern Rhodesia mines. Where the technology left off, blacks dug long and deep, to benefit white expatriates and enrich white South African mine owners and shareholders. Some black miners sent paltry wages home to families they had left behind. Little accommodation was afforded wives and children at Copperbelt mines. Their family life was discounted, their lives devalued on the mineral resource export line to Europe and America.

Africans were also traveling south by train from Northern Rhodesia through Southern Rhodesia, to flourishing gold and diamond mines in South Africa. There they met official racism under government apartheid laws. From parks to streets, separate facilities kept whites and blacks apart. Many who had settled in Johannesburg townships such as Soweto, never returned home. Many a family never knew what had happened to local men who disappeared into Harry Oppenheimer's Anglo-American company gold mines. And the West termed Oppenheimer a progressive!

I revisited Mudukulu to hear Benjamin again touch on his life as a young black preacher, who had tried to win a 10-mile race at the wrong time and place in America.

While attending religious school in Boston, he had learned more than I knew of the harsh treatment of black people in the United States and its history of slavery in the Deep South. He also knew a bit about the counterpart racial oppression in South Africa.

I met his nephew Peter, home from the Copperbelt for a few days with money to help his parents. He was using his brief time in the village to work the land. He came from the fields that first day of my second visit, to a supper I shared with the family. Nandi had cooked a chicken. Soon, Benjamin had offered me a bed in his hut and was telling me about family life in Mudukulu.

I learned that Benjamin had regarded Peter as a farm boy to the bone, but that Peter had other ideas. He had soon left home lured by earnings from Copperbelt mines. Peter's decision to leave had disappointed Benjamin. He recalled the day Yotham's brotherly support of Peter's right to decide his own future had angered him.

Chapter 13
All That Glitters

"Dig like an ant in the mines?" Yotham overheard his Uncle Benjamin put the question to his brother Peter, crouched silently at the table in his father's hut, his face buried in his big hands. It was not the first time Benjamin had lectured Peter and Yotham. To Benjamin's discomfort, Yotham intervened: "I think it a good idea to earn money in the mines. Peter may come home with some of the gold."

"Gold? It's not gold," Benjamin retorted. "Don't you know the difference between copper and gold? What would *you* do with gold? You are saying it is good for Peter to leave the village where he is needed. Good, you say. Good to return with a cheap watch and a smart suit, and God knows what ideas? Going off never to return maybe. Is that good? It is good for the mine managers north, where the copper is, and south, where the gold is, and good in both cases for their masters overseas. It is not good for Mudukulu. And Peter's little brother talks of gold as if gold were as good as the food we grow to stay alive!"

Having also told Yotham that Peter would make up his own mind, Benjamin, to his dismay, was met with: "Not when you are telling him what to do. It's the same with me. You tell me what to do, then you say I should make up my own mind."

Benjamin saw he was losing the thread of the argument. "You are upsetting me. I have no time for this nonsense. Get yourself ready for the dance. I must also get ready. I have a tale to tell tonight." His clipped sentences revealed his annoyance.

Yotham disobeyed with the spirited reaction, that years later would break the color barrier in sport in Africa and might have shaken corridors of white power in Southern Rhodesia, had he never gone to America to his death. Words flashed thoughtlessly and dangerously from within him. "Tell us tonight of the fight against the white man in Lusaka. The fight for Zambia!"

Benjamin's eyes opened wide, but he reacted conservatively. "What do you know of this? Never speak like that again. You are too young and your ears too big. This is dangerous talk…" Putting a hand on Yotham's shoulder, he cautioned: "Never talk of Zambia carelessly."

Yotham would have wriggled free, had the hand on his shoulder not fixed him like a vice; except, too, that his curiosity was stronger than fear of his uncle. "But why?" he glared back rebelliously. "Am I not a Zambian?" For a moment, neither lowered their gaze. Benjamin shook Yotham by the collar and urged compliance, unaware that Emmanuel had entered the hut and was silently watching.

Emmanuel hated angry words as much as he had hated the war in Burma. Grasping Benjamin's arm to release his son, he demanded: "What have you been up to, Yotham?"

"He was speaking up for me," Peter broke in. "I am offered work on the Copperbelt. Benjamin does not want me to leave Mudukulu. He says I am a farmer. Is that all there is for me here? I don't think so. Yotham says I should make my own mind up. That is all, Father."

Benjamin pulled his arm away saying there was more to it than that, then striding out of the hut before regaining composure enough to turn back, to say *he* had been wrong. "I agree that Peter must do what he thinks is best for himself."

Placing a gentler arm around Yotham's shoulder, he added: "Your father has sense from his years in the British army. See his corporal's uniform in the corner and his medals. He will advise Peter, not me." Benjamin used this piece of flattery to make peace with the older brother he admired, as one who had bravely served as company runner from behind Japanese lines.

Benjamin added: "Listen, the drums herald this evening's celebration. They socially summon our neighbors. The dance of peace will soon begin."

Peter smiled: "We will enjoy your folktale and song tonight, Uncle Benjamin. This is not the time for an argument over me."

"Amen!" said Benjamin adding. "Tonight, I will talk about our disappearing traditional territories of 900 years of Tonga settlement, due to the Kariba Dam displacing people. I will display your father's walking stick handle depicting *Nyami,* the Zambezi River God."

Drums reverberating down centuries of tradition had soon assembled young and old from a wide area, around a bonfire warming the night air. Benjamin directed games and songs,

69

warming up to his serious criticism of a government betraying promises made to River Tonga people, as a result of their rich fishing and hunting land lost to the Kariba Dam.

The *Makeya,* a dance of wild abandon to crude gombey drums, hand and leg percussion anklets, wooden whistles, shaken rattles and song, drew young and old into a wide circle. As darkness fell, the children cuddled together with their parents closer to the dying fire.

Beds that await them, are poles laid across forked stakes raised above the ground. There are no windows in the round huts, like the one Emmanuel had built for his family. The furniture comprises beds, table and wooden stools. Pots, baskets, hoes and axes are also kept inside.

A lamplight flickers on Emmanuel's khaki army uniform. The light illuminates the corporal's stripes he keeps white with Blanco, and jacket buttons still glittering from Brasso. His beret is up there too. His Burma Star, his 1939–45 National Service medal and regimental badge are pinned to his army jacket. So is his Military Medal with its red, white and blue ribbon, awarded for bravery on that day when British soldiers behind Japanese lines were encircled, telephone lines knocked out and by nightfall, a region of Burma almost taken from them.

At crack of dawn that day, Emmanuel's platoon was told only fast runners could avoid Japanese snipers and deliver an urgent message to regimental headquarters. Emmanuel and a comrade had volunteered for the run through monsoon rain. The two were peppered by Japanese shot and shell, as they ducked and ran. Emmanuel saw his comrade fall.

He got through to regimental headquarters by skin of teeth, to deliver the report of where lines had been cut and reinforcements needed, to save British troops cut off stemming a Japanese advancement on their supply line. Emmanuel did not, to my mind, exaggerate his military exploit. He had no reason to make up a tale of wartime bravery. Service in Burma spoke for itself, as did it for all who had served on the fabled road to Mandalay.

Much of his story is about how his luck ran out. He was half asleep, sheltering from sudden rain in a tunnel leading to his barracks, when a shell exploded inside the narrow entrance. Hit on the chest and leg by rocks and evacuated to a field hospital, a doctor stemmed his serious wounds and gave him an on-field blood transfusion.

Emmanuel urges his lieutenant to let him stay in Burma. Lucky for him the lieutenant has no say in the matter. A medical officer ahead of his time, he knows better than to judge Emmanuel's injury only by the chest wound. Soon he is detailed to embark overland for Assam, India, and with other severe casualties by air to England and the Star and Garter Hotel, located above the Thames, near historic Richmond Park, and converted for injured servicemen.

The comfortable white beds, brisk sisters and older doctors, were such a peaceful change for him after running for his life in the Burmese jungle, that he could hardly lie still in bed. Solitary walks in Richmond Park, where British prime ministers, poets and philosophers had once strolled, improved his mind. Under the warm sun that autumn, he brought in sheaves of wheat from the fields, and heard American refugee Paul Robeson sing of the ploughing and sowing so important for food in wartime Britain.

Eventually his health improved, enough that he was found a berth on the *SS Rhodesia Castle* bound from Southampton to Africa. His homeward journey was by way of Cape Town harbor, where for two days he was confined to ship. At the wartime neutral port of Beira, in Portuguese East Africa, he disembarked to find his own way home by army train pass to Salisbury, then to Lusaka, and finally by bus to Mudukulu. Benjamin recalled the welcome-home lunch, at which he told elders he had kept right on to the end of the road.

Recuperation healed the defined war injury. The chest marks disappeared. More serious was a lingering malaise of the mind. He was still shell-shocked. Less than a decade after Emmanuel's war service, the British government, with the help of enlightened medical knowledge, would provide free national health services and pensions for veterans with such affliction. Emmanuel knew nothing of Post-Traumatic Stress Disorder, as it officially came to be known. PTSD was hardly in the military medical textbooks. In World War II, some high-ranking military officers still regarded such affliction as cowardice. In WW I, cowardice had meant a firing squad.

That night before bed in Mudukulu, I told Benjamin that Yotham's death had sank my hopes of depicting his nephew as a non-racial sports hero, and me as an author, writing about a young African breaking through racial barriers on the running track.

"It is to no avail!" he shot back, riveting me in silence with his depth of feeling. "Go back to your journalism. Report the election fairly. Help Zambia achieve freedom. Africans no longer want to live like mice in their country!"

Chapter 14
Merely a Legend?

I nevertheless decided to stay another night at Mudukulu, since the next day was Sunday and the weather fine.

As the village wakens, children, near-naked in sewed cotton rags, are seen and heard. Babies are kept warm in treated animal skins in colder weather. Young men turn out in mostly short pants and grey shirts, and women with pieces of black cloth around thighs and breasts, chatter in the Chitonga language.

Younger women, bound for chapel with the children, are colorfully adorned in cotton dresses and beadwork of red ochre, reflecting the influence of traders who once took cheap beads and gaudy cloth up the Zambezi, to exchange for white ivory and even black slaves. Older women wear blouses and skirts bought at the trading station, while some men wear crumpled suits and shirts.

Sundays mean Sunday school for the children. Out for a morning run, I vividly imagine Yotham running to get to the church in time. I see him jog down village paths between huts, pick his route, stone to stone, across the almost dried-up stream, then sprint past emaciated cattle over sunbaked pasture, to the little flat-roofed chapel on a hill opposite his home that also serves as school.

Pastor Benjamin relates to Sunday school children his perception of future events: visions of impending upheaval for his country, fear of an unknown political future in wondering how protected are the majority of people.

Benjamin's sermon comes across to me more for an older congregation than for children. His booming voice relates adult life unfolding before their innocent eyes. He tells them to always question the truth of what they are told.

Judith Muleya is almost sightless, as a result of infection from the *mbwa* fly. So slight is her body, it could be that malaria has taken periodic hold. Yet, like her late brother, she is a good runner when well. She listens intently to Benjamin's sermon, after chattering in whispers with her friend Gladys.

Typically, Benjamin urges the boys to seek skill in woodwork, find easier ways to water the pastures, play, yes, but work in the fields, support the welfare association, respect parents. And the girls are to learn from their mothers, the best of family life and its needs. He quotes from the Bible: "Though a host shall encamp against me, my heart shall not fear; though war should rise against me, I shall be confident."

He even raises the image of Shaka, whose military skill he exaggerates above that of any other ruler in southern Africa. "In his day, Shaka conquered and united much of east, west, north and south. Were he alive, there would be no despotic rule in South Africa today."

One boy rises to ask how Shaka would have kept peace in a conquered land. "Peace comes through strength," Benjamin replies. "Shaka's strength came through discipline. My belief is that he fought valiantly and for *that*, I commend him. Peace will come to a future independent Zambia."

He ends the lecture by urging obedience, order, self-restraint, submission to authority, respect for elders, self-sacrifice and civic duty, that he says are akin to peace. The children are overwhelmed by his demands and so am I. Most prefer to sing hymns and recite prayers rather than hear of strife and discipline.

I had wondered about Benjamin's sermon, so alone with him, I ask the obvious questions.

"I did not praise Shaka," Benjamin responds perfunctorily. "I gave facts. The children broadly, on their terms, understand what majority rule means for them, and some of them, who Shaka was."

"You named this country Zambia."

"Soon it will be so. I have decided the children should get used to accepting this name. They already speak openly of Zambia out of school and, to my consternation, a few angry boys pretend to shoot white Rhodesians."

I was determined to know what Benjamin thought of the Hiawatha I knew well but of whom Benjamin actually knew more than me, in describing Hiawatha as peacemaker, teacher, statesman, and player in the formation of the British Empire by leading Indians forward in North America. "Hiawatha's influence assisted in five tribes burying the hatchet and wielding themselves into a powerful confederation, which became allied to the British and opposed Negro slavery."

He also answered with an extract from Longfellow's *Song of Hiawatha:*

> *None could run as fast as he could,*
> *None could dive as deep as he could,*
> *None had made so many journeys,*
> *None had seen so many wonders,*
> *As this wonderful Iagoo,*
> *As this marvelous storyteller!*
> *Thus, his name became a by-word*
> *And a jest among the people;*
> *And whene'er a boastful hunter*
> *Praised his own address too highly,*
> *Or a warrior home returning*
> *Talked too much of his achievements*
> *All his hearers cried, 'Iagoo!*
> *Here's Iagoo come among us!'*
> *He it was who carved the cradle*
> *Of the little Hiawatha.*

Model of Hiawatha by artist Augustus Saint-Gaudens inspired by Henry Wadsworth Longfellow's poem

He urged me to understand, that the *Song of Hiawatha* was a poem inspiring even white Americans. I told him Longfellow was known in Britain for exaggerating the facts.

"Listen," he hit back. "The poem's beauty, fact or fiction, lies in the cross-cultural love Hiawatha had for Minnehaha, he, an Ojibwa Indian, and she a Dakota. You must remember that Hiawatha was a man, as other men, and wooed and won sweet

Laughing Water, despite tribal differences. But we have more relevant things than Hiawatha to discuss."

I discovered that day, as I packed my return travel goods, that he had a copy of Longfellow's poems in a book he had purchased in Boston, and, inspired by Benjamin's romantic words, I reminded myself of my great uncle in London reciting:

> *You shall hear how Pau-Puk-Keesis,*
> *How the handsome Yenadisse*
> *Danced at Hiawatha's wedding;*
> *How the gentle Chibiabos,*
> *He the sweetest of musicians,*
> *Sang his songs of love and longing;*
> *How Iagoo, the great boaster,*
> *He the marvelous story teller,*
> *Told his tales of strange adventure,*
> *That the feast might be more joyous,*
> *And the guests be more contented.*
> *Sumptuous was the feast Nokomis*
> *Made at Hiawatha's wedding.*

I thought as we played chess, how my great uncle impresario, T.C. Fairbairn, would have enjoyed meeting Benjamin and discussing Hiawatha with him.

"Checkmate," Benjamin proclaimed to his distracted opponent.

To his surprise, as courtesy demands, I tipped my tiny chessboard King and, as comfortably as circumstances provided, lay back on the borrowed mattress and pillow, recollecting what had transpired that Sunday.

Chapter 15
Into the Political Arena

I had learned a great deal about Northern Rhodesia from my test trips to Mudukulu, and logically putting two and two together, decided that, throughout the land, native people were either praying for a peaceful independence from British colonial rule, or more and more siding with militant leaders urging action. I would use that knowledge politically, whenever safe, in my newspaper work.

On my arrival in Lusaka, the militants had gained the support of welfare associations that steadily, over time, developed into political organizations. The associations had reconstituted the Northern Rhodesia Congress and later the Northern Rhodesia African National Congress. I read in a leaflet that when the election writ was dropped, Congress was going to contest general elections that had for decades been dominated by white political parties. This was the policy when Rhodesian settlers and their leaders were telling the world, that Africans did not have the acumen to govern efficiently under "one man, one vote".

It was doubtlessly true to say, that the change from a simple African tribal life to an urban European life was tricky. But the change was not the coming-down-from-the-trees that I had heard some of my contemporaries insinuate. To begin with, it seemed to me the critics were missing the point. It was the freedom to make the change that was important to the Africans. Whether the change was worth it was something I pondered. Whether Africans had any alternative was debatable.

I had been unprepared for blatant racism when confronted by it in Salisbury, and by less open racism in Lusaka. I had become an open sympathizer with the African cause, by supporting progressive moves favoring Southern Rhodesian natives, introduced by the colony's former prime minister Garfield Todd, then curtailed by his successors. Todd had been run out of office by racists from within his own caucus and later confined to his farm. That had taught me to be careful about seeking to interview him.

The colony was, by then, being led by Southern Rhodesian-born Sir Edgar Whitehead, who had returned from public service in Washington to rout Todd's United Rhodesia Party. And Britain was dealing with more than Whitehead. There was a bombastic federal leader of Northern and Southern Rhodesia and Nyasaland in Sir Roy Welensky, who was attending Commonwealth prime ministerial conferences in London.

My accumulating knowledge was set back by an unfortunate murder, blamed on nationalists, that I had to report. At the close of Kaunda's United National Independence Party's first convention, a white woman was burned to death in her car up north in Ndola, and the murder tragedy hit the headlines even in Britain.

The murder was largely because of the frustration festering and simmering in all three white-dominated federal territories. On the African side, Hastings Banda, a doctor out of Nyasaland practicing in England, Harry Nkumbula of Northern Rhodesian Tonga extraction, and Joshua Nkomo of Southern Rhodesia were fighting peacefully at home and abroad, to convince Britain to bring majority rule to each of the federated countries. I projected that things might end in a cruel war, if Africans gained real patriotic military leadership promised by the newcomer Robert Mugabe.

Journalists used to say British arrivals in Southern Rhodesia eventually moved north or south, depending on their racial outlook. If they had a mind, the first thing they uncovered in Northern Rhodesia was that the southern federal partner was cheating the north out of its mineral wealth, and that the restrained Africans in the north were not aware of it.

I was particularly interested in the role of the British South Africa Police, the main Rhodesian police force, and by more than name, akin to the South African police. A mutual interest in track and field had brought me into contact with a young immigrant, South African policeman and runner, Julian Hall, one that I could approach for ideas, enjoy a run with, and an occasional drink after work. We became friends, mainly to my advantage as a reporter, seeking tips for stories from solid sources.

To me, an upcoming Northern Rhodesian rally of Africans, being urged to burn their federal *situpas* and wedding certificates, to protest federal rule, I viewed as potentially a cracking good story for my newspaper in Salisbury. However, I also knew any dramatic pictures I might take, could give my editors and the Rhodesia police nightmares, if they showed Kaunda again breaking the law. I considered, since he was newly released from prison and his party, UNIP, formed while he was incarcerated, that such photos might send him back to jail. What I did quickly discover, was that a policemen's role at a political rally in Africa was not a happy role, and that Kaunda's charisma had them mesmerized and on edge when he appeared before huge crowds.

Under the hot sun, girls flank the path leading to the platform. They chant praises of their leader. It is easy to see that the good-natured crowds regard such political rallies as open-air parties. Nevertheless, many of those present are wary of brown-helmeted African askaris, challenged by their role under white officers who looked strained and out of place. I knew that coping with this was one of Julian's predicaments. I watched him warily scan a sea of faces from the back of an open police van. Later, he told me that the cause of much of his trouble had been less the African demonstrators, and more the attitude of that day's superior officer. Since I was new to reporting a nationalist rally, I kept pretty close to the police van.

Through his binoculars, Julian scans the huge mass of African people sitting mainly knees-crossed in the burnt grass, dressed in an array of white shirts and pants, and colorful blouses and dresses. Speaker after speaker takes the platform, waving flywhisks or clowning in their own special way.

"*Kwacha*! *Kwacha*!" roars the crowd, as Kenneth Kaunda arrives. He smiles broadly and waves from the platform. The crowd quieten to hear the captivating politician speak. His first few words go unheard. Then those sitting in branches of surrounding trees seem to hush the wind, to hear his deep voice loud and clear in the open arena.

Kaunda speaks first as if from the pulpit. Then, taking the crowd along, he hammers out in clear and simple language, a road to Zambia's independence. He mocks policemen recording his every word. I can feel that my tension is also among the police near me. The senior officer looks apprehensively at the constables. Is violence being preached here? Then comes Kaunda's plea for peace and his message that after the elections, Africans will rule in their God-given land of Zambia.

"Zambia will be free!" he shouts. The crowd echoes his call. "Vote for UNIP!" he demands to chants of kwacha (dawn).

Platform leaders break into song. African women file forward into a circle to lead a dance. Their swishy red and white sisal skirts rise high, sweat rolls down their faces, breasts heave and feathers fly. They sing while dancing. Kaunda descends from the platform to dance with the women. I thought the police weak, in spite of their guns, when faced with a man like this.

Julian is gazing intently through his binoculars, when addressed by a glowering sergeant. "That's the second time I've asked why you're focused on that white girl in the crowd."

Returning the officer's gaze, Julian replies that he is merely watching her to ascertain that she is not in danger. "I'm looking for trouble in the crowd. I've seen her at African rallies. She's been in trouble before."

We watched Kaunda walk the length of a female guard of honor, bowing to one woman then to another. I figured he was heading for the bonfire, so instinctively I zigzagged my way through the crowd to get there before him. He did as I had anticipated, and he paused to smile as I clicked the camera the moment he threw what I knew was a federal certificate into the blaze. Others emulated him. I had good pictures. I returned satisfied to the side of the police van and took a quick photo shoot of the officer watching the bonfire through his binoculars.

"Why the hell are you photographing me?" he asked.

Julian rescued me: "Photographs of us will show security at hand, sir."

I kept quiet when the officer turned to face me then back to Julian. "Kaunda, huh! And this talk of Zambia! How can the people we see here govern themselves, never mind the country? I reckon Verwoerd has the right idea with his separate development. What do you think, Hall?"

Julian grimaced, before quietly saying: "Verwoerd's apartheid policies are condemned outside South Africa and hated by Africans inside."

The officer savored the remark as though he had expected it. "Maybe, maybe," he replied. "You see, Hall, what you forget is that I'm Rhodesian born and bred. You're *from* South Africa. What you say is true to form. South Africans call the blacks kaffirs. We don't use that term here. My ancestors worked like slaves building up Rhodesia. My grandfather fought in the Matebele wars, then came north to get himself a farm and put me where I am. He was a frontiersman-turned-farmer. I'm his grandson-turned-policeman. I'm not going to let that lot take what my ancestors won for me."

"Zambia, huh!" he went on. "This is Northern Rhodesia. It's part of the British Empire. I tell you, this Kaunda is an upstart native from Nyasaland who doesn't know what he's taking on in the elections. He shows no appreciation for what we've done for natives like him. We gave this country roads, schools, hospitals, trains. White South Africans went too far with apartheid."

"So, your old man came in a covered wagon with the British South Africa Company's Pioneer Column, looking for gold and a new country to take too far."

"My grandfather," the sergeant said, with a touch of annoyance at a constable drawing a bead on him. "Yes, he knew Rhodes. He knew about the Shangani patrol. Heard about it? A patrol of 33 Rhodesians took on 3,000 of Lobengula's warriors."

"And all 33 were annihilated, near the Shangani River, 100 miles from Bulawayo, in 1893," Julian interceded.

"You know your history from your South African university. Yes, true, but we crushed Ndebele and Shona revolts about the same time... but, hell, you're distracting me with your book learning. There's trouble among the crowd over there by the trees. Stop this talk and see to it before it gets out of hand."

The sergeant pointed to a growing crowd on the edge of a skirmish and told three black askaris to go with Hall and sort it out. Julian jumped from the police van. He got to the scene first, baton in hand, to find youths backing away from a black man lying on the ground, cut and bruised on arm and face, after defending himself from broken beer bottles. Youths turned and ran when the rest of the police party arrived with me in the police van. I took a quick photograph when Julian held his gun pointed horizontally over the man on the ground. One of the askaris grabbed a bystander.

"What do you know about this?" he demanded.

"Nothing!" the frightened youth responded, eyeing Julian. "I was just passing."

"So what happened?" Julian asked him.

"Fighting, *bwana*, fighting."

"Who were fighting?"

"UNIP and ANC."

"Who?"

"They ran away."

I wasn't taking shorthand notes, but I recall the words as if hearing them yesterday. The youth, protesting his innocence, was handcuffed and bundled into the police van. Another man on the ground said not a word.

"Take them both," Julian ordered the three African askaris. "Careful how you handle them," he added, noticing he had become the center figure of a mob. "Okay, disperse," he ordered waving his gun. "The fighting is over."

The onlookers moved sullenly away. I was given a lift downtown in the police van, knowing my newspaper colleague would have taken off in the press car.

"Bloody savages," the officer cursed a couple of times, before we got to the city center police station. "We'll likely just question these two and let them go," he quietly added.

"Can I quote you?"

"No… well, maybe. As police spokesman, say I stopped a riot."

"I have photographs showing that."

The officer laughed, then surprised me. "The photos are your business. Why, tell me? I know nothing of them."

The tussle between rival African political party members led my *Rhodesia Herald* story. I also sent to Britain's *Sunday Observer*, pictures of rioters facing the police along with Kaunda burning his pass, and one was published on the front page. If used prominently by the *Herald*, I judged the article would give its white readership a taste of what was in store for them in Zambia, if they did not come to terms with the nationalist majority that could very well sweep elections behind Kaunda. I thought my work might also caution Africans from taking militant political sides. Then it hit me! I was subconsciously using the new name, Zambia, for Northern Rhodesia. My work in revolutionary Africa had become big time for a former Scottish newsboy! An African wind of change had finally taken hold of me. Little did I know that the wind was about to turn into a hurricane, accepted and relayed by British Prime Minister Harold MacMillan, addressing the apartheid parliament in Cape Town at the end of a tour of Africa.

Chapter 16
The Louis Riel Connection

Finding information about the dark-haired white woman among the crowd at the Kaunda rally was easy. A file on Marianne Cleroux, and even a photograph of her, was in my Lusaka newspaper branch office library. So, thinking I might have satisfied my editors in Salisbury with my rally story and pictures, I decided to take a day off to look the lass up. I thought I might find a feature story on education. I also longed for a woman companion.

I discovered she was a Canadian schoolteacher originally in Northern Rhodesia for her non-governmental organization, Canadian University Service Overseas in Ottawa. It was the less-known equivalent, on a smaller scale, of British Voluntary Service Overseas and the recently formed American Peace Corps. The biology and English-language teacher had returned on her own accord, after a first two-year stint teaching at a Northern Rhodesian college.

My reporter's curiosity was rewarded, when I tracked her down to a township school 20 kilometers from Lusaka, where she was teaching English. She was not, what I first thought, typically Canadian. She showed not the slightest surprise when I turned up. She had noticed me at the rally but surprised me by soon asking how well I knew the policeman with the binoculars. I merely said he was a South African friend and dismissed her interest.

Off the top of my head, I mentioned that I admired Canadian Prime Minister John Diefenbaker. She said she hoped Mike Pearson and the Liberals would replace both him as prime minister and the Conservatives as the governing party. "Like you British, we have a socialist party, too, but far from gaining power."

"I've been in the news before," Marianne boldly said, while showing me around open-air classrooms, sheltered by only a roof, and introducing me to colleagues and a couple of pupils. Then, without telling me the news story she had been connected with, she cut my visit short saying she now had classroom work to do. To my delight, she agreed to talk more over a lunch date in Lusaka the following Saturday afternoon.

My delight was tempered by a growing unease about my relationship with the editors in Salisbury. I feared some newspaper staff would be discussing my work up north. I had filed only three real stories in two weeks. Then, to my surprise, the chief editor phoned, saying to stay longer on the campaign trail. He said my protest rally story and pictures would be in the next day's newspaper, and suggested I write a profile on Kenneth Kaunda. I regretted that as editor he was to be replaced by his deputy, with whom I enjoyed no such good relations.

At last, Saturday came and I quickly found out over lunch, why Marianne had sought a promise not to feature her in my newspaper, although I had no intention of ever doing so. When prompted, she told me that during her first two-year stint, she had come to love the simple life of the Africans, and in letters home and to the editors of Canadian newspapers, had argued their case for freedom from minority white rule with a conviction rooted in what she believed was right. She had seen injustices meted native Indians in Canada, and both Indians and blacks in America. I told her I, too, was sensitive to discrimination.

She qualified her concern saying: "I'm Métis, you know. My people suffer in Canada too. My first language is French, but English rules. The English ruthlessly settled with Manitoba's provisional Métis ruler, Louis Riel. Have you heard of him?"

I had not even guessed she spoke French, since she not only spoke but taught English. I could make no judgment of her background. I knew nothing about Louis Riel's tragic place in Canadian history, following the havoc the Métis leader had caused Canadian leaders one hundred or so years previous, by declaring the Canadian province of Manitoba independent and becoming its leader. Nor did I know that John A. MacDonald, Canada's first prime minister, subsequently had him hanged for treason during Canada's Northwest Rebellion.

Marianne told me her Métis people believed MacDonald destroyed Riel, following a rigged trial resulting from his armed defense of the Métis nation. She said MacDonald stood by the dock when Riel was sentenced to death. I was a fellow Scot who had long admired MacDonald for his pioneering of the Canadian railroad that opened up Western Canada. It would take more than a young

Canadian schoolteacher to change that piece of cronyism, no matter how lovely she was.

"Métis," she repeated, as if I had forgotten what she was about. Then to the pretty black waitress: "Omelets for two."

"Who and what is this maytee?" I asked.

"The Métis people are the prodigy of aboriginal Canadian women and white men."

"Where in Canada are you from then?"

"I'm from Winnipeg."

"They speak French in Winnipeg?"

"I do."

I was later to lament that no geography or history teacher in Scotland had taught me about the Métis people. No Scottish high school book to my knowledge mentioned them in Canadian studies. I had turned down university but doubted its books included, or its professors ever discussed, the Métis people. While the ebony-skin waitress was serving us, I urged Marianne to tell me about maytee.

She smiled: "As I said, my folk were the result of liaisons between French-speaking *couriers de bois* and native women. The trappers took indigenous Pawnee women, like my grandmother, as sexual partners, had children with them, then often deserted them. My family history records this. On the other hand, some of the couriers forged alliances and built families with natives. Louis Riel was Manitoba's first leader. He was also, for a while, a member of the Canadian Parliament in Ottawa, but he clashed with MacDonald and with the North West Mounted Police riding westward from Ottawa at MacDonald's bidding, to teach him a lesson."

She continued: "My great-grandfather and great-uncle were both murdered at Batoche, Saskatchewan, in 1885. Should I be more sensitive about this forgotten tragedy when talking to a Canadian newspaperman?"

"A newspaperman like me?" I asked wondering what she was on about. My Scottish high school had overloaded me with debatable facts, about the Scottish victory over the English at the battle of Bannockburn. But Batoche!

She did not stop there: "You're so very Scottish. Some of my Métis ancestors were from the Orkney Islands."

"From the Orkneys? I was born in the Scottish Borderland, historically sometimes called the Debatable Land, and as far away as you can get in Scotland from the Orkneys. You say your forebears were from the Orkneys?"

To my dismay, instead of answering this she asked me to explain what I meant by the Debatable Land.

"Well, a few centuries ago the English used to claim ownership of part of my Scottish Border homeland. When that happened, the Scots replied that ownership was debatable. Traditionally, we Scots on the border with England were cattle thieves or traditional plunderers. To me, the English were ravishers of lovely women like you. This belief came my way as a youth and again fairly recently. I may never get over it."

My unguarded compliment made her laugh, I think, contemptuously. "So, you border Scots don't get on with the English over the border. Well, let me tell you more about Canada, right back to the first Canadian prime minister and you must know who he was."

"Wait! I was joking. I don't think you are. My father and my siblings live in England. I did most of my journalism in England. I served two years as an army corporal in England. Tell me," I asked, thinking changing the subject might get me out of the Métis quagmire. "Tell me what happened to bring you to my newspaper's attention."

She deftly outlined the court case. One of her college pupils had retaliated against a white youth who had called him a kaffir. His punch had damaged one of the white youth's eyes. The black boy was found guilty of assault and placed on probation, despite what she said was a sincere apology. The magistrate had warned him that the next time he used violence, he would be sent to jail or to his tribal home.

Marianne vividly recalled the hurt look in the boy's eyes, when the magistrate sternly pronounced him guilty and warned him in somber tones. She had spoken up in his defense, pointing out the aggravation of the racial slur and noting the boy's usual peaceful nature. Prosecution witnesses had spoken up just as strongly for a conviction. Apparently, the backlash had been tough on her due to newspaper publicity. "I just wish you reporters would always tell the whole story."

Marianne said she had lost some of her white friends, and the black boy's flight into the bush had inflamed her hurt from headlines when his body was found. Her college headmaster had advised her to concentrate on teaching.

"The newspapers implicated me to the extent that I was politically involved."

On returning from Canada to work in Northern Rhodesia, she had been virtually shunted to a small native school. "That did not worry me," she contended. "Look, Garfield Todd was hounded out of the prime minister's office in Southern Rhodesia because he sought African advancement. Southern Rhodesia is now under Rhodesia Front rule, with Winston Field and Ian Smith on top of the heap they call civilization."

She continued: "I have as much time for them as they have for a Canadian Métis teacher who supports African independence. They're a bunch of white farmers taking over a British colony, though the British don't mean much to them unless they get their own way. You see my genes are not lily white like theirs. I'm a half breed. Had I been a nurse like my Canadian Métis friend Giselle, whom I originally came here with, or like my Cree friend Maria, they would have sent me to a leper colony. Why do you think your editors sent *you* up here?"

Her verbal onslaught on me and on herself left me groping. "My editors sent me here on open assignment to cover mainly the elections. I like Garfield Todd too."

"They sent you because you were not fitting in down south. You'll end up permanently here like me."

"And *you* are throwing a black and white Quebec toque at press, politicians and yourself," I joked. "In Scotland, they used to foolishly throw their bonnets in the air for joy, or sour grapes when aiming at politicians. You can't blame journalists for what happened to you."

My sarcastic use of the French-Canadian word "toque" was unforgivable, although she had drawn it from me. I later realized that I was turning Marianne into a Manitoba plate of Quebec pea soup. My face felt like it had turned scarlet. I tried to dismiss my mistake by asking, with a smile, how she was enjoying her omelet. But she was having none of it. There was no going back.

"Like all those who come from a cold part of North America, I was born with a toque on my head. Maybe you need a toque around your omelet-head to help you write and speak more intelligently on African affairs."

Reminded of *La Belle Dame Sans Merci,* I laughed. "I'm sorry– it was just another jest."

Marianne at that moment disclosed her real aversion to journalists: "I watched the police and you at the rally, and saw Julian watch me through his binoculars, while you were glued to the police wagon as if the black crowd would eat you up like the egg on your plate…"

"That's not true. I was never afraid. I took pictures of Kaunda at the bonfire. The policeman you refer to, my South African friend, was ready to help *you* if there was trouble."

"That was nice of him to worry about me. I agree that the police nearly had a serious riot on their hands, when they arrested two innocent men."

"Innocent? How do you know that? How close were you? Even I didn't know that when photographing the fighting."

"They let them go, didn't they? That's what I learned from Julian."

"Then you know Julian Hall well?"

"Yes."

That shook me to the core, but I didn't pursue it. Instead, I brought out my newspaper from my carrier bag and showed her my report on the rally. Increasingly mercilessly, she said she had read my story and that it put African political parties in a bad light. "You think Kaunda has anything to do with ruffians fighting? You'll be writing in a different way soon because Kaunda is going to win power here. Your *Rhodesia Herald* won't like it and the Southern Rhodesia government even less. That government has it in for Kaunda. Is that news to you, Mr. Reporter?"

I retorted that maybe *she* should have been the newspaper reporter. I requested aloud what had set me up for her verbal assault. Then I toned things down by asking: "What makes you so sure Kaunda will win?"

She looked right through me. "Just watch him. Or ask Julian. I've a feeling he might know from his experiences down south."

"You know he is a South African?"

"You told me."

I capitulated by changing the subject, to mention that my editor wanted me to interview Kaunda.

"You think Kaunda will want to be featured in *The Rhodesia Herald?*"

I saw her point and felt even more helpless. "I tell you what. The Americans, the Russians, even the Scots now seem to boost non-racial images through the Olympic Games. Why not the Zambians? I'm going to write a book about that!"

"There *is* no Zambia!" she retorted so loudly, it made me glad we were the only ones left in the café but the waitress, whom I suspected was listening in. "Northern Rhodesia is a third-world territory. Before Africans here tackle sport, they have to fight for freedom. Look, I've said too much. I must do my shopping before the shops close. Thanks for lunch."

It was clearly the brush-off of a kind worse than I had experienced in Scotland's historic Debatable Borderland. Buried in the back of my mind, were hidden thoughts of the night, a visiting English lad had moved in on my lass during my home town's annual festive celebration, of that almost solitary ancient Scottish victory over a raiding arm of the English army. I was scatterbrained enough to think of that reporter in Derby, almost kissing his young girlfriend in a place, where in my adolescent view at the time, he should never have dared go. I decided I had deserved to be jilted, by the slip of a woman I had taken to lunch and by all other women I had lost.

The waitress, her name Shua embroidered on her sleeveless pinafore, approached me sitting rejected at the table. I ordered a fresh pot of tea, mopping over my pitiful performance with, by then, only one positive thought: the originality of Marianne's novel description of Northern Rhodesia as a third-world territory. I dismally reflected that I was a third-world newsboy who had left school at 15. Had Marianne, as a teacher, concluded I was an ignoramus? I had to admit, she knew more than me of Africa and probably of life itself.

"So, you lost your friend," the waitress observed sympathetically.

I found this rather forward for a waitress and was tempted to give her a dressing-down for impertinence, before she dressed me down saying: "You don't have a clue how to treat a woman. Anyway, the café is closing."

After paying the bill, I made for the door turning to hand her a tip. I placed it on the table instead.

"There are more fish in Lake Victoria," she said impudently.

"The phrase, Shua, is more fish in the sea."

The thought of rejection was painful, the next few late nights in my Ridgeway Hotel room in Lusaka. I conjectured that my loss was due to stupidly talking politics on our first date. Yet I had to conclude that Marianne, not me, had done the talking, and that she was not a polite Canadian teacher at all, but a live-wire woman who had mesmerized me. A week later, shock hit harder when I learned from Julian, that Marianne and he had engaged to marry!

Chapter 17
Into the Transvaal

Shua's "more fish in Lake Victoria," held me together while I floundered like one of them. This quick capture by a Rhodesian policeman, of an attractive Canadian supporter of African independence, totally amazed me.

I figured they might have had *something* in common, if Julian had related to her his South African upbringing in the same way he had told it to me. Barriers would have melted. Nevertheless, Julian clearly knew far more about women than me. Maybe they were fighting for something and I was a trained observer.

I assumed Julian had told Marianne, of the heartbreak he had found in his South African home in the Transvaal town of Krugersdorp, and that she had told him of her racial struggles as a Métis in Winnipeg. They in common, no doubt, harbored deep resentment.

When I eventually visited Krugersdorp as best man at their wedding, I found that the town lay in mountain footholds at the center of cotton, fruit, tobacco and sugar cane farming. Some of the most productive asbestos and iron ore mines in the world, were located across the nearby mountainous border in Swaziland. Rich in resources but poor in human relations was Krugersdorp.

"The bosses profit from the cane I cut and the stalks I burn," said an African farmworker I encouraged to speak up. It had occurred to me that Africans knew of the exploitation of their bodies but were powerless to resist. I enjoyed a sweet cup of tea with thoughts of sugar cane, possibly first exported to Britain by Scottish settlers using black labor. The underlying tone of black violence, emanating from the town's prison and from judgment of its white counterpart of an English magistrate's court, also set me thinking.

I was aware that only white people owned the smart bungalows, such as the Hall residence around the park. The black people were house servants or worked for meagre earnings on the farms and lived in outhouses.

Julian's parents knew little of Marianne's background, but she was Canadian and accepted as wife for their son. Marianne had gracefully accepted my presence. I could hardly believe she was the same woman who verbally had destroyed me in Lusaka. She could well have played Robert Louis Stevenson's Dr. Jekyll and Mr. Hyde.

I escaped Krugersdorp as soon as I could and drove a hired car across the border into Swaziland, where I watched, from a distance, black workers in open cast iron-ore mines sweat under the surveillance of British overseers. Near the capital, Mbabane, I bumped into a platoon of British soldiers, marching as I had marched when I was an 18-year old national serviceman in England. I invited myself to their British Army barracks to take in a dance. Invited local white women, made it seem like being at the dances I had enjoyed as a soldier in Britain.

"I was once an infantry corporal," I boasted to one partner. She preferred the uniformed private who tapped my shoulder and danced off with her close up.

Soon I had crossed into Portuguese East Africa. In Lourenco Marques, I lodged with a Portuguese family and from the window of my room, watched runners of all colors run a marathon through city streets. The peaceful capital of Portugal's huge overseas territory, hardly reflected the fact that Eduardo Mondlane had formed the Mozambique Liberation Front and in northern Cabo Delgado province, was launching an aggressive armed struggle against the Portuguese. His freedom fighters had formed a border alliance, with Zimbabwean freedom fighters training to fight white Southern Rhodesians.

Lourenco Marques was lively as well as peaceful. I was later impressed to see the black African marathon winner presented with a trophy. The Portuguese had also introduced the bullfight for their leisure. They prided themselves that unlike the Spanish, they did not kill the bull. Instead, I saw matadors armed with sharp flagged pins, torment bulls in front of cheering crowds of all skin colors.

I knew well that irrespective of organizing a non-racial marathon, Portuguese rulers had banned Africans from education beyond Grade 4, effectively reserving skilled jobs for fellow countrymen coming in from overseas.

Sitting at a table in a dockside pub, a black woman handily tried to seduce me, almost in front of a huge ocean liner rearing up in the window as it docked. Having downed a few beers, I was tempted by her warm hand. It could hardly have happened in chaste Southern Rhodesia or cold Scotland.

I filled a notebook with rough notes, of how Julian's grandfather had left the coalmines around Newcastle, that gritty northeast England port, to try his luck in the Cape Colony of the late 18th century. He had married a Dutch woman in Cape Town, and together they had crossed Orange and Vaal Rivers, not long after ancestors of Transvaal-bound Afrikaners in lines of carts, had left the Cape to escape British rule. Some eventually would fight British and Canadian soldiers but lose the Boer War, as the Brits called it, and some land up in British concentration camps.

Julian's grandparents had farmed their homestead in the Transvaal and even made money from gold diggings around Krugersdorp. Their only son had attended university, studying to become a chemist. That son had married an Afrikaans woman who had mothered Julian. Julian's father, still lean in later life, related to me how his parents had come from the same part of Britain as me, though I reminded him they had come from the English side of the Scottish border.

Julian's mother had much of the toughness that characterized Transvaal families in an area whose ancestral womenfolk had fought alongside their men, when British soldiers again turned up with a mission of their overlords to add gold riches to their Empire. His mother was warm and welcoming and treated her African servants well. I summarized in my notebook that Julian was a third-generation South African, whose Dutch-English forebears were liberal compared with many of their countrymen and women.

On the other hand, his wife Marianne was a Canadian schoolteacher of Métis ancestry. I knew little more of her background than that. I personally kept my distance. I barely knew her. I had already figured Julian and she were of an ilk, carrying colonial grudges on their shoulders from their different homelands. I was merely a recorder.

Books had told me that the legacy of comfortable living in Krugersdorp was easily traced back to early gold rush days that had put the town on the map with an excitement that had become embedded in Transvaal folklore. I read that the town got its start around 1885, when two weather-beaten tents of the Kruger family were quickly surrounded by a thousand others, after news spread of the biggest gold strike ever. Wagons were soon all over the place.

Where they first pitched tents, men erected shacks that soon became streets.

Almost every nationality was there for the taking of gold. Dutch, English and German men predominated. Dynamite exploded in the surrounding hills. Methods of getting to the gold were sometimes ingenious and always laborious. Africans provided much of the labor and received little in return.

Small time prospectors would pan rubble for gold, in water from mountain streams. The boastful diggers looked for up to a fabulous 17 ounces of gold within a ton or so of rubble. The average strike was a fraction of that. Each day, new discoveries fanned the frenzy of what had become a gold town. The natives not in the forced labor camps, looked on in wonder. Others with dread, as their work conditions deteriorated.

Soon the Transvaal government had declared the Krugersdorp field a public digging, and a Dutch Reformed Church priest became gold commissioner. More than 2,000 gold bearing reefs were discovered and each one was named. Most went bankrupt. Several were exceptionally profitable. One, the Sheba reef, competed with anything American Klondike and Canadian strikes had to offer. "Not gold in rocks," the whisper went all over the world in the press… "but rocks in solid gold."

I read how gold frenzy turned into utter mania. Shares in Sheba rose from $1 to $11, when the mine was said to have yielded 50,000 ounces of gold from the first 13,000 tons of ore. Hundreds of adventurers rushed in. Claims were pegged along extensions and at deep levels of the Sheba reef in almost every direction. Companies were floated, some with lavish capital, merely on the strength of their nearness to Sheba. Land was grabbed from natives, who eventually became no more than worker-squatters at the whim of prospectors with their wonders of blowing pipes and metal ropes.

Other discoveries were also magnified in the excitement. Few people had much knowledge about geology or the slightest scientific understanding of the formations in which gold is found. There was just an uncivilized rush, and the wilder the rumor, the more attention it gained. New villages such as Krugersdorp and towns such as Eureka City sprang up. Swindling companies reached incredible proportions. Two stock exchanges became crowded day and night. Brokers, syndicate investors, and plain rogues, were all there in number. Newspapers overseas published planted articles and drawings of ships sailing up rivers to collect daily cargoes of gold from smiling workers. In this dream, the collapse was sudden.

Too much speculation in underdeveloped mines, too much investment in the remaining working mines, and plain swindling reached a climax. With the slump, the barmaids packed their finery, quit Krugersdorp, and followed the gold to jobs near newly-opened mines around Johannesburg. Adventuresome prospectors headed north, to look in vain for gold in Matabeleland, and eventually put a British flag over the land they would call Rhodesia.

It was plain to me that Julian had grown up apart from the African workers and servants on farms, mines and homes. Nevertheless, he clearly had seen, more than me, their second-class lives in their own country.

I learned from Julian, that he had been conscious of some black Africans hating those of their own people who accepted white supremacy. Dutch and English were also at odds, decades after the Boer War. Afrikaner victories such as at Majuba, had been expressed in bronze in Pietersburg, and triumphant British sieges like Kimberley, immortalized in England by the Boy Scouts led by Baden Powell. The Boer War was being called the South African War and Dutch Afrikaners beginning to take pride in their past fighting role and eventually the political party that represented them started ruling as it saw fit.

The English-associated United Party soon ran second to the Afrikaner Nationalist Party, and the Afrikaans language became more official than English in Parliament, though not in fields and kitchens where black Africans labored or served, as the whites introduced rugby and drank apple cider.

As a reporter, it interested me to find, that the national newspapers were also bound to decades-old division. The Transvaal's *Die Vaderland* was more extreme than *Die Burger,* organ of the Cape Nationalists. The Transvaal provincial administration was more extreme than the Cape Province, in keeping the African majority in place. The *Cape Times* was more supportive of the government than the *Rand Daily Mail,* which, from Johannesburg, opposed the ruling nationalists. *Drum* magazine was the only real literary paper the Africans in Soweto could rely on. For this I gave credence to its expatriate British editor, Tom Hopkinson.

Transfixed, I briefly researched at the excellent Cape Town Library, the story of the fight for freedom of the press in Cape Colony during the third decade of the 19th century. A dramatic clash in the 1830s, between Scottish settler journalists Pringle and Fairbairn, and Governor Lord Somerset, paved the way for press freedom at that time. The story of that phase in the cultural development of the English-speaking peoples of South Africa, is told in A. M. Lewin Robinson's study of the English periodical literature of the Cape from 1824 to 1834, entitled *None Daring to Make Us Afraid.* I acquired the book from a bookstore.

What caught my eye in a twinkling was the written work of an early settler poet who, stooping to parody the Robert Burns lyric, *My love is like a red, red rose,* had salaciously written:

> *My love she has a flat, flat nose,*
> *I long to see it soon.*
> *My love is like a blackberry.*
> *All of a sooty bloom*

I first judged that poem, titled *The Hottentot Beauty,* ugly racism. Yet, was it? It was soon clear to me that race had been a preoccupation in southern Africa for 150 years, and that I, too, had it on the brain. No wonder Julian had escaped a South African life of wealthy white people, living in fine houses with cars and swimming pools obtained from the work of blacks, who would return each night to the squalor that was making Soweto Township notorious worldwide. By some quirk, Julian had decided to become a policeman in Rhodesia. That challenged my brain.

For a while, the pull of the running track had vented Julian's frustration. He was fast. Soon he was selected for national trials. I knew that nagging doubts, over playing the apartheid game by joining segregated sport that favored the chosen few, had haunted him. I concluded Julian honestly hated violence and feared ending up alongside white South Africans in a civil war against black Africans, whom he knew had a huge claim to more than equality and partnership. How was he to prove to himself he was not a coward? By leaving South Africa and joining the police in neighboring Rhodesia?

On my last day of leave, I rushed back by air to a soon-to-be independent Northern Rhodesia.

I was determined to hook a fish I'd been thinking a lot about in a Lusaka restaurant.

Chapter 18
The Journey to Gonakudzingwa

Shua and I caught a crowded bus on the first leg of our journey to Gonakudzingwa in Southern Rhodesia. Thanks to her, I was onto a big story and, at the same time, helping her.

Over engine noise and chatter, she told me the background. Her pastor father had returned home from chaplain service in World War II, hoping to peacefully help unite the Africans in his country and one day bring about majority rule. The recent new government in Salisbury had opposed his mission and his crowded church. Seeing his popularity rise, police began breaking up meetings and searching homes. When the party he supported was banned, her father had struggled to link religion with trade unions. The authorities cut this short, on grounds he had taken up the reins of militant revolt and was an enemy of the state.

Shua had taken leave to make one of her periodic visits home, to find her father's Harare house empty. Her uncle, with whom for safety she was living in Lusaka, had told her that her father had been driven away in a police van. Her mother had followed him. A week later had come a censored letter from her parents, saying they were in detention and that her father was ill. "Did the police give a specific reason why they arrested him?" I asked.

Shua shrugged her shoulders. "He threatened their power. My father would have cooperated if the authorities had treated Africans fairly."

"Why Gonakudzingwa?" I asked, also wondering exactly where on earth the place was that we were traveling to.

"My uncle, who has connections with the African National Congress, suggested he might be there."

"You must think it is a detention camp."

"I know it is a detention camp, and I have a rough idea where to find it."

The town of Fort Victoria was our first stop. After a meal, we found another bus going east. All too soon we had to walk with vague direction. I cursed the fact that my Ford was off the road, awaiting new tires and mechanical repair in Lusaka. I promised Shua I would rent a car for our return.

The south-east part of Rhodesia we had ventured into, was hot and arid, the sandy road and low scrub, broken here and there by skeletons of trees arched up to a blinding sky and giving little shade. Our journey took us over riverbeds across the low veldt of Rhodesia. Animals had almost abandoned the area. Mosquitoes thrived where there was water. I felt sorry for Shua in this arid land. We hid as two truckloads of Rhodesian soldiers passed, leaving us swallowing their dust.

A cluster of brick homes and huts brought the revelation that people actually lived in the desolate region. There was a small lodge with rooms to rent. So we paid a few shillings and were shown to a clean room with bunk beds, mosquito nets and white walls. The lodge keeper was a diminutive Pakistani man with pointed face and sharp eyes. He showed us wash basins and gave us towels. "Put this lotion on your eyelids," he offered, "then come for a meal."

"How can we thank you?" Shua asked.

"Give thanks to Allah," the man replied before asking our destination. The Pakistani was a good listener at dinner. Over curried rice and thin slices of pork, we told him our story. He asked Shua her father's name.

"It is Simon Sararanyatwa."

"Is your father a pastor in Salisbury?"

"He was."

"If he is detained by the government, I don't believe you will find him at Gonakudzingwa. That future prison is reserved for bigger fish such as Joshua Nkomo and Robert Mugabe, not for the Reverend Simon Sararanyatwa."

The Pakistani man surprised us with what further he had to say. "I am Ali Khan," he introduced himself. "I am Muslim, but I once attended your father's church in Salisbury. If your parents are at Gonakudzingwa they will be overjoyed to see their daughter. To think that your mother may be detained with him shows unusual cruelty by the authorities."

"My mother followed him when he was arrested. The arrest was bad enough but now my mother too."

"Be brave," he urged her. "You have only a few miles to walk to the village of Gonakudzingwa. I will draw you a map. Another

97

man I know of, like your father, peacefully fought the vile inequity of racial discrimination."

He continued: "I speak of Mahatma Gandhi. He spent time in a South African prison, before returning to India to win its independence. I came to Rhodesia from South Africa because of its crackdown on government opponents and the terrorist trial that awaits Nelson Mandela and others."

At that point I told him of my policeman friend Julian, who had also escaped South Africa for Rhodesia.

"That tells a story," the Pakistani lodge keeper continued. "The writing is on the wall when even whites oppose apartheid." Realizing he had a rapt audience, he continued: "Gandhi fought peacefully against laws and customs that keep mankind apart. After his first resistance campaign, he marched his followers into Pretoria's central prison."

"You say he marched into prison!" Shua exclaimed.

"Yes," Ali continued, "he was…"

"Who would be so foolish?"

"Foolish? Gandhi marched in with head held high."

"Then he must still be in prison. I know what goes on in South Africa. I have never heard of this Gandhi."

"Gandhi was assassinated in India before your time. Assassinated by hatred and bigotry. His fellow Hindu assassin opposed Gandhi's policy of communal and religious tolerance."

"But why did he march into prison?"

"It was his way of fighting apartheid. The South African–no, maybe more the Transvaal police were arresting Indian people for little things like not carrying their passes. New laws were taking land and votes from Indian people, just as they had disenfranchised Africans and made them register; as though they were common criminals or communist enemies, when many of them, like me, had been born in South Africa and had nothing to do with communism. Black people were being treated badly by white farmers, and by the police who were moving black or colored people like me from their homes. They do it officially with more vigor today under Verwoerd."

He continued: "Gandhi and his followers filled the prisons so full, they could hardly function. When some of Gandhi's supporters were killed, General Smuts turned a blind eye. I think he wanted Gandhi out of South Africa, so Gandhi obliged him by leaving. India's independence came in 1947 and, although Gandhi had fought peacefully for Indian freedom from British colonialism, he was assassinated at a rally in India that very year."

"Did your Muslim people kill him?" Shua asked.

"No! Didn't I tell you his assassin was Hindu?"

Ali continued: "The white settlers in control here fear the black people they discriminate against. Most white settlers want Rhodesia and its riches passed down from father to son. If they only looked north, they would see that the days of their dominance are numbered. Tanganyika under Nyerere, and Uganda under Obote, approach independence from British colonialism. Kenya will follow under Kenyatta. White Rhodesians ignore peril, at a time when they could sensibly partner with the black majority through multi-racial sport and allow majority rule."

"Tell us about Robert Mugabe," I asked.

"I know who Mugabe is!" Shua rebuked me.

Ali Khan ignored her interruption: "Mugabe is a Southern Rhodesian teacher, home from Ghana with his wife Sally. He is one of a few well-educated black Rhodesians. I believe he attended Fort Hare University in South Africa. In his wide travels, he reached independent Ghana and learned ideas from Kwame Nkrumah on how to win freedom from colonialism."

"Do you think Mugabe can help win Zimbabwe's independence?"

"Possibly."

"Let me enlighten you," Ali Khan continued. "Mugabe was not just teaching in Ghana. He was, as I said, learning. He became a disciple of Nkrumah. Ghana was one of the first African countries to oust British colonialism. His struggle was long and difficult. What Mugabe learned in Ghana, he will put into practice here. He is more a political leader than a guerrilla fighter."

Ali continued: "Mugabe will not lead the growing Zimbabwe army of freedom fighters on the field. The man who holds the key to defeating Rhodesian colonialism militarily, may be the young Josiah Tongogara. He leads patriotic fighters who have liberated zones of Zimbabwe bordering near here, freedom zones in Portuguese East Africa. Tongogara could lead in any widespread future war. He can tell political leaders, like Mugabe, what the fighters need, and the fighters, what the political leaders want. His big problem is the tribal split between Mugabe's Mashona tribe and the Matebele led by Joshua Nkomo. Tongogara is stuck between Mugabe's ZANU and Nkomo's ZAPU. Those political parties now have growing military backing. And who gains by their rivalry?"

"Of course, Ian Smith," I proclaimed. "Surely they should unite."

"I read the newspapers," Ali said. "Do you plan a story on Gonakudzingwa?"

"You seem to know everything."

"Don't believe everything you hear. Judge wisely. Obtain knowledge, love and happiness. To me, sport is important if freedom is to be won peacefully. The Olympic Games will soon be banned to South Africa over its race tendencies. I have talked too long. I've been talking you away from the good night's sleep you both need."

Shua and I retired with Ali's words in mind. We agreed he was a wily old bird we could trust. Bed was welcome and we fell asleep immediately.

Morning dawned cloudless and potentially sweltering, so we stayed at the motel until late mid-afternoon when it was cooler. A maid had served us breakfast and handed over the map Ali had promised us. He also told us over lunch, to return to him if we faced probable difficulties at Gonakudzingwa.

"What do you think he meant when he said, 'Run so that you may obtain?'" I asked Shua, as we left the motel to walk the road mapped out for us.

"How should I know? He was blathering on about sport. He seemed to see a love of sport as a way ahead for Zambians and Zimbabweans. That sounded odd to me since it is freedom Africans seek."

"The Olympic Games are where the world's best athletes compete in dedication to peace. That's what he was getting at."

"Do Zambians compete?"

"No–not yet. Well, maybe as part of the British team if they are good enough."

"Will our runners play at those games when freedom comes and Southern Rhodesia is independent Zimbabwe?"

"Marathon?"

"A race of more than 26 miles."

"Okay–race you to that tree!"

A quick sprint by Shua took me by surprise. I levelled with her, despite carrying both our rucksacks, then strode a pace ahead. She grabbed my shirt tail, knocking me off balance. We landed on sandy ground beneath the tree. Neither of us was hurt. I laughed. That set her laughing too. I called her Laughing Water, as we drank from a bottle of water Ali had given us. The tree offered shade. I hugged her. She hugged me! I was in love.

I confessed: "I wanted to hold you like this last night, but Ali kept on talking."

She smiled: "You fell asleep the moment your head touched the pillow."

For a brief moment we lay in each other's arms. I thought I had at last found a woman. Next, a big dark brown and white bird alighted on the tree above our heads. "It's a fish eagle," Shua whispered of the bird perched majestically on a stout branch. "It will not harm us if we move slowly away."

"Does the fish eagle eat fish?" I asked.

My question left Shua smiling. I picked up a flat stone. "I present you with your gold medal."

"For the marathon?"

We were so absorbed that we had not seen an approaching car until it was abreast. I stuck out my thumb for a lift. Too late, I noticed the word P-O-L-I-C-E written on the blue and grey vehicle. Shua pulled down my arm, but the car had stopped. Two policemen called us over. "I did not see it was a police car," I whispered to her. "Let *me* answer their questions."

Chapter 19
Going Where?

"Who are you and where are you going?" a police corporal asked.

"To Gonakudzingwa."

The policeman paused as our destination sank into his brain. "What business have you there?" he asked.

"We hope to find someone there."

"At Gonakudzingwa?"

"My parents may be there," Shua nervously said.

"Why were the two of you rolling on the ground?"

"We were having fun," I replied. "That is why my friend here is smiling. I sometimes call her *Laughing Water.*"

"You threw her to the ground!"

"She threw me to the ground!"

"You were running away. Then you hid under the tree," he charged. "So you, a white man, are going to Gonakudzingwa, hoping to find this black woman's parents. Am I correct?"

"We did not hide. We moved slowly from the sheltering tree when an eagle perched above us," Shua said.

"What's that stone doing in your hand?"

Shua had forgotten about her gold medal and quickly placed it on the ground.

"You were ready to throw that stone."

"I am searching for my parents. You must believe me. That stone was only part of a game we were playing."

"A game?"

"The stone was a gold medal for running a playful marathon."

The officer stared at her dumbfounded.

"Your passes," he requested holding out a hand. Shua delved into her shoulder bag and handed over a pass she had obtained from the authorities in Lusaka. I had only my British passport to show. The corporal scanned Shua's pass and returned it with a nod. He voiced upset with me. "Why are you with this woman?"

I felt fear creep up my spine when the constable gingerly poked at my trouser pocket, where Ali's map bulged like a hernia. I saw that the policemen had guns. He pierced me with his eyes as I coolly explained that the map showed our route to Gonakudzingwa.

"Shua is my friend. She needs help to find her parents. This map tells us where to go. Shua playfully raced me to the tree as she said. We had been idly talking about the Olympic Games and we were having a drink of water. I playfully presented her with an Olympic gold medal–in fact, only a flat stone. I'm actually a reporter on the *Rhodesia Herald*."

The constable stared at me for a moment, then delved into the back of the car and came up with a copy of the *Herald*.

"You will find my name in the masthead on the editorial page."

He found the page and read it aloud.

"So you, a *Herald* reporter, and your friend, are headed for Gonakudzingwa. Are you intending to write about Gonakudzingwa in the newspaper?"

"Yes."

"What's your father's name?" the corporal asked Shua.

"It is Oliver Sararanyatwa. He is a church minister in Salisbury."

"Holy smoke!" The constable broke in to the corporal's obvious distaste in ordering us: "Get in the car. We're headed to the camp where you say your parents are detained." To the constable, he said: "She has a pass and appears to be looking for her parents. He is a reporter, and his passport and the newspaper confirm this. We'll let the Gonakudzingwa police sort this out. It's their job, not ours."

Half an hour later, after passing through guarded gates, our police car drew up outside a low wooden building. Heavy shovels were scooping out soil around us and bulldozers leveling it. Dormitory-style wooden barracks had been erected. The corporal, with my passport and Shua's pass in hand, told the constable to guard us, then left the car to enter the police building. After five minutes, he returned. He motioned us out of the car and led us into an office.

Chapter 20
Inquisition

"So, Mr. Fairbairn, you work for *The Rhodesia Herald.* What brings you to Gonakudzingwa?"

"I was accompanying my friend Shua."

"That was not my question. What brings you here?"

"I'm a reporter on a story. That's my job. My friend needed help. It was my duty to help a woman best I could."

He turned on Shua. "So what help do you need? And why are *you* here?"

"I am looking for my parents."

"Oliver Sararanyatwa and his wife?"

"The Reverend Oliver Sararanyatwa, my father, and my mother."

"Do you expect to find them here?"

"I had hoped to find them here."

"Well, they are not here. So what will you do now?"

"Keep on searching."

Turning his eyes on me, he stated: "So you are a reporter on a story?"

"No harm in that is there?"

The police officer stared intently. "Maybe not. Is this African woman your means to a story?"

I first ignored the implication, saying: "We have committed no crime. You cannot hold us here. The Reverend Oliver Sararanyatwa may not be here as you say. But he is being held somewhere by police. A woman has the right to openly look for her parents. I have the right to help her. My search for a story is a means of helping her. I left word of where we were going with my newspaper and with a hotelkeeper in Fort Victoria. Either of them, or both, will raise the alarm if we do not return this coming weekend as intended."

"What do you know of ZAPU?"

"Nothing more than it is an African political party."

"But your friend is the daughter of a man linked with ZAPU."

"I am with Shua to help find her father who was taken somewhere by police. She was told her parents might be here. She is worried about her father and mother. Will you help her?"

"Where did you meet Shua?"

"In Lusaka."

"What were you doing in Lusaka?"

"I'm a reporter assigned to report the Northern Rhodesian election campaign."

"Report the elections from Gonakudzingwa? And what more have you to say, Shua?"

"I am saying a prayer."

With that, the police officer drummed his desk with his fingers. He indicated bewilderment thrusting two palms in the air, before calling in two African askaris and telling them to lock up our two bags, lock us up in a secure room with two single beds and a washroom, and serve us beans on toast for supper. To Shua and me, he said: "I have other things to do now. Since I now seem to be your hotelkeeper, sleep well. My superintendent will continue this discourse in the morning."

Shua and I were shunted off. The askaris carried our rucksacks away and took us to a room furnished with two single beds, a table, two chairs and an open barred window. I judged that one constable was standing guard outside, until 10 minutes later, the other served us supper. He closed the door from the inside, then whispered that he had overheard our interrogation. He asked Shua to listen carefully. "Your father and probably your mother are in Bulawaya. I shall return here at 3 a.m. with your bags and documents, and drive you from this place to wherever safety lies. Be ready for me!"

He next shouted out, telling us to give him our shoes and socks. He threw a blanket at each of us. With that, he left with a salute that left me stunned.

"What's going on?" I whispered to Shua. "How can *he* save us? Is this a police trap?"

"I trust him," she said softly.

"I don't."

"We must."

"He may lead us into worse trouble."

"If he comes, we should go with him."

"But if caught, there will be no mercy from the police. They will leave us defenseless, saying we escaped after we were served supper. The noise of starting a car will raise the alarm. There is risk to us in his sudden decision to help us. You are won over. Yet, if we *were* to trust him, and he returns our property and takes us to Fort Victoria in whatever vehicle he has, we could head back to Lusaka in a hired car."

"So you will trust him?"

"Yes," I said, swallowing lingering doubts. "We will await his coming. I'm not speaking about Jesus by the way!"

"It seems like a miracle to me."

Excitement was enveloping both of us as I took advantage of her nearness to embrace her. She pressed against me saying she loved me for doing what I was doing. I clumsily tried to raise her blouse from her skirt and slip my hand below it, but she stopped me.

"No," she admonished me. "I said I loved you for helping me. You are white and I am black. That is a mix that only time and God will resolve. But I now know where my parents are."

"Wow!" I replied. "Which university did you say you went to for that turn of speech?"

"Fort Hare in South Africa. Mugabe also studied there. My father, as a clergyman, once had influence and money. I had a good education with a degree in sociology and religion. No more talk though. Let us rest until our saviors come."

That night, as the camp slept, the askari crept back. Another askari quietly loaded our belongings and Shua into a police car. The three of us, with Shua at the wheel, pushed the car 150 yards before starting the engine. The askaris agreed to drive us to Ali's rooming house rather than distant Fort Victoria. "From there you can go on your way by bus. We are heading east to train at a guerrilla base, with the new Patriotic Front freedom fighters on the Portuguese East Africa border. We have been planning this since word of unity. You gave us reason to do it earlier than we intended."

He said the Gonakudzingwa camp was being prepared for the detention of Joshua Nkoma and Robert Mugabe, now allied in the Patriotic Front. Learning this plan of the Smith regime had angered the askaris into absconding. Acknowledging our thanks for services rendered, the askari added: "All we ask is that you, as a journalist, tell Zimbabwe's story to the world."

106

Chapter 21
Great Zimbabwe

Shua and I huddled together in the cold for hours outside Ali's lodge, until his maid answered our knock on the door.

"You are back and no doubt in trouble," Ali greeted us.

We told him our story over breakfast. "You say the police may be after you? Where will you go?"

"We will go by bus to Fort Victoria, then I'll hire a car and drive to Lusaka."

"Tell you what. I have reason to drive to Fort Victoria. I will take you, provided you tell no-one."

Ali then surprised me, by suggesting that on leaving Fort Victoria we should visit the historic ruins of Great Zimbabwe, to hide from any police chase that day, and leave me with a safe and ready explanation of a newspaper assignment there. He took the words from my mouth, because that was the intention my newspaper knew about.

Fort Victoria had been established in *her* name, by the Pioneer Column in the footholds of Empire, after Cecil-Rhodes-supporting military pioneers marched from South Africa into the domain of King Lobengula of the Matabele nation. The town was an important stronghold during the Matabele War that founded Rhodesia.

We booked into an inn rather than the bigger hotel, and in the town library, buried ourselves in the history of the Great Zimbabwe ruins. The car hire company had told us we could have a vehicle the next day. So, next day, our route took us to one of Africa's great land mysteries near Masvingo. Legend said Zimbabwe was built by African hands based on gold trade with the Arabs; a tragic city plundered by colonial treasure hunters, to compound the mystery and deny anything like an African civilization before the white man arrived in numbers.

An antelope meandering near our car, bolted when we arrived at the Zimbabwe ruins parking lot. A giraffe blended almost invisibly into the background. I gave no thought to reports of white rhino and lions said to be in the area.

A small museum was our first call and we had it to ourselves. We learned again that the Great Zimbabwe ruins had functioned as an international trading site, built between the 11th and 15th centuries. A curator guided us to a display of excavated articles from China and Arabia. He said the most mysterious finds on display, were soapstone Zimbabwe birds that may have been totems. From a lofty vantage point, we looked down on the *Valley of Ruins* dominated by the Temple of Great Enclosure, with walls more than ten meters high. Its most striking feature was the dry stone Conical Tower. We were told its purpose defied explanation, although scientific observers believed it was associated with fertility rites.

In the reconstruction of a Karanga village, a potter showed us how he made pots by the ancient African method without the aid of a potter's wheel. A witchdoctor, crouching on the ground, threw bones and told Shua her fortune: "You will overcome misfortune and find happiness in the church of God," I recall writing his words in my notebook, and photographing Shua and him displaying the bones.

Before leaving the parking lot, a squealing warthog charged, forcing us to dive into the car. Luckily, I had not locked up. We watched the pig apparently furious at missing us. Only then did I question the safety of visitors.

I knew many hectares of agricultural land had been developed around nearby Lake Kyle, being built with catchment dams across the Mtilikwe River. The precious water, hitherto lost after short rainy seasons ended, was now stored and used for agriculture throughout the year. Side by side with virgin bush, were orderly fields of wheat and sugar cane. The white man had brought about agricultural riches and increased black bass fishing. Plans for a scenic road skirting the Nyuni Mountains and a new game reserve were being considered.

"What will you write?" Shua asked me. "A story about Gonakudzingwa would risk retribution by the Rhodesian government or police."

In Fort Victoria, I had already written memos in my notebook: *There are no detained persons at Gonakudzingwa yet. But there soon will be. I found out from an African askari, that they are building the restriction camp to imprison Joshua Nkomo, Robert Mugabe and may be other patriots.*

The memos included a fairly verbatim account of what the interrogating police officer had asked us. I recalled that Shua, when questioned, had mumbled back: *I was saying a prayer.*

Also, in my notebook: *That night we heard the clumping of heavy boots on the wooden floor outside. It was an askari with blankets and supper. I nodded thanks. Then he startled me by shouting at the top of his voice, to get our boots and socks off and lie down on the beds. He took them away. But that night, when the camp slept, the same askari along with a comrade, unlocked our door and returned my money, clothes, diary and other documents as well as those of Shua. He drove us to Ali's lodge, telling us the two of them planned to join guerrillas training to fight for Rhodesia's freedom from a base further east. He said that the Gonakudzingwa camp was being prepared for the detention of African leaders, Nkomo and Mugabe, and this had angered the askaris. They had left a note with the BSAP saying they were joining the freedom fighters. Shua and I promised allegiance to their fight for freedom. Before we broke company, he urged me to get Zimbabwe's story out to the world.*

Chapter 22
The God Nyaminyami

The trip north was uneventful through Salisbury. There was nothing to relate except a flat tire for which I blamed the warthog. A garage hand fixed it and I filled up with gas. I was mentally prepared to crash roadblocks. The anti-climax demanded a reason. I could not at that time come up with one. There was just a nice drive to hit the great north road.

I knew my editor in Salisbury might be under government pressure because of me. I also knew that he was being replaced, that very week, of the Northern Rhodesian elections. With this in mind, I decided to take the northern route to Lusaka across the Kariba Dam. It was shorter and quieter. We proceeded steadily towards the border, unhindered. I wondered if I had exaggerated the reaction by the police to our escape from the detention camp.

The bush around us became dry, harsh and rocky. Though the heat was stifling, there was a breeze and we had an open sunroof. We passed through tree-dotted plains where giraffe and kudu grazed almost hidden. The plains gave way to swampland where baboons swung from trees and soon we saw waterbuck romp on a half-drowned islet, approaching the man-made dam that was Lake Kariba.

"The home of my mother's ancestors is near here," Shua said, breaking a half hour's silence. I wondered what she was getting at and suspected fear of getting her uncle into trouble in Lusaka. I immediately found out I was right.

"I will have to tell my uncle what happened at the detention camp. Maybe I would be safer from Rhodesian policemen if I hid in my native village."

That irked me so much, I drove the car to a stop at the side of the road hoping to settle things. "Shua, I love you too. I'll take you to Scotland. I have never been in love like this before. Are we not white and black fighting the same war on racism?"

"Yes."

"Is our relationship not important?"

"I told you I loved you for helping me."

"Just for my help?" I cried out. "I need more. Am I asking too much of you? I thought you really loved me. Where will you end up if you hide? You'll just be someone who ran away. I won't hide and I refuse to let you hide. You, the daughter of a detained African clergyman, are likely too much for the already overwhelmed police to take on. My theory is that though police can arrest your father on false charges of enemy of the state, they will back off arresting a daughter looking for her parents, or, a journalist seeking a story. They may also be embarrassed by two askaris deserting them to join the liberation struggle. Think about it!"

I revved up and drove slowly across the highway atop the Kariba Dam that had been built some seven or eight years earlier for hydro-electric power. For the first time I saw close up, the vast valley where the Zambezi was held back to form Lake Kariba. A few workers, on either side, were shoring up giant concrete pillars. The predominantly Italian skilled workers who had built the dam, were there for only the years of construction. The rising water of the dam had forced many River Tonga tribesmen out of their homes. A few had drowned, along with animals not saved in time.

We stopped on one side of the highway to take in the panoramic view of the turquoise water and green landscape. "This is needed," I told Shua. "The generators send electric power into a grid that stretches from Bulawayo to the Copperbelt. Skilled dam builders labored alongside your people. They overcame the spirit of the river!" I immediately regretted that remark, because until then I had known little about what she knew about that spirit.

It set her off telling me that Tonga elders had commanded their god, *Nyaminyami*, to come down in wrath and destroy the dam. Indeed, for successive seasons, floods had set work back. Eventually, concrete had subdued a less angry god.

"Shall I relate a poem?" she asked, her dark, shining eyes bewitching me but fixed on hills beyond us. She was back in the days of her childhood.

O Zambezi, O my river
O Zambezi, thou art my mother
Thou dost make the trees to flourish
Whence I fashion out my boat
To the birds thou dost give succour

To your reeds they trust their eggs
Through the gift of thy pure waters
Dost thou bring my children food?

Thou dost quench my thirst and hunger
In thy hand bear my canoe
O Zambezi, O my river
Truly are thy waters blessed
O Zambezi, O my river…

"That tells you what the Zambezi means to my people."

We crossed on foot to the other side of the road. What we saw stunned me. Controlled water gushed out of two huge low holes in the wall. It looked to me like massive jet pees of dinosaurs. "People lost their homes and government did not keep promises," she said softly. "Did your English queen know this when she declared the dam open?"

I pointed out that it was Britain's Queen Mother who had declared the dam open, and that she must have ascertained that those uprooted by the water would have new and better homes.

Shua was doubtful: "Traditional land, where some of my forebears are buried, is now under water. These were sons of the river. That's to say sons of the Zambezi that provided food for their families. The river gave my people fish and fertile mud, to grow crops as well as a route for their boats and water to drink. It was called *The River of Life.*"

"They will now fish the lake," I argued. "There will be more and easier catches. The river is reasserting itself. Those sons of the Zambezi now have a lake and water still flowing downstream. The important thing is that people will have electric power. You see tradition and progress clashing. I say diversity improves life."

"Black and white diversity? What *are* we Africans? What do we *want* to be? I overheard my uncle say, we are weary of drinking our tears and must fight back against white men to find out."

I swung round, rattled and confused. My hitherto polite voice snapped: "Whit the hell d'ye say? Whit's gang into ye? Can't you just love me?"

She mocked me and not lovingly: "What schooling did you have? Why are you talking like that? I'm not blaming you! I blame Ian Smith and the Rhodesia Front for the troubles. Swearing like that tells me that you don't know how to speak to a woman!"

I tersely explained that she had not been too polite herself: "Women working in my Scottish hometown hosiery mills handed me down my accent. It's the worst in Scotland. Those women shouted out on top of noisy machines that wove beautiful clothes, the likes of which women wear all over the world, if they can afford them."

I ranted on unmindfully: "Zambia needs electricity. Ask Kaunda! He knows towns and villages need power for the welfare and comfort of his people. The way you're reacting, you would think the Zambezi had disappeared from the face of the earth. Your mighty river of life is heading towards the Kafue, and these two rivers, as one, head to the sea. They make trees flourish and cool the hippo. What's your problem?"

"As if I can answer that here and in a few words."

I shrugged and walked over to the car, glad through my tired eyes to see her follow suit on the passenger side.

I drove Shua to her uncle's place in Lusaka. She said he would probably not welcome me in, taking into account the trouble we might be in. I carried on to the Ridgeway Hotel, took a room and booked a call to my newspaper office in Salisbury. I owed them it.

I was enjoying a shower when the return call came from the newsroom. "What the heck are you doing back in Lusaka?" the news editor asked tersely. "I thought you were in Fort Victoria doing a story on the Great Zimbabwe ruins. Our new editor, Malcolm Smith, whom you probably have not met, wants a word. Be careful what you say to him."

I forgot his advice when the editor came on the line, actually asking who I was and where I was. I introduced myself as one of his staff reporters, adding: "I'm in Lusaka. I had to bring a needy friend to her home here. I helped her seek out her father and mother who are in police detention. I have my Great Zimbabwe ruins story in my notebook and also an exclusive story on a place called Gonakudzingwa. It's a detention camp, meant for enemies of the state, where no other reporter has been."

"Well, Fairbairn," he replied tersely, "that may be true. What is also true is that the Special Branch visited me today. I told them you were doing a story at the Zimbabwe ruins. Nothing more. I must be honest and say, I prefer you do *not* return right now."

That took my breath away. "You know about Gonakudzingwa then?"

"Yes, I do. Rumors have been rife for months at my previous post in Umtali. Rumors we did not rush after for the paper. My predecessor here thinks you are a good reporter. With this self-assigned Gonakudzingwa affair, as I know it, he might have been mistaken."

"So, the policy is to censor a scoop!"

The blast from the other end had me later thinking about a desk editor's job in Nairobi that was being advertised.

"You numbskull! Even your colleagues say you see Southern Rhodesia through the eyes of a Scot. I've a couple of generations of Rhodesian pedigree behind me, and now you convince me that what they say is true. Since your previous editor told me you were good at your job, I'll give you one more chance to live up to it. We're transferring you to work under Rowland, now that he is editor of the *Northern News* in Ndola, and I editor here. Be there in a week, at his consent, to start on the desk."

He continued: "The politics you're up to can't go on. I'll assign another reporter from here to cover the Northern Rhodesian independence. The time for the black man has not yet come in the Rhodesias. That's pretty liberal of me, because some people here say it won't ever come. I won't lecture you any more on race relations or anything else. Go north, young man."

Before putting down the phone, he seemed to hesitate, then justify himself with a single phrase: "We here fear government censorship!"

I snuggled down under the sheet on my bed, head whirling, back sore and still damp from the shower. That night, I had a nightmarish dream about trying to put a newspaper to bed.

In the morning, I phoned the *Northern News* to ask my far friendlier editor, whom I by then wasn't surprised had been sent north, if I could stay in Lusaka for a couple of weeks to be present for the big day at Independence Stadium.

Rowland's reply raised my spirits: "I'd like you to cover the independence ceremony and anything else of importance, before coming to Ndola in two weeks to work on the desk."

Chapter 23
Kwacha!

Zambia gained its independence on October 24, 1964. Queen Elizabeth's representative, the Princess Royal, elderly but serene, stood beside Prime Minister Kenneth Kaunda during the last seconds, before another part of a British empire, on which it was said the sun never set, gained its freedom. The Union Jack was lowered in darkness and seconds later, the fish eagle emblem of Zambia was spotlighted, fluttering in the soft breeze above the heads of thousands of revelers in Independence Stadium, Lusaka. People of all races celebrated in peace and joy, the birth of the new nation.

I listened as the voices of the crowd watching, joined those of a choir of women singing Zambia's new national anthem, written only a few weeks earlier to the music of *Nkosi Sikelel i'Africa*:

> *One land and one nation is our cry*
> *Dignity and peace 'neath Zambia's sky*
> *Like our noble eagle in its flight*
> *All one, strong and free*

Fireworks lit up the dark night as thousands also sang the English version, *Stand and Sing for Zambia*.

Earlier that day, garden party guests ranged from President Julius Nyerere of Tanzania to Harry Oppenheimer, boss of the huge Anglo-American mining company headquartered in Johannesburg, with interests in Zambia. I watched the Princess Royal, standing beside Kaunda, graciously welcome guests both young and old.

On that day of independence, athletes ran around the stadium track. They circled once, before halting at the dais to salute seated dignitaries. Having only that day assumed the office of prime minister, Kaunda addressed them on the theme of a future, when clashes between people would occur only on sports fields and freedom from oppression would be universal. A loud cheer erupted when he exhorted them to carry that freedom ceremonially to all parts of Zambia. Soon the athletes lined up to climb a hillside, one by one, to light freedom torches.

Each mounted steps to the hillside flame overlooking the cheering crowd. The cheers reached a crescendo when they appeared near the top, to mount the final steps to the Flame of Freedom.

They plunged their torches in and raised flaming symbols in gestures of triumph, that I, among thousands, shared. I watched nostalgically, knowing they were on their way on the first legs of relays to all parts of the country. Red flames contrasted vividly against blue sky. The flame of freedom was alive in Zambia. It seemed to me that hardly a thought was given to dark clouds gathering in a sullen Southern Rhodesia.

I looked almost everywhere for Shua but could not find her. I dared not go to her uncle's house. That evening, I typed out my independence story on my portable typewriter kept at the hotel, wired it to London and telephoned it to Ndola. My journalism career was almost out of control and my love life again at a standstill.

Chapter 24
The Katanga Affair

I completely lost touch with Shua while continuing on the respected *Northern News* in Ndola. It seemed that I would never find a woman I could call my own.

Ndola was interesting, with a swimming pool and a small library. In contrast, there was little for editors to do at night after the newspaper's midnight deadline expired, except throw darts and drink beer. Even in daytime, card games predominated for desk editors, while reporters wrote their stories. Soon, I was a dab hand at cribbage, no better at darts, improving at chess, easily winning at snooker.

The Belgian hotelkeeper, my host for a short time when first in town, loved chess. When he was not on some nefarious and dangerous trip over the border to run-down Elizabethville in Katanga, where he was winding up business affairs, he and I would sit through the wee hours after my paper's deadline, resolutely moving our pawns, knights and queens, as though we sought a stalemate. When your opponent takes 15 minutes over a move, it encourages sleep. He would invariably win after tedium gripped me.

I would return to my lodgings wondering if I should take the trip with him to Elizabethville that he had suggested. I turned him down. It was too dangerous to go with a Belgian who had left Katanga and was back there on business.

Katanga's Premier Moise Tshombe, with Belgian compliance, had led the mineral rich province to unilateral independence. He personally, once or twice, had come across the border from Elizabethville to my newspaper office, alleging maltreatment in news or editorial.

Southern Rhodesia's government, along with the West, had branded democratically-elected Congolese Prime Minister Patrice Lumumba a communist. The Rhodesians regretted when suddenly Tshombe disappeared but were delighted when he reappeared as prime minister of all of the Congo under President Joseph Kasavubu.

I had spent a year in Ndola's humid heat and was considering a break southward by train to Cape Town in the middle of the night. I was considering going home by ship to Britain, to escape the increasingly violent atmosphere and the boredom of darts and cards, along with my confining contract with the Rhodesian newspaper company that I considered had been broken by its management of me.

One night, seated at the editing desk, conjuring up headlines and laying out pages, a desk colleague invited me to go with him to a track and field meet in nearby Luanshya. That town's copper mine complex had a running track, a little distance from whining turbines and mine-head wagons. The mine sports club chairman had set up a team of athletes from the mines, to compete against a team chosen from runners working over the border at Katanga mines.

"Come on," my colleague said, "the match-up is long-standing and tagged international. There is more than athletics to it. I heard that the mine's new cook at Luanshya, by name of Pierre, is from Katanga, and that he smuggled his wife and children from Elizabethville. Apparently, he is well-educated, and in both English and French, tries to rally Zambians against Tshombe. There may be a story for you as a stringer for the *Sun,* and me for the *Times.*"

The cook, Pierre, indeed, was native to Katanga but had his wife and children with him in Zambia.

"Those runners are helping Tshombe," the cook said in Luanshya, when we caught up with him and asked about the international athletics challenge match.

"Tshombe is back from Spain, where he fled when troops of the *Organisation des Nations Unies au Congo,* or, the Blue Berets as you might say, were thought to have defeated his secession bid. He was recalled by President Kasavubu to deal with the Simba tribe.

"The mine owners in Katanga still support Tshombe. I cooked for the Katanga gendarmerie when its police and troops skirmished with Congolese troops. They may not now have their Katanga national hymn, flag, map, coins and stamps and other independence bits and pieces, but I doubt the rebellion is over. I understand huge quantities of Katanga money were recently burned as fake in a furnace near Ndola, while troops of foreign nations serving with the UN restored Katanga to the Congo. But rebellion is not over," Pierre predicted.

As a journalist I knew about the fake money going into the furnaces. I had tried and failed to cover the story, when two friendly police officers filled me with beer at the airport restaurant, the night the money was flown in. Nevertheless, the story broke. I regretted missing a scoop at the get-go.

"That did happen," I whispered, as we listened to Pierre speak.

There were no more interruptions as Pierre directed remarks to me: "Tshombe used Belgian troops, white mercenaries and Katangese soldiers to betray the Congo, then he came back as premier. He murdered our leader, Patrice Lumumba."

"You say Lumumba was murdered?"

"You don't know that?"

"I know he is dead and heard rumors."

"He was murdered in the way United Nations leader Dag Hammerschold was killed, when his plane came down from the sky near Ndola during a mission to bring peace to Congo. Many believe it was an accident, and truth to tell, maybe it was. Lumumba's death was no accident. He was delivered to his enemies in Katanga after his capture by Mobutu's troops, while fleeing across the river to his northern stronghold of Stanleyville. His body ended up in the bush with bullet wounds. Right now, UN troops are replacing Belgian troops in Katanga. While this is going on, the Katanga secessionists are running a track meet in Zambia at *international* level! Who set up this track meet?"

I did not know, but he did.

"The idea came from Union Miniére some time ago, when Katanga was consolidating unilateral independence. The Belgians, who still run the mines, are up to their necks in capitalism and willing to put on any show of supporting Katanga's independence. A track meet fits the bill. The meet is loaded propaganda. Union Miniére executives have influence in Zambia too. The company never supported the Congo. It supported Katanga and Belgium. What a mess we are in!"

Pierre broke into a colloquial French that told me that, though his English was good, he spoke French too. *"Sans fais rien… peut-être je ne suis certain de rien."*

"What?" I asked puzzled.

"Maybe I am certain of nothing," he spelled out in English. "I hate Tshombe and Kasavubu. But worse is Mobutu. You may well ask who he is. He is the army officer who helped capture Lumumba. He has American and Belgian backing to finance his army. Some say he actually named himself president of the Congo, while standing on a beer barrel, surrounded by loyal soldiers!"

"Did you see him do that?"

"I know Katanga is dangerous for people like me to proclaim the truth, but it does not change who I am. I don't have to see to believe."

"Surely you are exaggerating, Pierre," I ventured. "I never heard of any beer barrel accession to the presidency by Mobutu."

"*Je n'ai pas mes yeux dans ma poche comme vous. Pourquoi est-que je suis ici?* While Congo starves, Katanga reaps rich mineral harvests, and this has angered local tribesmen who are now rebelling along with *Force Publique.* When times are hard, people turn to religion or war. Copper, uranium, plutonium, provide Belgian cash for white mercenaries on Tshombe's side. I was a fool to cook for those mercenaries after Lumumba was executed."

My thoughts were that this outspoken cook was an idiot if his family's survival was important to him. But there was no stopping Pierre.

"I have word from Elizabethville that further insurrection is in the air. Many of my tribe are returning to their Katanga homeland from Angola and Brazzaville. That means fighting and killing. It is hard for you to know what is going on, because I can see you don't speak French!"

I had no idea what to say to that in the shadow of this man who, like a radical politician, spoke wise and foolish words.

"On one side," he ranted on, "you have the shadow of Tshombe, the influence of Union Miniére and a bunch of white mercenaries; on another side, you now have General Mobutu and his Congolese, Belgian and American capitalist supporters; in the center you have UN troops from America, Canada and the Soviet Union; on top of all, you have refugees trying to get out of Katanga."

"Enough!" I exclaimed.

Pierre was momentarily quiet, then said: "I tell you these things only because as a journalist, like my father, you can judge and write about it."

His last words for a long time left me in disarray. Then Katanga physically came to my boarding home in Ndola, and I learned that what he had said was true. There was a road exodus of Belgian settlers. The Ndola airport was crammed with mostly women and children carrying suitcases, hoping to get to Salisbury and on to Brussels. The Southern Rhodesian government set up a system of emergency aid for their Belgian friends. United Nations troops ended Katanga's second secession. Tshombe gained exile this time in Franco's Spain, and Mobutu *did* become the new Congo military president.

I met refugees at my Ndola lodging house, telling of looting, murder and rape in Katanga.

Zambian mines were gaining markets from the chaos across the border. I predicted war north and south, and cowardly or sensibly, left Ndola by train in the darkness of night.

Chapter 25
Ian Smith's War

Rhodesia has struck a blow for justice, civilization and Christianity... in the spirit of this belief we have assumed our sovereign independence

Prime Minister Ian Smith's broadcast that November morning, a year after neighboring Zambia had become independent, was what many Rhodesians had expected. The announcement had been planned in advance. White people had awaited it with support or with a mixture of fear and excitement, black people with anger and dread. So, people crowded around the few television and many radio sets in Salisbury homes and in black townships such as Harare.

The prime minister later stood up, tall and lean, in the banquet hall of Meikles Hotel, to address leaders of Salisbury society. They had raised glasses in a toast to their Queen, but nodded approvingly when he warned that they might soon be leaving her realm.

Smith read from the eve-of-battle speech of England's King Henry V. *"That he which hath no stomach to this fight, let him depart. He today that sheds his blood with me shall be my brother; and gentlemen in England, now a-bed, shall think themselves accurs'd they were not here."*

When he had finished speaking, the Salisbury Municipal Orchestra played the British national anthem, *God Save the Queen.*

Immediately after Ian Smith issued his Proclamation of Independence, Governor Sir Humphrey Gibbs issued a proclamation declaring the government illegal and removing Smith and his ministers from office. But censorship had been introduced that morning, and the governor's proclamation was neither published nor broadcast within Rhodesia, though it was broadcast by the British Broadcasting Corporation.

For white Rhodesians there was much at stake. I used to reflect, in one way admirably, how few communities in the world could match the sun-drenched affluence that descendants of Rhodesia's hardy settlers had achieved for themselves. Lions still commanded distant escarpments, and elephants, baboons and rhinos, foraged in valleys of rivers bulging with hippo. But on rolling high veldt, brushed with elephant grass and flowering with jacaranda trees, the whites had carved out a tidy empire of modern tobacco farms and cattle ranches.

Taxes were low and so were prices and, for whites, wages were high enough to permit all but the most menial workers their own cars, homes and servants. Salisbury's white population, spread out over 30 square miles of more private swimming pools than any other city of its size in the world.

Only a week after unilateral declaration of independence (UDI), black protesters thronged the tarmac of Salisbury Airport. They had struggled there from their homes outside the city. They had crowded on balconies, perched in jacaranda trees, and clung to flagpoles around the airport building. More than 6,000 of them were squeezed in a tight mass, hemmed in on one side by a 12-foot wire fence and on the other by a cordon of police and their dogs. When an RAF Comet whistled to a stop, and a chubby man appeared at the cabin door, they erupted with thunderous cheers.

"Mambokadze tinoda nyika yehu!" roared black Rhodesians, there to greet Harold Wilson, Labour Party prime minister of Britain. "Your Majesty the Queen, we want our country," they demanded. "We want one man, one vote."

Wilson had come to Rhodesia to prevent the white-supremacist colonial regime of Ian Smith from seizing independence.

Wilson's chances seemed slight. In talks with Smith, the previous month in London, neither side had made meaningful compromise on the fundamental issue. The British had said the government would give Rhodesia its freedom, on condition that the nation's four million blacks were guaranteed control within the foreseeable future. Most of the whites interpreted this as their suicide. The white Rhodesians were determined blacks would never rule the country. They claimed violence in the Congo, autocracy in Ghana, Mau Mau in Kenya, and communist penetration everywhere in Africa, ruled against the blacks.

Wilson gained little ground from his talks with Smith, but he was determined to keep on trying.

I watched another form of Chamberlain's peace in our time with Hitler, as Rhodesia's unilateral declaration of independence reverberated around the world.

In South Africa, Prime Minister Hendrick Verwoerd proclaimed South Africa impartial, but secretly authorized ministers to do all they could to see that Rhodesia had the means to carry out its independence declaration. South Africa's apartheid policy had kept blacks and whites apart for years, by such legislation as formal education for natives in the Bantu language and making government permission necessary for blacks to live in urban areas. It had taken away political rights and brought in identity passes. Blacks in South Africa were being hauled off to jail and plans underway to move as many as possible to any of eight remote Bantustan republics, where they would live segregated from whites. Divide and conquer was the rule. In two decades of power, the South African regime had handed down 55 major laws to restrict Africans in everything they did or held dear.

I knew that decrees from parliament in Cape Town were moving in on whites too. Enemies of the apartheid regime had been confined to their homes or jailed without trial.

So, South Africa supported white supremacy in Rhodesia as well.

In Tanzania, President Julius Nyerere called a cabinet meeting that urged Britain to stop the white minority in Salisbury from taking over the country in the South African way.

The Zambian government offered Britain a base for its troops to launch an attack on Rhodesia and end the rebellion.

Wilson ruled out use of force.

I took a vacation in Britain and found British youth hypnotized by four mop-haired pop singers seeking to hold someone's hand. England's chance of winning the World Cup Football Championship, being played out in Britain, was another conversational option in an atmosphere of Beatlemania. During a dance one evening in London's Piccadilly, a young singer demanding satisfaction left me dissatisfied. I found out later who that singer was.

"She loves you, yeah, yeah, yeah" and "I can't get no satisfaction" topped the music charts.

When England won soccer victory over Germany, the minority white takeover of a country of four to five million Africans was lost in sport and music. The Rhodesian UDI also competed with Charles De Gaulle's blackballing of Britain from the European Common Market, an oil grab by Biafra province of Nigeria and the Chinese Cultural Revolution. The stage was set for a British debacle in south-central Africa.

Worse were new British laws that determined immigrants were to be allowed into Britain largely on the basis of race. Conservative Enoch Powell was sounding off about rivers of blood and directing his diatribe at black and colored immigrants. One had to search the papers to hear Tariq Ali demand action against Ian Smith's self-pronounced gift to civilization.

I wrote letters to the editors of *The Times* and *The Guardian*. One of them became the subject of a heated British Press Council debate on racism and fair comment. The result cleared the *Guardian* of racism but reprimanded the editor for publishing my letter. I was furious at the press council judgment that I had spotted only by chance in the newspaper.

There were no lack of demonstrations and counter demonstrations at Speaker's Corner in London that year. One such demo took me to Trafalgar Square.

As I left the Tube station, a newspaper billboard caught my eye. The *Daily Mirror* was blasting out its Chinese lead story:

RED
GUARDS
ON
RAMPAGE

I silently complimented the editor who had written the terse poster.

An hour later, a more dramatic poster replaced it:

VERWOERD
MURDERED
IN SOUTH
AFRICA

I hurried to buy the special edition of the *Mirror* at a Tube corner newsstand.

The apartheid prime minister had been murdered beside his parliamentary seat in Cape Town, by a messenger drawing a knife from a cloth-covered silver tray. The news, sensational as it was, made that day's protest rally against Rhodesia's white regime ultra-sensational.

I was not the only one buying the *Mirror* that cold morning. I saw copies of the newspaper being handed up to the official platform party in Trafalgar Square. Nearby, the traditional

Christmas tree was in place, ready for festivities later that month, and from high above, Lord Nelson, representing much of Britain, looked down with a blind eye. As I lowered my eyes, I recognized Judith Todd, daughter of the former Southern Rhodesian prime minister, as one on the platform.

Commotion reached a climax when she rose to speak. "Now we are seeing them in their true colors, their racist colors," she shouted, pointing to the nearby South African High Commission building. "Rhodesia must not be allowed to go the apartheid way of South Africa. Smith must be stopped. I want to see in Zimbabwe a prime minister who represents the people, before another Christmas. I want to see majority rule throughout southern Africa."

A crescendo of cheers and boos almost drowned her words.

"Look what has just occurred in South Africa–a founder of apartheid murdered in his own parliament," she exclaimed, holding up the *Mirror*.

Her words were met with near silence because the news was a revelation.

"There must be no sell-out of the black majority in Rhodesia," she insisted, at the same time, no doubt, uneasily eyeing one heckler trying to break through police to get to the platform.

As her shrill voice shouting freedom for the oppressed Africans reached a crescendo, a man roared out: "Ian Smith has the answer."

"No," she retorted. "Into the Tower with him!"

This time cheers drowned boos. Fighting broke out as hecklers tried again to reach the platform. I saw two being dragged away by police.

I was demoralized by this reaction. Yet I had to grin when two mini-skirted young women, wearing badges, urging people to make love not war, canvassed my support of the anti-apartheid cause. I had been accustomed in Africa to long skirts and short hair, but here were short skirts and long hair. The cultural difference with Africa was before my eyes, in Britain's 1960s world of youth and fashion. I wondered if the short skirts would ever reach Africa.

I accepted a button and made a contribution to the cause. "Those who fight are never right, eh? Is that slogan what you're saying?"

"Mind me bloomin' legs!" the short-skirted Cockney girl jolted me. My head rose to meet a friendly smile.

"Have you two visited southern Africa? Have you experienced apartheid?"

"No," they chorused. "But we know what's bad there."

126

"Then how can you denounce war to defeat apartheid, without having seen if war is justified. I live in Rhodesia and have seen what peaceful resistance gets you."

"We believe Ian Smith can be defeated by economic sanctions. Harold Wilson will stop Smith dominating the Africans. Britain doesn't have to go to war."

"Smith's not dominating anyone," a voice broke in over my shoulder. "He knows the natives are not ready to govern Rhodesia. Look what happened to African countries given independence. Look at the mess in the Congo. Look at Nigeria, Chad, Sudan and Ghana. See what's happening in East Africa where Kenya, Uganda and Tanzania can't see eye to eye. Britain won't go to war against Rhodesia. That woman on the platform pontificates like her father. He's rightfully confined to his farm."

"You a Rhodesian?" I turned to ask.

"No."

"A South African?"

"Yah, that's right."

"The woman you refer to is, as you say, the daughter of former Rhodesian prime minister Garfield Todd. She's the good daughter of a good man. Are you against good women as well as black Africans?"

The interloper mumbled out something about my possible background. "You should support Smith if you're a Scot like him," he said.

"You know a lot about me! Are you by any chance with the South African government building over in the corner? If so, think again about what happened to Verwoerd." I thrust the *Daily Mirror* in front of his face.

He was abreast of the news and nearly had a fit. "They murdered him!"

"Where does South Africa stand on Rhodesia?" one of the girls broke a moment's silence.

"We don't interfere in another country's business," the South African recovered enough to say. "Wilson and Smith should get around the table and iron out their differences."

"That's what you girls are saying too," I pointed out. "In fact, Smith won't, except for his UDI, discuss Rhodesia's future in meaningful terms with Britain." I said this knowing Wilson was trying to pin Smith down, to the extent of meeting him this time on *HMS Tiger* on the high sea at the end of the year.

"But the Africans…" one of the girls broke in to be silenced.

"Ordinary blacks don't care," the South African said thrusting the newspaper back at me.

"They don't want the chaos of the Congo. They don't want communism taking over in the shape of East Germany moving into Tanzania like they moved into Zanzibar. The blacks are content with wives, huts, food and land. Blacks are better off in Rhodesia and South Africa than anywhere else in Africa. They're better off than the blacks in America or even here. My country's policy of black homelands and separate development will work in South Africa. Continued white leadership will work in Rhodesia, until the blacks are ready to be partners in government. Wilson won't pin down Ian Smith!"

"Like hell!" I hit back by then, convinced this guy had South African High Commission connections. "Did white leadership work for Verwoerd? Look what it got him. A knife in the throat, from a colored messenger discontented with the treatment of natives in their native land."

"Cut down by a cowardly half breed assassin," the man hit back. "That's what happened to Verwoerd. You would never call his policies wrong, had you experienced his policies."

"He's from Rhodesia," one of the girls said of me. "He may have seen more than you think."

The South African saw he was losing the argument. He threw a fist when I thrust up a thumb in support of the girl.

"Stop, or I'll whistle for the police," the young woman exclaimed holding a whistle to her mouth.

I waved his arm aside and melted into the crowd, regretting losing the company of the two attractive young women.

From the speaker's platform came the African voice I had nearly missed hearing.

The tall speaker apologized for having to refer to people as black or white–blaming British colonialism–then went on: "We, in Zimbabwe, seek self-determination. We seek the right to live free in our own country. That is why more and more are joining the Patriotic Front guerrillas and even sacrificing their lives for majority rule. Your government tells us to protest peacefully. Well, it has not worked. Zimbabweans will take arms from Russia and China, not because we want to, but because Britain and the United States of America will not help us. Let me emphasize loud and clear. We have reached the stage when we believe only armed struggle will gain us freedom."

"He's a warmonger," came a roar from the crowd breaking a momentarily near silence.

In the British House of Commons next day, the Labour Government set six conditions for giving Rhodesia independence. "But Rhodesia *is* independent," scoffed a member from the opposition Conservative ranks.

I was in the public gallery, wondering if I was dreaming, as British parliamentarians played politics, while Zimbabwean liberation forces gathered strength and individual Africans faced execution for fighting for freedom.

Inside closed doors in London later that week, a distressed President Kenneth Kaunda broke down in tears, as he warned British peers of the House of Lords and British MPs of his vision of a world split on racial lines. He said Zambia was on the frontier, committed by geography and principle to supporting liberation movements and non-racialism in southern Africa.

"Send in British troops," he urged. "End the rebellion. Arrest the traitors in Rhodesia."

The British prime minister's action was to again stress his invitation to Smith, to meet him on the battleship *HMS Tiger,* off Gibraltar, for conciliatory talks and, as if it would help Africans, open a radio transmitting station across the Rhodesian border in Francistown, Botswana. Its object was an airways offensive that the British government hoped would help bring the Smith regime to heel.

Chapter 26
High Court of Rhodesia

Andrew Smyth was one of the best criminal case defense lawyers in Rhodesia. Yet he had a glum face, as he stood waiting for police permission to enter Rhodesia's Supreme Court building. Maybe it was because Smyth had been defending blacks for years and that day was to appeal against the execution of Oliver Sararanyatwa.

"Save my father," Shua had appealed to him. Smyth knew it would not be easy. He feared it was a question of time before the Rhodesian government would deport him to Britain, or make his stay in Rhodesia untenable.

This little man with a grey moustache, walked solemnly into the courtroom and sat down on the right side of the front bench. The dock, where Oliver would stand, was a few meters to his right. Policemen and other lawyers shuffled in. A girl sat down quietly at a table with a small machine to record the proceedings. The public gallery was filling with people of all races. The fact that at least the appeal was being held in public, must have been in Smyth's thoughts as it was in mine.

I had returned from England convinced that country would let Zimbabwe down. I managed to catch his eye from where I sat on the far side of the public gallery. I was pleased to find he recognized me with a wave, from a short meeting when I earlier had passed through Salisbury on my way to London. I had not risked drawing attention to myself in the section of the courtroom reserved for the press.

"All stand!" shouted an usher, as three bewigged judges entered from a side door and sat down on red and gold chairs by the wall facing the courtroom. A minute later, Oliver Sararanyatwa was brought in. He appeared tired and haggard, standing handcuffed between two policemen.

The court clerk stood up: "This man is appealing against the death sentence passed on him by the High Court of Rhodesia. He seeks leave to appeal to the Privy Council in London, England. Mr.

Andrew Smyth represents him. Opposing the appeal on behalf of the government of Rhodesia, is Mr. Harvey Willoughby."

Smyth rose in curt formal acknowledgment. "I represent the prospective appellant, Your Honor," he said to the presiding judge.

Willoughby also rose: "I oppose the appeal on behalf of the Attorney General and government of Rhodesia."

The judge addressed them: "I understand you are merely making statements supporting your respective cases." He then turned to Sararanyatwa: "Do you understand the proceedings? We have the evidence from your trial before us. This is not exactly an appeal to us. It is an application to appeal to the Privy Council in Great Britain, which your lawyer says is the last lodge of judicial appeal. Do you understand?"

Oliver said he understood.

Smyth was fast to his feet. "I beg to point out that permission to appeal is as significant as the appeal itself. I also ask the court to give my client a chair. He is sick and standing may aggravate his condition."

Willoughby supported the request, so Smyth sat down.

"No doubt a chair can be provided," the judge declared, before beckoning Smyth to state his case.

Smyth rose again. "Thank you, Your Honor. I seek permission to appeal to the Privy Council in Britain, against the conviction of this man of God on a capital punishment charge. He is to be executed if this application for appeal is rejected. Refusal of permission to make an appeal will have that dire result. The basis of the appeal is that the man's alleged offence is of a political, not criminal, nature. Even if he threw the grenade, which he denies, but on which charge he was found guilty, my case is that this was the result of unprecedented political circumstances in this country in which a rebel government…"

Smyth's words were lost in booing that erupted from that part of the public gallery where I was sitting. The judge thumped for silence. Smyth continued "…I repeat, as a result of unprecedented political circumstances in which a rebel government…"

This time Willoughby jumped up: "Objection! My learned friend has called the Rhodesian government rebel. But it is the *de facto* government as ruled by this Supreme Court and, as such, is responsible for law and order in the country."

There were murmurs of dissent then shouts of support from the public, bringing the presiding justice's hammer down again. He held a short-whispered counsel with the two other judges. One nodded as

131

he spoke, but the other appeared to have a difference of opinion. He turned sharply to face the court.

"Objection upheld!"

"Thank you, m'lud," Willoughby acknowledged.

Smyth, unmoved by the ruling, plodded on: "Nevertheless, it is my submission that the Act under which my client is charged, is an enactment made after the illegal unilateral declaration of independence on 11th November, 1965, that is at the heart of this case. This Act, by terms of a Privy Council decision, is null and void. The judges in this courtroom are bound by that judgment. The judges are Her Majesty's judges–as pointed out by the Privy Council–and cannot give effect to any enactment passed by the present Southern Rhodesian Legislative Assembly."

The presiding judge waved him to a halt. "But, Mr. Smyth, who is making it possible for this court to sit, by virtue of the payment of salaries to officers, the provision of a defense and other matters of that nature?"

Smyth appeared to be racking his brain. "I must point out that the government has not paid me to defend my client."

The judge peered over his spectacles: "I was not referring specifically to this case in which you are only one factor."

Smyth nodded. "Be that as it may, I maintain the court was constituted under the British-approved 1961 constitution. I submit that the court is bound by the decision of the Privy Council. The fact that judges, among many others, have been put in a difficult administrative position, cannot justify disregard of legislation passed or authorized by the British parliament, by some local introduction of what I can only term an apparent doctrine of necessity."

Smyth took his spectacles off and looked direct at the presiding judge. "It is for the British parliament, and that parliament alone, to determine whether the maintenance of law and order would justify the recognition of laws made by our usurping government. The instruction from the Queen's representative in Rhodesia, is that every individual should go about his lawful business and that no support should be given to last year's unilateral declaration of independence. It is clear that a refusal of permission for an appeal in this case will help the rebel government."

Noisy scenes again erupted around me. Downstairs, two policemen strode the length of the courtroom to where a man stood shouting at Smyth. There was a scuffle. The man was led out. The judge thumped for silence.

"This very disturbance," he said, "clearly illustrates the point that we cannot regard maintenance of law and order in a vacuum. An essential regard is the provision and the means of enforcing law and order."

The judge nodded to Willoughby sitting in his chair.

"M'lud–we have ceased to recognize the Privy Council in London. Rhodesia is now a sovereign independent nation owing allegiance to no other country. There is no appeal from this court to the Privy Council."

Smyth jumped up: "Objection! The Privy Council in Britain has been the ultimate court of appeal for Rhodesians, and the rest of the Commonwealth, for at least 25 years. To reply to Your Honor's point–there are grounds for believing there is a bigger threat to peace in Rhodesia today, than there was before the unilateral declaration of independence. Growing numbers of Zimbabwe guerrillas, a race war, an international boycott, a threatened shortage of oil are the real disturbances. These are results of UDI."

The judge pondered his reply: "We are getting into questions beyond this court's jurisdiction. You will have to confine yourself to the appeal, Mr. Smyth. A fundamental question remains for this court to settle: Is the Privy Council the court of appeal for Rhodesians today? Have you anything more to say, Mr. Willoughby?"

"Yes, m'lud. I submit that the Privy Council is no longer the court of appeal for Rhodesians. I ask that this request for permission to appeal to Britain be refused, as were previous similar requests. An order of the judicial committee of the Privy Council would have no force in Rhodesia today, so appealing is in any case pointless. We have a precedent for refusal. I repeat that the Privy Council is no longer the final court of appeal for Rhodesians."

He continued: "The 1965 Rhodesian constitution does not give right of appeal to the Privy Council, and proclaims that judges of the Rhodesian courts derive their power from the *de facto* government of Rhodesia here in Salisbury. Unless the Privy Council and the Supreme Court of Rhodesia have the same source of authority–that is, the recognition and enforcement of their orders by the Rhodesian government–they cannot remain in the same hierarchy or court, because each will declare the law according to different criteria. The one will judge according to the legal norms of the government in Rhodesia and the other according to the legal norms of the government in power in Britain."

Willoughby paused to quench his thirst after his long legal submission. He continued: "The appellant, Sararanyatwa, escaped from detention and tried to form base camps for a military style invasion of Rhodesia…"

"Objection! This is evidence from a doubtful source as stated in court earlier. My client, the *Reverend* Oliver Sararanyatwa, is too ill to invade his own country. He suffers…"

"Objection overruled."

Willoughby continued: "The guerrillas, belonging mainly to the banned Zimbabwe African People's Union or to the National Union–ZAPU or ZANU–are out there in the bush, in conventional military lines with platoons, divisions, headquarters, and reforming themselves into an army. Their aim is to indoctrinate and train tribesmen and infiltrators, and on a given date attack Rhodesian security forces and civilians. Sararanyatwa and two other terrorists were caught after a grenade was thrown into a Rhodesian military vehicle. The death sentence is mandatory.

"We believe some of the terrorists were trained in Cuba, Algeria and Tanzania. Some surrendered after they were dropped ultimatums by the Royal Rhodesian Air Force. Others escaped into Northern Rhodesia and Mozambique…"

"Point of information, Your Honor–the name Northern Rhodesia mentioned by Mr. Willoughby, is legally and constitutionally the republic of Zambia. Another point of information–my learned friend refers to the *Royal* Rhodesian Air Force. Does this mean the government of Rhodesia, or at least its military, recognizes Queen Elizabeth as Queen of Rhodesia?"

The judge focused on Willoughby, who was already consulting a colleague. "Well, what do you say?"

After the whispered conversation, Willoughby straightened up. "M'lud, I request a short adjournment to take instruction."

"Oh, very well. Since it is lunch time… court adjourned for an hour. All rise!"

I took a deep breath of fresh air outside the courthouse. I watched Smyth do much the same thing and inwardly thanked him for valor in the face of the enemy.

Willoughby's adjournment, nevertheless, had left Smyth smiling. I dug deep in my brain for a reason. Ah, yes! An hour to confirm a government recognized its Queen. Were the circumstances not tragic for Shua and her father, it would have been humorous. I realized what Willoughby's riposte would be. He would come back and say Rhodesia recognized the Queen, but not the authority of the British government. He would tell the judge the appeal to the Privy Council was a government affair, since privy councilors were appointed on recommendations of the British prime minister.

Sure enough, when the court resumed, I congratulated myself on my foresight when Willoughby, having said Smyth rightfully corrected him on Zambia's name–"although it was possible the incidents occurred before that country's change of name"–then told the court just what I had expected on recognition of the Queen.

"Does that answer your question, Mr. Smyth?" the judge asked.

"I seek to establish that the government of Prime Minister Ian Smith recognizes the Queen."

Willoughby appeared to be still in two frames of mind, knowing he had already answered indirectly. He again put his head down for advice. "Yes," he said, "Rhodesia recognizes Queen Elizabeth."

"Thank you."

"You may continue now Mr. Willoughby... but, where were you?"

"When interrupted, I was saying that after the terrorists were captured others surrendered. Their lives were spared and they are in detention camps. The appellant, Sararanyatwa, did not surrender. In a statement, one of the surrendered terrorists said: 'I was told in Lusaka that ZAPU, ZANU and the ANC were combining to fight in Rhodesia.'"

Smyth jumped to his feet. "I object. This is merely collateral evidence and not relevant to my client, the Reverend Oliver Sararanyatwa."

"Objection upheld. We have heard the trial evidence, Mr. Willoughby. Are you calling this witness for cross examination?"

"No, m'lud."

"Is that then your case?"

"Yes."

"Anything more from you, Mr. Smyth?"

"I notice Mr. Willoughby addresses you by the term m'lud. This is short for My Lord. Did the British government make you a lord, Your Honor?"

"Are you being contemptuous, Mr. Smyth?"

"Merely curious."

"Well, if you are curious enough, check out my credentials yourself. I will hear no more of this."

The judge turned to the prisoner in the dock. "Stand up!"

Sararanyatwa no doubt was taken by surprise. He must have thought the judge had forgotten about him. Had he not been handcuffed between two policemen, he could have sneaked out of the courtroom by the side-door.

"Have you anything to say on why this court should or should not allow you to appeal?"

Smyth stood up to intervene on his client's behalf, but Oliver was already replying.

"My lord," he said with an ironic twist. "Your honor, m'lud…" he was interrupted by laughter that forced the judge to bring down his hammer with loud thuds. "Yes?"

"I would like to say… that I, too, do not recognize the British Privy Council. I told him that," he said gesticulating at Smyth. "He did not agree with me. I seek only justice in a court of justice. In all due respects, My Lord…" More laughter forced an official demand for silence. "You are not representative of the black majority. What I say…what I say…is that Zimbabwe will one day be free. I am willing to die in the struggle against you."

Smyth stared blandly at his client before sitting down. There was a hush as the click of the stenographer's keys silenced. A wail sounded out from the public gallery. It had to be Shua's mother. Her father broke into a tribal dialect she would understand. It struck me, this was the only time during the trial that the old man lost his composure. The judge rapped for silence. He turned to Oliver, and asked: "Have you more to say?"

Oliver's silence answered him.

There would be no sanctioned appeal to the Privy Council.

The test case was lost.

Smyth did not look up as they led Oliver from the courtroom. The defense lawyer stood up as the prosecution lawyers filed out, then he sat down again head in hands. My hand on his shoulder brought him to reality. "A penny for your thoughts?" I challenged him. "Sure, it's bad. But don't let it get you down. Have you any moves left?"

"Yes–the Queen."

"The Queen?"

"You see something wrong in an appeal to the Queen?"

I turned when a short stocky man with a bullet head and greying hair came up from behind. "You know your next move, Andrew."

"The Queen."

"Yes–it will give them something to think about. I would appeal direct to Buckingham Palace. Meet me in the Meikle's bar in an hour and we'll discuss it. Watch you're not tailed. Park away from the hotel. Go in the back door. I'll do the same thing." Turning to me, he surmised: "You know the danger you're in."

"Danger?"

"Go to Meikle's with Andrew and we'll discuss that too."

With that, he strode out of the courtroom. I wondered who he was and what he knew that had made him warn me.

Leo Wolfson's stride was a hint to his character. He never would have won acceptance as a Member of Parliament in Rhodesia, speaking up for blacks, had he not had guts. Officially, he was an independent MP, but almost everyone knew he was a thorn in the side of the white government. To the Rhodesia Front he was a turncoat. To Africans he was a supporter of majority rule in the wake of Terence Ranger. He knew his time in the Rhodesian parliament would be up at the next election, when new boundary rules came into play.

This went through my mind as Smyth drove warily in the direction of his home, while I watched out for any car tailing us. The lawyer put on a burst of speed along the highway, then turned up a side road that led to his house. He accelerated, then drove into his neighbor's driveway. A quick semi-circle and he was waiting concealed by trees from the road, and ready to drive out and turn in the direction whence we had come. A police car duly passed and turned into Smyth's driveway. Smyth gave it ten seconds then he sped back to the city unseen.

"Know who was in that car?" he asked me. "It was the superintendent himself. First time I've had that honor. I hope my wife makes him a cup of Earl Grey and puts arsenic in it."

When we reached Meikle's Hotel, we found Leo Wolfson waiting at a table near the bar in the lounge. "Andrew, I saw the police superintendent take off after you. Did you give him the slip?"

"I believe so," Andrew said. "And he may not be enjoying my wife's company."

"Where will you go?"

"To Britain–where else? I'm a British citizen and I have a date with the Queen."

"I wish I could join you. Anything you need to do with the appeal, I will, of course, help you with."

"You will?"

"Give me an address and telephone number in Britain."

Smyth produced a pen and paper and wrote a London address down.

Wolfson memorized it then tore it into small pieces. "My information is that they intended to deport you as soon as you lost your case."

"Did you hear Willoughby refer to the judge in the archaic term m'lud?"

They both laughed, then Wolfson turned to me. "Do you know the danger you are in?"

I told him I would be heading north as soon as I had completed assignments in Salisbury.

"Back to Zambia?"

"Yes–then north to Kenya. I'll be looking for a job in Nairobi, while white journalists are clearing out before independence."

"Is there anything I can do for you?"

"I want to write an article contrasting Salisbury's top establishment figures with death row Africans. I hate to ask for help to do a job as dangerous for you as me. What I aim to take with me to Nairobi, is the inside story on The Salisbury Club, in stark contrast to the prison where guerrillas are being held for trial and some for execution. I read an article by Clyde Sanger in *The Guardian*, entitled, *Country club revolutionaries.* It gave me the idea. He said talk was wide open in those clubs. I'd like to hear it. I need help to get inside."

"You'll never get inside the Salisbury Club. Ian Smith is a member."

"I could challenge him to a game of billiards."

"Terrific idea–only you would never get inside, never mind inside the mind of Ian Smith. You must think the Rhodesia Front leaders easy to take in. They're not. Nor will you get into the prison, unless…"

"Unless what?"

"I was going to say unless you break into the club and you're arrested."

"Thanks, but no thanks."

"You stand out like a sore thumb to the Rhodesia Front."

"You must be kidding. I'm only a glorified newsboy!"

"They've already arrested journalists here."

"I wouldn't actually need to get inside the club or prison if I were told from reliable sources what goes on inside."

"Tell you what. Maybe I'm underestimating you and myself. I *can* help. I can produce a young lady who will take you as a guest, to a fairly representative Rhodesian sports club, this very weekend. Not the Salisbury Club, but a club here in Salisbury. Play tennis?"

"Badly."

"That's all the better. I'll lend you my tennis racket and a partner will take you to the Milton Park Sports Club. You'll get a good idea of white Rhodesian thinking there. It's actually one of the more liberal clubs, with multi-racial soccer but a segregated tennis section. You know how stuffy tennis players are. Actually, racist there. I resigned from the club when they voted against accepting black members."

"That sounds like a good story in itself."

"Now–about the jail," he cut in. "I doubt you'll get an interview with the recently retired hangman, though you can try and he would be the man to talk to. Information on executions is rather secret you know. I think you'll have to settle for second best again. I know a former warden who may talk to you. After that, you can try your chances with the retired hangman. He's the man who used to press the button on death row as the Americans talk about. You may be lucky. Trying to land him may be risky though. He may hang you!"

"Look," Andrew interrupted. "I should move on to meet my fate. I'll take a rain check on dinner until we reunite one day. I'm anxious to spend the evening with Emily. We'll probably pack our bags in advance. Maybe I can keep the police busy while you two are planning your blockbuster series. I'll look forward to reading your stories if I get the chance," he said, direct to me.

To Wolfson he said: "Next year in Jerusalem!"

Wolfson stood up. They clasped hands. Smyth turned and left.

I felt I had caused an early departure, so I apologized. Leo brushed my words aside, saying they knew their unfinished business could wait another day. With Smyth's departure, I was left with the Wolf–as I had named him–my mind pondering over his offer of a weekend date with someone at the tennis club.

I improvised to explain the four-part series of articles I planned for the *Sun*. I explained to him that the *Sun* was a new middle-of-the-road London newspaper that had taken me on as a stringer, as it tried to match circulation with the *Daily Express* without rivaling its sister tabloid, the powerful *Daily Mirror*. Adding to reports on the Salisbury tennis club and jail, the series might include a day in the life of a Rhodesian tobacco farmer and a Rhodesian policeman.

The Wolf nodded in approval, suggesting I might try to find out how the subjects of my stories reacted the day unilateral independence was declared. "That day will be stuck in their minds. The series could be important, if it prods the British government into

139

direct action instead of hemming and hawing with Smyth aboard battleships off Gibraltar. I could write a book on that tomfoolery."

"Now what about this date with a tennis player," I asked.

"I had my daughter Penny in mind," he said. "She stayed on as a club member."

"Wow!"

"Then I'll set you up for Saturday. I warn you not to get Penny into trouble. She'll know what we're doing, so play along carefully. Now listen, because my idea is that you must have club members believing you're an acquaintance from her holiday in Scotland last year, where along with my wife, the four of us played golf and tennis together at St. Andrew's. They know about our visit there. Rehearse your part in the story. Of course, keep Penny and me out of what you eventually write. I would never endanger my daughter if it were not important to the future for so many people."

Chapter 27
Love-all at a Salisbury Tennis Club

The weekend weather looked just right for the country club, though the forecast was a bit hot for tennis. Lying in bed early that morning I wondered if the club had a swimming pool. I thought I would take my swimsuit just in case.

Doubly nervous over Penny, I cut myself shaving, then had to hunt high and low for my tinted glasses that I thought might help disguise me. Eventually, I had washed and dressed in shirt and shorts, and was off in my rented-for-the-occasion car to pick Penny up at her home.

She came out in a flowery dress, carrying a sports bag and waving a tennis racket. She also carried her father's sports bag and a racket for me. This dark-eyed brunette coolly suggested: "We could go for an ice cream first and talk. It's important that we get to know each other."

We drove to a little-known wayside café, because as I explained to her, I did not relish my former editor or publisher coming along unexpectedly and likely tackling me about a contract dispute. Soon, Penny and I were discussing my characteristics and hers at an inside table. She was bright and cheerful, and I was intrigued at her complicity. It did not bother her at all when I told her my tennis was poor. "If by some bad luck, someone seems to have recognized me at the club–and I'm not a complete stranger here in Salisbury–I'll let you know by putting a thumb in the air," I told her.

"It's hardly likely, because I've never been near your club. I've been working up north mostly in Lusaka and Ndola for the past three years, and actually, I'm just back from a holiday in Britain, so I'm well up on Scottish affairs. My next newspaper job, I hope, will be in Kenya in two weeks."

"Oh, I never gave a thought to fear of recognition. Daddy didn't mention that possibility. If it happens, I'll excuse us and we'll clear out. I'm just taking a new friend to my club for a game of tennis. I think I now know enough about you and your Scottish-English family. So let's go."

"Hurry up!" we heard a club member order the barman, when we entered the clubroom and sat down in comfortable seats at a table. "Let's have some service." Behind the bar, a round-faced African wearing a white jacket fumbled around. It indicated to me that he was either new to the job or intimidated by his surroundings. I guessed both. But it made me wonder, why the club had hired him or had failed to train him.

"This new boy's no good at the bar," one member complained within the barman's hearing, as the man returned tardily with drinks. "We hired him rather quickly. I'd rather we'd kept Joshua."

"What went wrong?" I innocently asked, after Penny introduced me.

He repeated that Joshua had been fired and went on to tell me why. Above the bar were two portraits, one of Zambian President–his official position by then–Kenneth Kaunda, and the other of Rhodesian Prime Minister Ian Smith. LOVE ALL was written below the portraits. Joshua apparently had wondered about the meaning, in context with the photographs he could not avoid seeing whenever he dipped beer glasses in hot water, then hung them open end down above his head to air dry.

He had asked a club member about the pictures, and sometimes Joshua had taken newspapers, left lying around the bar, home to read. So he knew the political situation. He had concluded there was some political joke hidden behind the expressive words. He also knew Kaunda and Smith were bitter opponents. More dangerously, he knew why.

One day he had conversed with a club official who had asked him which of the two politicians he admired most.

I envisioned Joshua as a brave but honest man. He would have kept his job had he said Smith. He might have kept it had he said he preferred Kaunda because Kaunda was black. What he bluntly said, was that he preferred any fighter for majority rule.

Joshua, his wife and twin daughters, were forced to leave their *shamba* on the club grounds and move to who knows where. To be sure, Joshua would be now looking for work, probably without even a character recommendation from the club. It had been easy to find another to fill the post.

The story was told to me as Penny and I sat in the clubhouse sipping drinks served by Joshua's successor. I, by then, knew of her work for blind children in Salisbury and that she wrote Braille. This was a safe conversation piece for us to latch on to. I was the Scot she had met in an Inverness hotel, who had taken her to a theatre play one night and later joined her family for golf. We had written one another and I had come to Rhodesia to visit her. There was no hint my cover would be broken by anyone in the club, so I relaxed. I stressed my Scots accent and the company enjoyed it when I told them to call me "Scottie".

"Anyone for tennis?" a bronzed Rhodesian youth called out, poking his head round the bar door and chuckling at his cliché.

"We'll play, Alan," Penny said, acting normally because she was a keen player, rousing me from a bout of lethargy that was, to me, natural after drinking alcohol on a hot day.

I was introduced and Alan guided me to the court. "You're Scottie. A friend of Penny?"

"Aye. We met in Scotland a year ago."

"And you came all the way here to see her?"

"I wanted to see Rhodesia."

Alan spun his tennis racket to start the game, leaving me nonplussed on a call. Penny came to my rescue. "Smooth!" she exclaimed.

The spin turned up rough.

It meant I was first to serve and unluckily have to smack the ball into the sun. I recall the game from Love-all to Love-40, as I tried to serve a ball my keen young opponent could not kill with one passing shot over the net.

"Bit out of condition with the serve, Scottie, eh?" Alan remarked, after he had passed me down the alley for the third time and we were changing sides. At least the switch put the sun in our opponents' eyes.

"It's not like Scotland here," I replied. "The altitude may have got tae ma lungs."

Penny roamed the court like a tiger to keep our end up. I wondered if good fortune might bring her to my hotel room in the evening. I was hardly a beginner with women anymore and thought perhaps an interest in Braille might do the trick. My mind had wandered so much in her direction that I completely missed a return of the next serve. That made the score 0-2 in games.

Penny smacked two aces while serving, to win the third game. I detected some return to form when I volleyed a ball that came straight at my upraised racket. Alan shouted, "Well played, Scottie!"

I was too aware of Penny's crouching figure at the net or else had forgotten the best spot to serve from, when Alan, anticipating my weak delivery, ran craftily round his backhand and with forehand smashed the ball past my racket, hitting me with excruciating pain on the crotch. I gripped my vital parts with both hands and staggered to the bench. All three players commiserated.

"Can you walk to the clubhouse?" Penny asked.

"A'll try," I said. "Alan… can ye gie me a shooder?"

Alan misheard at first, but on Penny's translation, was delighted to help, since it was he who had hit my balls. "I say Scottie, old pal, I'm so sorry. Certainly, you can lean on me. What with you just getting into your game and my forehand finishing you off."

Was I wrong in thinking he smirked? I wondered if he fancied Penny and was disguising a touch of jealousy. I was not badly hurt, but I had disguised it to get off the court. I understand he later asked her where the Scottish clown had gone.

I was one of the most popular men in the club for a while, as the story of my mishap did the rounds. Drinks flowed in my direction and conversation flourished. I had to call a halt, or else risk saying something I might regret. I sorely missed my notebook and pencil.

"We had hoped to go back to Beira in a couple of weeks," one club member sitting with his wife said across the table. "I don't think we should–what with this threatened petrol rationing."

"The old country's letting us down badly," said another. "Surely Harold Wilson is not serious about blockading the Indian Ocean to stop tankers getting through. For how long will the socialists rule England? What do you think, Scottie?"

"They dinna just rule England you know. They will lose the next election if Ian Smith has his way. Yet Wilson's a tricky beggar."

"South Africa will see you through," said a third member named Tony, making no bones about his nationality. "Man, my country is strong enough to insist Britain leaves Rhodesia alone."

"Aw thought South Africa was neutral on Rhodesia. That's whit the papers say. And aw thought Smith thought the same thing on the relationship. Ye'll have to watch out for the United Nations though."

"Hell, no, Scottie. Think again. You just don't get it. Britain can't dictate neutrality to South Africa. And as for the United Nations!" The man made a rude gesture that raised a laugh. "South Africa is sending petrol to Rhodesia so we can drive south or across for a holiday in Beira. We tennis players will serve sanctions right back at Harold Wilson. Hit *him* on the balls. You know what that feels like!"

"There's a rebellion going on in Portuguese East Africa," I pointed out. To stir the pot, I added seriously: "It seems to me Rhodesia is facing international sanctions backed by the Security Council. Maybe you should keep your friend Britain on side until an arrangement about the long-term future."

"Which side are you on?" Tony challenged me. "We don't let the thought of an embargo on Rhodesian tobacco worry us. You can still get Cuban cigars in New York, despite an embargo there. Rhodesian tobacco will lose its identity as it goes through Amsterdam."

"What will happen if the Dutch middlemen join an embargo?"

He reacted with a contemptuous shrug but could say only that it was unlikely.

I decided to mix things further. "I heard the Rhodesia government banned the *African Daily News,* that broadcaster John Appleby was sacked and chief sub-editor John Parker given suspended imprisonment."

"You know a lot for a Scot just arrived in the country," Tony charged. "You sound like a journalist. What do you do back home?"

"I read the papers."

"Well, there is no censorship here, except for religious books that show intolerance and pornography. Ask Penny. She should know."

Penny took the heat off by changing the subject: "Come on, Tony. You know I'm not into politics like my father. Scottie can't play tennis, but he teaches golf." I thought it fortunate they had no golf course at the club to find me out!

Turning to the couple that had started the discussion, she went on: "You should holiday in Cape Town instead of Beira. A cruise through the Indian Ocean is really nice. Deck quoits and table tennis, then dancing under the stars."

"That's right," Tony broke in. "Sail, as I did in the other direction from Cape Town to Beira. Once we strike oil in South Africa, no bloody sanctions or blockades by Britain will worry you or us. Look at the investment the West has in South Africa and Rhodesia. You think they'll hand it over to the blacks? Money talks. Smith just needs to bide his time."

"You believe there's oil in South Africa?" I asked.

"Not so if you have it your way," he replied, no doubt feeling pissed off with me. "Do you realize that the consequences of any British reprisals for UDI might mean the economic destruction of

Zambia? We could cut off coal and power supplies, and block the railway."

I kept silent at that assertion. I was beginning to think the conversation too hot when Penny, bored with the political talk, asked who wanted a game. "Have we a four? Or even just the two of us?" she said to me in a London accent.

"The spirit's willing but the flesh weak," I replied.

I had detected no real discontent among most of the members sitting around Penny and me. Considering the fate of Rhodesia and its four million people was hanging in the balance after an election by only 108,000 voters, I had expected to find a bunch of rebels scowling as they questioned their future.

To my relief Tony took up the tennis offer, possibly to get away from me.

I ordered a round of drinks as they parted. The conversation was too good for me to waste time playing tennis.

Yet I couldn't resist bristling the hair on another South African's red neck, by complimenting the African barman. "Hope they're treatin' ye right," I said to him in the broadest lingo I could muster.

He hardly understood a word.

"Dinna be nervous," I urged him, placing a tip on his tray.

He smiled and in his best English replied: "I am not nervous. I try to please."

"Well, we have to leave," Penny said turning to me on return from the courts. "Remember our dinner date with my father. He doesn't enjoy late dinners."

After we walked past the courts we came to outdoor bowling lawns, thronged with white people in white trousers and skirts, floppy hats and caps. The white Rhodesian institutional bowling tournament was in full fling. As many women as men played. I drew Penny over to a seat to overhear them chat about the weather, servants, and the following week's round robin. Talk of politics I guess was frowned on. Most of the time they just rolled the bowls in arcs and chit-chatted. Towels came out on a tray to wipe perspiration off foreheads.

"I should have taken you bowling," Penny remarked when we were alone. She then shook me: "A bowl would hurt only your foot. You went a bit far and could have got me in trouble. You tried to draw Tony out. He's with the government you know. I'm politically hot as it is. Tony is wondering about you!"

146

"I have my story for the newspaper. That's what this is about. By the way, you know my golf is as poor as my tennis. Brilliant of you to intervene though! What bothers me is that about two kilometers as the crow flies, two men are concentrating on another game. They are playing draughts. Unlike the bowlers they have no time for idle chatter. They are playing out their last hours on earth."

"I'm quoting the former fired prison warder your dad put me on to. The two draughts players and 10 other condemned men are in Salisbury prison. The rest of their story is in my notebook. I shall tell your dad more about it over dinner. He's a brave man."

That evening my story went like this:

"Give us a drag," calls out a man dressed in prison shirt and shorts. The others sit around in similar clothes and soft shoes, watching the draughts board.

"Give the warder a shout. He will give you a drag! And then keep quiet. We're concentrating," protests the man with a cigarette. He lowers his head to stare at the checkers. It's his move. The spectators silently watch.

The nearest warder swishes his baton through the air, studiously looking the other way and pretending not to hear. The smoker makes his move. Disgusted snorts erupt from one prisoner seeing the smoker's opponent sacrifice a checker to take two. "When will someone teach you how to play?" asks another prisoner, breaking the golden rule of silence around the draughts board. Rebuffed, he picks up a book and settles down in a shady corner. A clergyman, hoping to comfort men confined to games of draughts on what might be their last days on earth, had brought in books, mostly about religion.

The prisoners have been sentenced under Rhodesia's Law and Order Act, which makes death mandatory for anyone found guilty of bombings, sabotage or carrying weapons of war. They await their fate in a prison surrounded by high walls, with wire that allow sunshine into the courtyard for only four hours a day. Seemingly watching over them on the ground, are only three warders.

One more warder is on duty at the gate, where a notice signed by the chief warden warns people that nobody is allowed in unless on official business. The warders are lightly armed with baton and whistle. That's only half the story. Above them, where walls meet at right angles, a machine gun is trained on the prisoners. There is little chance of escape. Perhaps mercy can come only from their Queen across the sea in Buckingham Palace. Provided she is still their Queen.

"The one-eyed hangman has gone," one prisoner tells another. "He is retired and a man with a black beard has taken his place."

Another rumor is that they bury executed prisoners inside the prison yard. This time it is true. The graveyard lies just within the main gate. Fear rather than hope dominates prison life. Through hours of boredom, the draughts board helps dispel the thought of death. Last Wednesday, two condemned men were taken upstairs to a dark cell to wait out their last hours. From down below, prisoners shouted up to them. "Appeal, call your lawyer."

On Wednesdays, the day executions are carried out, prisoners refuse to eat although those due to die are offered a feast. Any hope prisoners harbor, is expressed when listening to news they are allowed from the controlled local broadcasting station. Eagerly, they grasp at snippets about the political situation. They often discuss the case of Johnston Ibrahim, a chief who was the first man to be sentenced under the Act. He had escaped death after his sentence was reduced to one of life imprisonment. It was Ibrahim who had introduced a religious element. Twice a week, Anglican ministers or Roman Catholic priests visit the prisoners.

Often there is talk of Chief Rekayi Tangwena, who marched down to Salisbury from his tribal land near the Mozambique border, and was fighting in the law courts to keep tribal land. Prisoners ponder what they would have tried to do.

One prisoner recalls that prisoner Harry had tried to win an order in court allowing people of all races to use the Salisbury public swimming pool. "Yes," says Harry, with a smile. "I took the city to court to try to win my right to swim in the pool. I won my case. But do you think I won the right to use the pool? They just closed it down until they could pass another law keeping me out. I went berserk and joined the guerrillas. They will make a monkey of this chief. Why should he have to go to court to keep what belongs to his people? But I do not hate the white man. Todd is good and Ranger helped me win my case but was thrown fully clothed into the swimming pool by Rhodesian rugby players."

I can quote the former chief warder, saying that shadows over prisoner faces reflects the calm way they discuss politics. There is rarely violent argument over which African political party to support. They know that to them, either could mean a new chance of life. They grasp at political news like thirsty men. The news worsens.

One man talks of the love he left behind. Charles tells a tale often repeated. He had just eloped with the love of his life when he was arrested on terrorism charges going back a year. He had already told her parents that he intended to marry their daughter. Now his father had returned the girl to her parents. "I wonder what she will do now," he muses.

It is older prisoners who play draughts like they used to with their children or grandchildren, and even one of the wardens has a game. This sympathetic warder told me he also allowed prisoners to kick a football about the yard. "They chose teams, appointed me as referee and sweated out the boredom. My bosses took the football away. They fired me saying I was too friendly with the prisoners. I'm appealing."

Oliver Sararanyatwa has been in the condemned cell for two months. Confinement and his illness have left him haggard. Fellow prisoners pity him. Some remember his fiery church speeches. They recall his articles in the newspaper that is now banned. If he is beaten, they are beaten. They know his lawyer's appeal to the Queen was futile.

So, two kilometers from where white tennis players shout "love-all", black draughts players await their time on earth to run out.

I lie next morning in my hotel room bed with a slightly bruised crotch, pondering the paradoxes of life in Rhodesia.

Awaiting dawn, 160 kilometers from the city in the countryside, Douglas Amos rolls his shirtsleeves up his brawny arms on that first day of Rhodesian independence. He stands tall and lean on the stoop of his rambling homestead, watching the first morning rays cast light on his tobacco crop. He has done well over two decades on his farm.

Amos goes inside to listen as his radio gives a repeat broadcast of the prime minister's declaration of independence, then he whistles along with the light music that follows.

"Smithy had to do it. Can't understand why Britain's acting this way," he remarks to his Dutch-born wife, Paula, over breakfast. She is an early riser too.

"Are you going to Salisbury?" she asks, while doing the servant's usual job serving pancakes and pouring tea.

"Maybe or maybe not. Tell you what. We promised the farm boys a holiday to celebrate Rhodesia's independence. Let's do it."

Paula shrugs. "They may not like it."

Amos ignores her. "C-H-A-R-L-E-S! Charles... tell the boys outside they are on holiday today."

"Okay, *baas.*"

149

"Tell them it's Independence Day. No work today. Say there is meat to roast tonight."

"Independence Day," the houseboy repeats, with a glum face that disappoints Amos. When the boy starts sweeping the floor, he grabs the broom.

"I said it was a holiday! Go tell the boys to have the day off. NOW!"

"Yes, *baas,*" Charles repeats, padding barefoot from the house.

"What do I do without *you* here if there's trouble?" Paula asks, assuming he may be leaving for the city. "UDI is not so good for them and they know it."

Douglas Amos turns to his wife with a frown and roughly takes her hand. "Okay," he decides, "I'll not go to Salisbury. I'll merely send a telegram of congratulations to the prime minister. I'll take you out to dinner in Umtali. It's a holiday for us too."

Paula smiles back. She puts up with him but fears his political cronies. She also fears for their safety. Like her Scots-born husband, she is a person of few words, rarely openly emotional and, though romantic love might be dying, still tending towards affection for him. Her fidelity in the past went down well in white Rhodesian circles. Nobody was concerned if they spent evenings alone, reading or attending to what the servants could not do for them. Some nights, they used to give the cook and houseboy the night off. Dutch-Scotch evenings, he called them. The whisky bottle would come out and they would retire to bed early, without even locking the door. Things have changed and Paula fears the turn of events could end in bloodshed.

She might once have been the good wife of a tough Rhodesian settler-farmer, but they have grown older in different directions. She had never entered into political argument like so many daughters of Dutch settlers, even if her way of cutting through political sophistry had helped Amos in politics. Nor had she sought the pseudo-sophisticated life of the city. Amos often wondered, if in an emergency she would take up a gun and shoot the black terrorists he now knew were there. But where?

He still finds a beauty in her that in the earlier days of their marriage, had roused Amos to tell her she came from the racial mix of her adventurous sea-going Dutch forebears. He rarely thinks this way in the quagmire of events that have come to his doorstep with the rise of African nationalism. With the changing times, such talk would be embarrassingly dangerous to a Rhodesia Front branch chairman with a half-colored wife.

Charles pads back in. "Paper, baas."

"Have you told the boys it is a holiday?"

"Yes, *baas.*"

"That pleases them, eh?"

"No, *baas.*"

"Why?"

"They say UDI is not for them."

"They call it UDI?"

"Yes, *baas.*"

Amos takes a deep breath and rolls himself a cigarette, before sitting down to read the newspaper. He gets up again as Charles leaves and, unaware of his wife watching him, unlocks his gun cupboard built into the living-room wall. He makes sure his guns are loaded, then locks them up again. He had so far never had reason to use guns, except when one evening lions attacked his stock, and even then, he had also called in a game ranger.

Satisfied he could defend the farm, he picks up the newspaper.

RHODESIAN INDEPENDENCE CHALLENGED

The front-page headline in huge type hits him in the eye, and the text annoys him.

Amos knows, before reading the article, where the challenge was coming from, and it does not please him to read that Britain's government is again proposing trade and oil sanctions against his country, to end the administration in which he plays but a minor role.

A white space where the inside editorial usually appears, next catches his eye. Ah-ha, he thinks, the printers must have slipped up. He grins at the idea then, perplexed, frowns. He chides himself for being slow on the uptake, when he sees that set in the center of an otherwise white editorial space is a small notice inside a black border:

**This edition has been subjected to
government censorship**

"What the hell!" he explodes. "The bloody paper's full of blank spaces."

Paula, this time, scolds him for swearing. He passes the paper to her as understanding dawns on him. "It's those damned journalists. Why can't they print the right news, or stop their subversive editorials by not printing them at all."

Paula spells it out: "Obviously the editor and the government disagree on how to run this country."

"It's the editor up to his tricks. That's why his paper has been censored. Does he think he can get away with undermining Rhodesia's independence before...I mean... already. This editor would hand our farm over to black agitators. Don't you see that, Paula?"

Charles comes back into the living room so quietly that it startles Amos. "Did I not tell you it was a holiday?" he shouts.

Charles disappears.

"I'm not so sure about that," Paula replies, "the editor is white you know."

Amos reaches for the newspaper and screws the front page into a ball.

"Why did you do that?" Paula asks. "I was about to read the paper."

"Well, I say we cancel our order and buy the *Express.*" He tosses the crumpled paper to her. It barely crosses his mind that the unilateral independence he supports, will in a short time lead to their separation and divorce.

Paula leaves him for the kitchen, pointedly saying: "There are many more Africans in this country than there are whites, and they were here first. I think our marriage is over, Douglas. We're split in two, like colored and white."

Soon she leaves him for an apartment in Salisbury, where she is a willing subject for an interview.

Independence does not start well either for Patrol Officer Julian Hall of the British South Africa Police. Julian, for one thing, has a troublesome sore throat after a training exercise in a thunderstorm the night before. He is roused at dawn, by loud shouting and banging on the door of the barracks to which he has been posted for military training. Julian is fully roused by an officer unhooking his steel helmet and throwing it on his bed, shouting: "Wakey-wakey!"

Word gets around that the military police are under orders to break up a demonstration against UDI near Government House. Carrying riot shields and batons, 30 men, with officers drawn up at front and rear, move off at the double. Traffic sheers on to sidewalks. Julian, not as keen as usual, slows down. The crash of a truncheon on his helmet, resounds in his ears. An officer grins at him. "Keep up the pace!"

The squad crunches its way down Stanley Avenue towards Government House. A crowd of Africans expressing sullen displeasure at UDI has gathered. They wish to take their protest to Governor Sir Humphrey Gibbs. Julian has seen several such demonstrations. He knows protests, generally, can be broken up peacefully and does not share the sublimely happy look of a fellow quasi-military conscript, whom he knows is an ex-Katanga mercenary.

The demonstrators are starting to disperse, when one of them with a loud-speaker horn demands what he says is his right to protest against UDI at Government House. Protestors gather around him, proclaiming their rights and thrusting placards at police batons. It's just the opportunity the ex-mercenary needs to make an arrest. Minutes later, there is a full-scale riot. A senior officer waves his men back as reinforcements with Rhodesian ridgeback dogs arrive. The demonstrators hurl stones and a gun is fired.

Julian is hardly out of the way when tear gas grenades explode among a group of Africans herded together. They run in different directions, coughing and spluttering, with dogs at their heels. Shots are fired above their heads. A few arrests are made.

When the smoke dissipates, the demonstration is over. Police pile a few stunned demonstrators into police wagons and round up their dogs. Ambulances roar up for the injured. Paradoxically, the first to arrive is for injured blacks only. Eventually, an ambulance for an injured military policeman arrives.

The next day, Julian learns he is on 24-hour standby call to active duty helping the Selous Scouts combat terrorists infiltrating into Southern Rhodesia. African townships are shocked into recognizing that they are subject to emergency laws, turning policemen into soldiers.

So, I write this series of articles that I hope my newspaper in England will print. I am almost ready to head to Nairobi, hopefully to a new job and maybe interest an editor there in the same series. Meanwhile, I stay a while longer in Salisbury with my friend Julian, pledged never to reveal he was the subject of one of my interviews. This is real journalism from the real McCoy for a newsboy, from a wee town in Scotland!

Chapter 28
"Destroy the Enemy"

I knew Marianne sensed something wrong at home following the heightened tension. She had been waiting for Julian to tell her what was going on in Rhodesia's war on terrorism, but to her mind, he was holding back. So she asked me what he was hiding. In turn, I asked Julian to square up with her.

"Yes, there is something serious that I must now explain, Marianne. It's a transfer to active army patrol duties with the Selous Scouts in Rhodesia's southern or eastern border. I expect to be there for two months. You can come to Umtali or Bulawayo with me for a while, depending where I'm posted."

"I doubt I would want to go there. Patrol duties you say?"

"That's the word."

"With the Rhodesian army? So what's a policeman doing with the Rhodesian army?"

"On two months of secondment."

"I know what's going on, so don't shield it from me. The call-up is under the national emergency law. If you're going to fight Zimbabwe guerrillas or South African freedom fighters, then I'm keeping away," Marianne said.

Julian considered her reproach.

"When do you go?"

"I'm not certain."

Marianne drew close to her husband. "Let's soon make a break for Canada. I wanted you out of the police force and now they have you in the army. This fighting is madness. Do white Rhodesia Front politicians know anything more than white power and conflict in the middle of a black continent?"

"They apparently can call up policemen. I agree with your misgivings. We'll find a way. Not just yet, though. I'm not going to kill anyone if that's what you fear. Nor am I going to lose my nerve and run away. We'll make that break for Canada after my two months are up."

"I didn't say you would kill."

"I know."

"So have you no idea when you report?"

"Probably next week."

"So soon!"

"Well, it's a bit rough, but I don't want to raise suspicion by complaining."

"We must then make the most of the next few days."

"Doing what?"

"With an emergency law in force, you could be called in at any time."

"I'm on notice."

"I thought as much."

"After this is over, we'll head for Canada whether this government likes it or not. Security is tight at this particular time," Julian said.

Marianne's face turned whiter. "Do they expect an invasion by insurgent Africans?"

"All of this will soon be behind Julian and you," I tried to tell Marianne.

From the kitchen, she characteristically demanded we tell her why they could not send Ian Smith to fight, since the unilateral declaration of independence that caused the crisis had been his idea. Then she changed her tune: "You'll need to be careful, Julian. I'll give you the lucky charm my Métis mother gave me. It's because of this, I'm afraid," she said, patting her belly. "Can't you get off for domestic reasons? Does the superintendent not know your wife is four months pregnant?"

"Darling, the superintendent is not in charge. It goes higher than that."

"Of course. Except that you're not a trained soldier."

"I can't do anything about that."

We sat down to supper and Marianne's demeanor improved as the night wore on. There was no more talk of fighting or killing. Just an acceptance our togetherness would be broken for a cause none of the three of us believed in.

A loud rap at the door disturbed the tranquility. Julian answered. Marianne and I heard the deep voice of an askari mumble something, before Julian returned saying: "It's sooner than I thought. I'm to report for a late-night briefing. I have an hour's notice."

Half an hour later, Julian kissed Marianne goodbye, promising Canada would soon be their refuge and, after shaking hands with me, slipped into the night.

He told me the next day, that a former British Royal Marines commando was the lecturing officer, who had stressed that the terrorists were trained and disciplined and warned that on patrol any tree might hide danger. Among orders he chalked on the blackboard, were: "Contact, engage and destroy the enemy."

Chapter 29
Mosquitos and Muck

I had no good reason to stay around in Salisbury or visit the newspaper office where I was more than likely not welcome. So I returned to Lusaka quickly by train.

A bulky letter awaited me at my Ridgemont hotel. The askari who had rescued Shua and me from the police at Gonakudzingwa, had found out where I could be contacted. He had written an account of his training, essentially asking if I was keeping my promise to tell the world about what was going on in Zimbabwe. A freedom fighter from Portuguese East Africa had mailed his letter uncensored from Biera. He wrote:

"Our training with wooden rifles and dummy bullets has ended. We are now armed to the teeth with real rifles." He gave details of the guerrilla training he had gone through on his Mozambique border base. He praised his good sense in keeping the use of his askari boots.

"The only pants available, used to be so short that our calves showed. Now we have uniforms and long grey stockings. Black caps that sagged around our heads when training in the rain and drooped over our brows, have been replaced. Our soldiers are spoiling for a fight. We are singing liberation songs as part of the struggle.

"We have Bob Marley to listen to:

> *Every man gotta right*
> *To decide his own destiny*
> *And in his judgment*
> *There is no partiality*
> *So arm in arm with arms*
> *We will fight this little struggle*
> *Cause that's the only way*
> *We can overcome our little struggle*
> *Africans liberate Zimbabwe.*

The training, including runs with pack on back, dummy weapons trained on targets, charges with bayonet and rifle into sacks of straw and grizzly shouts when making a kill, was tougher than that of askari training."

"I had undergone bayonet rush and thrust, as a soldier in the King's Own Scottish Borderers. It seemed the African guerrilla leaders had copied British basic training as well as British army ranks.

"The askari revealed that the colonel of the regiment had read out a list of things freedom fighters shouldn't do: desert posts, traffic with the enemy, or disobey an order from an officer or non-commissioned officer. They were told that rules of war meant attacks directed against enemy soldiers, should do as little harm as possible to civilians, who likely were their friends.

"Our barracks are decent," he wrote. "We each have a bed, a cupboard and good food. Kerosene lamps gave us light to blacken our boots or write this letter. We have reading material in the shape of crumpled manuals about arms and paperback novels in a makeshift quiet room.

"Each morning as training progressed, recruits like me first drilled in a compound and then with rifles aimed at targets in a quarry, until under the hot sun, we were soaked with sweat. We advanced with dummy Sten guns down the range. There was enough ammunition to fire rounds and one of us was punished for firing indiscriminately. A short but astute sergeant and a lofty lieutenant taught us to snap our rifles from left shoulder to right, and how to keep our rifles clean with a piece of rag attached to a long string."

The askari-turned-freedom-fighter wrote that recruits knew that officers and sergeants had been civilians before volunteering. They had been so quickly promoted that they were learning as they went along.

"The evening before our passing-out parade, leader Tongagoro visited us and told us we were now trained soldiers. We would soon be on a mission to sabotage Rhodesian resources and kill the Rhodesian enemy, to free Zimbabwe from colonial and settler rule and put Robert Mugabe in power. 'Remember you are not alone,' he told us in a note. 'The vast majority of our countrymen believe in what you are fighting for. The objective is freedom for Zimbabwe.'"

With that he implored me, as a journalist, to tell this to the world. I wondered how I could possibly do that and packed his letter deep in my suitcase.

In catching the Blue Train south all the way to Cape Town, my intention was to leave Africa and sail home on one of the P&O liners that regularly left the Cape for Southampton. It did not take much to change my plan when in a Cape Town youth hostel, I bumped into a South African late of East Africa, who told me white journalists were leaving Kenya for fear of Jomo Kenyatta. The likelihood of a job there, coupled with my by-then-beloved Africa, set me on a diametric about-turn. Instead of sailing to Southampton, I hitchhiked up South Africa's beautiful east coast to Durban on my way to Kenya.

Surviving a lift by a drunken American, who started driving on the right instead of the left side of the road, I reached Durban and there boarded a liner for Dar es Salaam in Tanzania. The ship's captain had been informed in advance of a strike by cargo handlers in Dar, so he astutely took his ship to Zanzibar to unload cargo, hoping the strike would be resolved later to allow him to dock in Tanzania. Sullen Africans met my eyes in the town of Zanzibar. The air was foreboding, ahead of a black revolt and the flight of Arab rulers that would eventually ally the island to an independent Tanzania.

Tanzanian authorities gave me two weeks in Dar es Salaam, on my telling them I was headed for an interview at *Newsweek* magazine's bureau in Nairobi. This stretch was based on the one article of mine used by the American news magazine, but bringing it to attention in Tanzania served its purpose.

I booked in for a week at the Pan-Africa Hotel in Dar and was shown into a large room with two beds, a cooling fan, mosquito nets and a view of the Indian Ocean. Showering before walking down Independence Road past shops and buildings, I stopped to admire Asian women, graceful in colorful saris. I took advantage of an African barber snipping away on a street corner and he gave me a haircut and a shave with an open razor. Along the road an Indian tailor, seeing me admire his shop window display, came out to tell me he made clothes for *Mwalimu.*

"Mwalimu?"

The tailor seemed surprised. *"Mwalimu* is President Julius Nyerere–our teacher. You must be a visitor."

"Yes, from Zambia," I responded. "Will the suit in your window fit me?" I was thinking of job interviews in Nairobi and my need for a smart suit.

"I doubt it–come in and I will measure you for a suit at a good price."

After jotting down my measurements, the tailor said the suit would be ready in five days.

"I'll be spending a week here, so that will be fine."

I continued my promenade, taking in everything and everyone and breathing in the salt air deeply. Imposing new government buildings were going up beside charming old edifices dating back to the former German occupation of Tanganyika. I admired Dar es Salaam's natural Indian Ocean harbor, in which dhows and the ocean-going liner I had disembarked from the previous day, still rode the waves. The sparkling blue sea, fringed with yellow sand and tall feathery palm trees, delighted my eyes.

Away from the ocean and into the Asian quarter, I came across a hive of bustling activity and a mosque here and there. Small business shopkeepers and traders dominated, and washing had been hung out to dry from balconies. Through the narrow belt, I reached a sprawling city district with mainly African residents. I found houses of plastered mud with corrugated iron roofs, shops with goods heaped in windows, on tables or stacked on stoops. Transport was by bicycles, swerving in and out among children and heaps of garbage. Cars sprawled in yards, and it looked as though they would remain forever useful to only scrawny pecking hens.

Singing led me up a street and to a sign indicating the headquarters of the Tanganyika African National Union. The party had come to power with 70 of 71 seats in parliament at independence. TANU was already in virtual control of the vast independent country, of what I had read was nine million Africans, 75,000 Asians and Arabs, and 25,000 people called Europeans.

Conducting the choir of children was a slightly built man, possibly in his early 40s. He had a cheerful face with a moustache and curly hair. He wore sandals and a dark green TANU shirt. It took me but a moment to recognize President Julius Nyerere, helping a choir learn a party song. I returned to my hotel fulfilled by what I had seen, and after picking up my new suit a week later, confidently took the bus to Nairobi.

The *East Africa Standard* was my first newspaper stop. But my luck was out. The assistant editor told me his editor was in London recruiting journalists and that I would have to await his return.

So, with little ado, knowing that journalists really were needed in Nairobi, I approached *The Daily Nation*, arriving in the newsroom in the late afternoon. I was introduced to Joe Rodrigues, the chief sub-editor, and Jack Beverley, the Sunday edition editor. After examining my references and hearing of my experience to the south, they told me to sit down at the editing desk and show them what I could do.

I passed a half hour long on-job test and was taken to publisher Michael Curtis, who offered me a two-year contract with work starting the following Monday afternoon. I silently blessed the journalist in Cape Town, who had said newspapers in Nairobi needed staff as a result of Jomo Kenyatta and fear of Mau Mau warriors. I even learned on reading my new newspaper that the Duke of Edinburgh would soon be on his way to Nairobi to preside over ceremonies of independence from Britain. What a time to start work on a Kenyan newspaper, with the biggest event in Kenyan history pending!

For accommodation, Rodrigues had directed me to the YMCA building, on Hospital Hill Road, where I found a room for rent. My rental agreement included meals and use of a swimming pool in full view from inside the dining room. Seeing attractive young women in bikinis from my dinner table heightened my senses, despite the presence of sun-tanned young men and the drawback of a religious Scottish YMCA manager, who I feared would pray for this fellow countryman, alone and single in Africa.

I did though wonder if I would ever find a life-mate and could not but recall my grand adventure with Shua, and how circumstances had forced me to leave her without the opportunity to say goodbye.

The next Monday afternoon, I met my *Daily Nation* colleagues on my first nervous day at work on the news desk.

John Platter was originally from the Great Rift Valley agricultural area of Kenya. With the new black government in power, he had seen the future on the land as bleak for a white farmer's son. Using his university education and charming personality, he had moved from farming into journalism.

Tyler Myers, a recent United States settler, knew lots of journeyman journalism tricks, but he was equally involved in unlawfully sending ivory and wooden African animal carvings back to his American homeland, as a black-market business to make money.

The chief sub-editor, Joe Rodrigues, was an Ismaili Muslim follower of the Aga Khan who owned the paper. He was experienced and sober in his approach to journalism and friendly to me.

On another side of the desk was Harry Sambo, a black African working on *Taifa Leo,* the Swahili language edition of the *Daily Nation,* and to me, reserved and inscrutable.

The four of us completed our editing a half hour before midnight. Joe had already briefly introduced me to the reporters, proof readers, librarians and downstairs layout staff.

"We usually go for a drink at a nearby pub. Are you game?" he asked me.

"I owe you a beer," I replied.

There were just the four of us in the Chez Joie place, each with a glass in hand, and they wanted to know more about my background and ambitions. After a couple of beers, I was foolish enough to ask Harry and one of his black African reporter friends, why one of the two had a lighter skin than the other. Reporter Helen Shapiro came to my rescue by breaking the silence that followed my question, in asking, with a laugh, why I was not wearing my kilt.

"It's no Robbie Burns night," I drunkenly defended myself.

Overlooking my indiscrete question, Harry Sambo asked who Robbie Burns was. I ended up reciting his poem *To a mouse!* That made everyone laugh even more when I said Burns also wrote a poem entitled *To a louse!*

I gingerly walked home in darkness to the YMCA, where bed awaited me in my tiny room. I looked forward to a morning swim before breakfast, then to reading the headlines this former paperboy had now written for the *Daily Nation* of Kenya.

Chapter 30
Elsa and Me

I again soon sought the role of reporter, assigned to writing news and meeting people, rather than editing stories written by others.

I had missed out on seeing Prince Philip turn to Jomo Kenyatta, when the Union Jack came down and the Kenyan flag raised, to ask him if he was sure of his decision to break with British rule.

I longed to be out and about, rather than sitting around drinking tea and editing.

Opportunity knocked unexpectedly, when I flew down to Mombasa for a vacation. I learned that scenes for the movie *Born Free* were being shot up the coast near Malindi. I arrived at the film scene hotel in time for dinner, and after sitting down, noticed principle actors Virginia McKenna and Bill Travers, dining at a corner table on the other side of the room.

The Open Roads Film Company of London had barricaded off one end of a long sandy beach at Malindi, with cliffs at the other end to guardedly film scenes, such as Elsa the lioness swimming to an islet a short distance out to sea. So I hired an African fisherman to row me past the barricade, to the tiny off-shore islet that I understood Elsa would swim to. But the film company's public relations officer (PRO) had deliberately misled me. The swim I sought to photograph for my story was not being shot that day but the next day. I learned later that the PRO had phoned my newspaper office in Nairobi to affirm my photographic credentials, and the newspaper's chief photographer had told him, quite rightly, that I was not one of the paper's photographers.

I was disappointed but not down-hearted, waiting in vain for Elsa to swim out to me. I asked the fisherman to row me to the beach and he did so. Hey presto! Who, but actor Bill Travers, George Adamson and Elsa the lioness, came walking toward me three minutes later. I clicked my camera as they approached, then clicked a second time when they were abreast. Elsa's ears pricked up, but I had my photograph!

The next scene, off the agenda, was never shown in the wonderful film. A fellow came running over the sand toward me, like Anthony Quinn bearing down on Peter O'Toole in *Lawrence of Arabia*. Reaching me out of breath, he managed to exclaim: "You ruined that scene trespassing on our beach!"

I introduced myself as being from the *Daily Nation* newspaper, adding that the beach was public and I sought a photograph of Elsa swimming in the sea.

"What?" he demanded with incredulity marking his face. "That's the photograph we want for the cinema billboards. Get the hell off our production area!"

He was no bigger than me, so I retorted in kind: "You can go to hell!"

We wrestled for a short time and I was getting the better of him, when he toned down the argument and offered me a photograph of Bill Travers shaving with the lion's tail, if I would not disrupt production the next day.

At that comical point, I thought discretion the better part of valor. Instead of fighting we shook hands.

After retreating outside the wire, I bumped into Joy Adamson and told her of being herded off the beach.

"Oh, I know all too well what you are up against," she remarked about Open Roads. "Jump into my car to my place and I'll give you a story."

It turned out that her story was a rant about her view, that she should have been playing herself in the movie and not Virginia McKenna acting as her. All the while, a pet cheetah roamed around me giving me the creeps.

My photograph of Elsa on the beach appeared in the *Daily Nation* a few days later, along with a story headline saying the lion had never been more a prisoner. This prompted a letter a week later from the film company, to editors in Nairobi inviting news photographers to their camp in the Kenya Highlands. I was not chosen to go since I was a desk editor. The photographers took pictures from inside a cage, with the lions that played the different ages of Elsa, outside.

My article, nevertheless, was a scoop and I'm sure on account of it, I was soon switched from the news desk to reporting the news.

And what assignments, they were right around the corner every work day! I travelled to President Kenyatta's farm holding to cover a party rally, and there was told by my African photographer that the president's daughter, Mary, wanted to meet me. I was at home in my duplex near Government House the following Saturday afternoon, when lo and behold she came cycling along and knocked at my door.

Mary was a lovely lass of 17, and I was smitten by a young woman I suspected I could never be close to with Jomo's blessing, even if he had married and divorced a white woman in London. I had actually been baking scones, so I put the kettle on. As if she was a visiting younger sister, we enjoyed the scones with strawberry jam. I next brought out my set of checkers and showed her a few games. When this slim figure and beautiful face of a woman stood up and faced me, I did so want to kiss her. My courage deserted me. I later regretted I had not cast doubt aside. Instead, I suggested she leave for home or else her father would be after both of us. She stayed another half hour with card games and more strawberry jam!

Such had been Mary's impression on me that at work a few days later, I phoned Government House hoping to talk to her. Guess who answered? Yes, Jomo! I was stricken silent when in his deep growly voice he demanded, "Who is this?" I thrust the phone down shaken to the core. I often regret having not asked permission to court his daughter, but maybe I did the wise thing.

I was the only white player on the *Daily Nation* cricket team, often fielding near the boundary with Kenya's National Park located behind me. I knew there were lions there. I was a good runner and I also knew that the lions would have to be good jumpers to clear the high fence between them and me. I was also a keen billiards player at the Aga Khan Club. I beat the East African champion in a snooker tournament and the result went into the *Daily Nation*.

A standing joke repeated many times, told of when the *Daily Nation* was getting ready to publish its first edition in 1960. The publisher was awaiting a key item of machinery for the rotary press. When a plywood box arrived from England, he assumed that was it. He called the staff downstairs to ceremoniously open the box. He was shocked to find stationary from England along with pencils, pens and even type-measure rulers. However, the key gadget did arrive later, and the *Daily Nation* publishes successfully to this day.

What I did learn about journalism was the story behind the Brass Check. I was assigned to the opening ceremonies of the Pan-Africa Hotel in Nairobi, knowing the story would be supported by lucrative advertisements. The procedure has been popular with advertisers and newspaper management for a long time, and unpopular with journalists for just as long.

Prolific American writer, the late Upton Sinclair, wrote about it critically in *The Brass Check, A Study of American Journalism.* He said, an orator claimed that the empire of business, in this way, maintained a control over journalism and he linked the process to prostitution. He pictured a roomful of women displaying their physical charms and men walking up and down selecting one, as they would select an animal at a fair. One man, as others did, paid three or five dollars to a cashier at a window and received a brass check; then he went upstairs and paid the check to the woman on receipt of her favors. Suddenly, the orator put his hand in his pocket and drew forth a bit of metal. "Behold," he cried out, "the price of a woman's shame!"

So, having accepted the type of assignment that some journalists before me had resigned over, I cautiously took the elevator up to the hotel's fifth floor. In a social affairs room, I found Ugandan President Milton Obote telling a small crowd of his assistants and hotel management agents, his findings after having spent a night at the hotel. In a corner of the room, in full dress uniform, was Regimental Sergeant Major Idi Amin, there, I presumed, for the president's security. This soldier, who only a few years later would mount a coup d'etat overthrowing Obote and taking over as Ugandan president, was of little significance then. Had I known through foresight that he would topple Obote, alarming not only Britain but the world in his few years of presidential reign, during which he expelled numerous Ismaili citizens of Uganda, and opposed Israelis invading his land following the killings of Israeli athletes at the Olympic Games, my story would have been no brass check. That man, subject of *The Last King of Scotland,* a movie of that name with Amin played by Oscar award winner Forest Whitaker, looked anything but a king or president, but certainly a formidable army RSM.

I must say that I found the first two Kenyan-born black editors of the *Daily Nation* extremely capable. Hilary Ngweno, who had a French wife, and James Githi, formerly an aide to Jomo Kenyatta, built for a Kenyan future well beyond my powers.

So, in 1967, thinking of my own future, I was ready to move on. African students from the Journalism Department of the University of Nairobi had sat beside me at the editing desk, hoping to realize their career dream helped by my tuition. I knew I was training them to take white jobs. I judged this natural in what was their native land.

166

So I filled up my second-hand car and drove south to Cape Town and a liner to Southampton that, this time, I was determined to embark on.

It was not until 2015 that I again contacted the *Daily Nation*. I wished the newspaper well on its 55th birthday. The publisher reciprocated wishing me good luck too. This occurred close to my 80th birthday. Mary Kenyatta emerged from the past days, to again tickle my fancy by emailing me. She had obtained my address in correspondence with the newspaper and she said I had served Africa well. Memories to be thankful of are made of this, as Bob Hope used to sing.

Chapter 31
Reaching for the Top

While in Africa, I had freelanced for the *Sun* newspaper in London for four years, so my first stop in England was at that paper's doorstep not far from Fleet Street.

The interviewing editor was aware of my background and work as a stringer. He was also conscious that with the second biggest news story of the day, still the three-way tussle between Southern Rhodesian leader Ian Smith's white colonists, black African nationalists and Britain's Prime Minister Harold Wilson, the *Sun* needed Africa experience on the editing desk.

Of course, the biggest story in the London press, was Britain's ongoing blocked attempt to join the European Economic Community. In 1963 and 1967, France's president, Charles de Gaulle, had vetoed Britain's entreaties. His argument was that Britain had to choose between Europe and the open sea, meaning America and other Anglo-Saxon nations. He fought against what he wrote was "Washington's Trojan Horse."

After De Gaulle lost power in 1969, Britain applied for a third time to join the EEC, headquartered in Brussels, and won entry in 1973, but Brussels-bashing under the Margaret Thatcher government continued instead of her leaping gladly into European affairs.

There were these two top stories and many more on Britain's foreign plate, when the *Sun* had started up in 1960, and more critically, on my plate, when I joined the fulltime staff to eventually become foreign copy taster in 1966.

Sun sub-editors sat at a long, horseshoe-shaped desk on a wide-open floor also used by news editors, reporters and columnists. The subs often rewrote stories and penciled in headlines on numbered newsprint scraps of paper. The chief sub oversaw from the apex. I sat next to a Canadian senior foreign news taster, passing to him the best stories from the wires and from our correspondents, and spiking others. Senior backbench editors sat behind us at *their* desk, dealing mainly with possible page-one stories passed by another taster, while desk editors on the rim worked on inside-page stories.

Reporters and columnists could be seen typing away all over the floor to its farthest point, where a news editor handled assignments. The clatter from beyond the editing desk must have set pulses racing like mine, as Underwood typewriters handled work now done by silent computers.

The *Sun's* main Fleet Street broad-sheet rivals were Lord Beaverbrook's *Daily Express* and Lord Rothermere's *Daily Mail*, both bigger and more conservative. The *Sun*, then itself a broad-sheet, regarded itself as liberal until after my departure, when it became a right-wing tabloid *Sun* in Australian Rupert Murdoch's stable, and no friend of what had been the *Sun's* tabloid sister newspaper, the *Daily Mirror*. The *Mirror* then had the largest circulation in Britain, and for that reason, competition with the *Mirror* from the *Sun* I worked on was frowned on by decree of the International Publishing Corporation owners. The publisher had nevertheless warned us, that if the *Sun* did not reach a circulation of a million, it would go belly-up or be sold.

The open floor was something like a three-way circus with big shots Hugh Cudlipp, from the *Mirror*, and Ted Castle, husband of Labour Party stalwart cabinet minister Barbara Castle, occasionally sitting on the backbench near where I was making headway as a copy taster. I was not the only one judging incoming news. As I said, a *fine* copy taster advised the page-one senior editors. There were no women on the editing desk, but a few women, among many men, rattled typewriter keys on the open floor, writing reviews and stories of social events.

I was aware that Cudlipp, chairman of the International Publishing Corporation, had launched the *Sun* when, the solidly Labour, *Daily Herald* folded, and it was he who had quietly ordained that the *Sun* would not encroach on *Mirror* circulation.

Cudlipp, author of the book, *Publish and be Damned*, was scarcely acquainted with the Australian newspaper upstart Murdoch, to whom he sold the *Sun*. Murdoch, in my absence, turned it into a tabloid like the *Mirror*. With no holds barred he went head-to-head with the *Mirror*, including in his paper, bare breasts on page three. Murdoch's brash *Sun*, within a few years, came out a million readers ahead of the *Mirror*.

I left the *Sun* on a promise of a job with the Paris-based *Agence France Press*, provided I could improve my French. The opportunity to do so arose during a half-hour break in a pub across from the *Sun* office. I was by chance, seated beside an Indian gentleman, telling him of my previous work as a journalist in Africa and how my aim to improve my French was vital since I had been offered a press job in Paris.

"Well," he said, "why don't you rent my cottage in Menton for the winter?" He said Menton was located on the French border with Italy, at the eastern end of the Côte d'Azure.

"*Les Cicadas* is not really *my* cottage," he told me. "It belongs to my wife who is a doctor. If you are really keen, arrangements can be made for you at good rent, provided you leave Menton before the end of April next year when we arrive. I assure you of rest, relaxation, and the chance to study French in Menton or Nice." I treated him to a second beer, accepted his business card, and encouraged by the opportunity to talk further at his home, returned to finish my shift full of the idea of studying French in France.

At his home the following week, I learned that the chalet was empty because the British government had placed a currency restriction on overseas travel that winter, and the couple sought to use their cash allowance when summer came. They stressed that on the Côte d'Azure, winters were mild and tourists fewer, but told me that the currency restriction would apply to me too.

A four-month residence in Menton and a job with *Agence France Press* might be mine if I improved my French. I was soon commuting by train from Menton to Centre Universitaire Mediterranée in Nice, alongside many Italians who regularly crossed the border for work in France. Little did I know, that my job interview in Paris would be undone by an outburst of massive strikes by workers in the French capital.

Also, at that time, U.S. President Lyndon Johnson was sitting in the American Embassy in Paris, longing for a political victory. Protests against the American war in Vietnam were raging, and Johnson, the most associated with the war, sought a peace agreement.

Johnson had abandoned the idea of again running in a presidential election, but he wouldn't mind being remembered by some more attractive epithet than "murderer" and other unpleasant names being shouted at him. So he had ordered a break in the bombing of Hanoi and organized a peace conference. The fact that there happened to be another form of war raging on the streets of Paris, the city where the conference was to be held, was something

Johnson found comical, because it was President Charles de Gaulle who would have to contend with that conflagration.

Johnson had little time for de Gaulle. His view was that the French wartime leader had forgotten that the U.S. had saved his country from the Germans. On the other hand, de Gaulle thought the Americans had no time for him, and at one time, after the war, rumor said he had contemplated that they were trying to steal his country.

De Gaulle must have been able to hear the noise of the demonstrations from afar, as the riots raged in his beloved Paris. The Fifth French Republic had begun to wobble. First, it was students against the Vietnam War. That was okay for him to handle. Then the demonstrations became bigger and more violent. Trade unions were taking a million workers out. The country still recovering from World War II was grinding to a halt. At that point, De Gaulle disappeared!

Meanwhile, a letter to me from *Agence France Press* told me their workers were on strike and my interview was postponed. Even my college restaurant staff had struck. I had to do without the excellent low-price meals I depended on. Yet, there was another side to the coin. I could freelance strike articles to the *Sun* and earn a little money to tide me over until I would have to go home to Britain.

Police were edgy. I had just bought a French-English dictionary for my studies and was standing quietly, photographing a pigeon perched on a statue in downtown Menton, when an *agent de police* came up from behind and requested I accompany him to the station. A woman I had never before set eyes on quietly followed us from behind.

At the station I was asked for my passport. *"Mon passport?"* I repeated in my still schoolboy French. *"Vous l'avez ici!"*

The policeman went next door to check. He returned: *"Ah, oui! Il est ici."*

The woman who had accompanied us stood silent in the background.

"Mais, avez-vous le gout?" for something or other, the policeman asked.

"Le gout? Le gout?" I muttered, tearing the wrapper from my French-English dictionary and looking the word up. "Taste, liking, s-m-e-l-l!" I spoke out in confusion.

"Connaisez-vous la rue Corniche?" the policeman next slowly asked, reminding me of Peter Sellers in his hilarious role as an *agent de police*. I misunderstood his French words, thinking he had asked

me if I knew *la route a Nice.* "Yes, I travel by bus to college in Nice, though some mornings I go by train."

The *agent* frowned in a plainly puzzled way. His English was worse than my French.

The silent woman broke in. I understood little of what she said. She apparently cleared me since I was ushered on my way with profuse apology. A senior *agent,* who spoke English, explained that the woman had been assaulted on rue Corniche a few days earlier and had identified me as a suspect. He hoped I would understand.

The next time an *agent* stopped me I was quick to demand his identity card and station location, and he seemed happy to see the end of me as I of him.

My home in Menton was a dilapidated chalet atop a steep graded hill, stretching down to town and sea. The view over the Mediterranean was panoramic and immediately above me were hills rising to mountains. Lying directly within upward walking distance, was the historic village of Ste. Agnes. Lemons and oranges grew on trees in my back garden, as they did all over town. Delicious French pastries and baguettes were available at a *boulangerie* below my chalet, and I ran down the steps for bread each morning.

Les Cicadas was a rural paradise in every way, except one thing that had consequences. Two taps in the bare kitchen provided water. One was water for washing up and one for drinking. I continually mixed them up.

For a month I had the company of a lovely young artist from Amsterdam, traveling on the Côte d'Azure and supporting herself by drawing caricatures of diners in pubs and restaurants. There were two bedrooms in the chalet and she insisted that we use both of them. I couldn't but love Marian Reuter. She realized I wasn't the Lothario for her, but she was safe and appeared happy during the month she stayed at my chalet, until the time to part from me.

When April came, I had to drag myself from the cottage and reluctantly return by train to Britain, leaving the chirping cicadas behind and abandoning hope of a job in Paris. After a week in London looking up, but not finding a former girlfriend, then visiting my father, step-mother and my many half brothers and sisters in Corby, Northamptonshire, I travelled to Scotland to visit cousins, aunts and uncles. Turning down a job in Galloway, I found better prospects in Edinburgh editing foreign stories for *The Scotsman.*

A week after starting my new job, I was finding digestion and staying awake difficult. My limbs were weak. One nightshift, I felt particularly sick and a bit dizzy. Slick headlines were hard to come up with. With deadline midnight registering on the great clock in the editing room, the shift ended and I went straight to an Edinburgh emergency clinic. "I have a bad stomach," I told the emergency doctor.

Taking one look at me, he shook his head and smirked. "You have more than that. Look at your yellow eyes and face in the mirror. You have jaundice. You'll have to be admitted to hospital now!"

I had no intention of rising again after being placed in a hospital ward bed. Hepatitis was my second encounter with serious disease, since penicillin had saved me from dying of diphtheria in my childhood. At age eight, I had been one of the first civilian patients, after soldiers, to be prescribed the anti-biotic. This time I was in mental unawareness in the Edinburgh infirmary, with yellow skin and yellow eyes that were even unaware of the lovely nurses.

What came to my mind later, was the probability that the hepatitis was the result of the water supply in Les Cicadas. Yet, there was a lot of hepatitis around in Edinburgh that year of 1969. Even doctors were dying from it. The next day, my bits and pieces of suspected infectious clothing were cleared from my rented room and got rid of by my landlord, who, I later learned, deposited them in my suitcase at *The Scotsman* office.

I was hardly aware of my Aunt Margaret visiting me on the second night in hospital. I still hovered unaware of the pretty Scottish nurses.

When I came to, three days later, I saw a long ward with beds and patients on either side. Time passed slowly as the nurses helped feed and clean me. It was a week later that an auburn-haired nurse appeared above me. She asked if I needed a massage. She transposed me to heaven with her subtle hands on my back and thighs. I could have kissed her a hundred times, except that I knew she was just doing her job. Three hours later, I enjoyed lunch from a tray, sitting up, and thinking I was on the mend. I had writing paper and a pencil. My book on Africa was taking shape. Even the attentive chief male nurse was welcome at my bedside, and soon, me in his office.

Two weeks later, a senior doctor and two interns paced the infirmary ward floor. The doctor spoke only one word to me. "Out!" I wondered if he meant that very day. But no! The male nurse came quickly to my bedside when the coast was clear. "He doesn't mean now," he assured me. I sort of thankfully slipped down my comfortable bed, knowing I would soon be discharged. I was kept in long enough to date a nurse named Fiona. Soon after discharge, we went out for dinner, then intermittently met when we were free.

Still weak, I lodged with my Aunt Margaret and Uncle Charlie and returned to the *Scotsman's* editing desk. Charlie had visited the newspaper office to collect my belongings and make sure they would have me back. Doctors advised me not to drink beer and avoid fats for at least six months. But worse, my romance with Fiona was going downhill. Relations froze as a result of my night shifts and her day shifts. It took me months to fully recover from my illness and a repeat of love's labor lost. I soldiered on at *The Scotsman* newspaper, but I had lost my mojo for headlines.

I planned an escape back to Africa, where I had enjoyed perfect health for six years and was not unknown as a journalist, from my work in Southern Rhodesia, Northern Rhodesia and Kenya. It was an advertisement offering a job on the *Central African Post* in Lusaka that caught my eye. My application letter was acknowledged, but I was told it would take some time to arrange a work permit. Work permits for expatriates had been difficult to get since Zambian independence.

Then, in a café on Edinburgh's Royal Mile, I met Eileen Braidwood. My courtship was whirlwind after a first date to see Shirley McLaine in *Sweet Charity*. Nothing stopped our relationship and on our wedding day, I crashed my rented car on the way to church. I told no one but Eileen, and in the church parking lot, hid the bumped wing. The prosecutor never did charge me.

Our honeymoon in northern Scotland went askew, when we stopped for a drink of water at a well and I left my wallet on the rented car roof. This placed expenses on Eileen's shoulders. She must have decided she could improve my dottiness. She liked the idea of going to Zambia.

Bad news came in a letter that told me a job permit was unobtainable. The government of Kenneth Kaunda had Africanized journalism and other jobs. So we stuck a pin in a world globe, so to speak, and it pricked hard into Canada. Our passenger ship was to be the P&O liner *Oriana*. She was sailing from Southampton to Vancouver, via Bermuda, Bahamas, Acapulco, Panama City and Los Angeles. We booked to disembark near Los Angeles and catch a bus to Santa Barbara where my sister Isla lived. After nursing in northern Saskatchewan, Isla had married an American doctor, so our plan on reaching America was to take a holiday with Isla and Dr. Jerry Ecker in Santa Barbara, before going on to Vancouver.

The train from Edinburgh's Waverley Station to King's Cross was comfortable and we arrived in London in time for breakfast. We had three days before embarkation and found comfortable digs in West Finchley with my grandfather's brother, impresario T. C. Fairbairn of Hiawatha production fame.

Wasps spoiled our tea and scones in Richmond Park. I took Eileen to the wooden sculpture with James Thompson's recitation that I knew so well:

Ye who from London's smoke and turmoil fly
To seek a purer air and brighter sky...

Chapter 32
Our Happy Hunting Ground

Our last day in London started early, with an English breakfast fit for a king and queen at our West Finchley digs.

T.C. Fairbairn was already old and would live to the age of 103. He had recently moved in with one of his two sons after leaving his home on Shaftesbury Avenue, where I had tracked him down during my years on the *Sun*. In his nineties, he had shown me around London, pointing out where the scandalous Christine Keeler lived and one Saturday night, lending me a tie and a Panama hat to improve my dress.

His theatrical accomplishments included dramatizing and producing *The Song of Hiawatha* with a cast of 1,000 performers, 700 in a chorus, 80 in ballet and a full symphony orchestra. They played in Melbourne, Australia, from October 21 to November 4, 1939, in aid of war charities. This had followed performances from Scarborough to the Albert Hall in London. He had brought Indians from Canada to fill spiritual roles in the Happy Hunting Ground, some in wigs, beards and pall by Cyrano Costumes of London. He presented me with a souvenir program pertaining to the performance in Melbourne. One written scene for Hiawatha's wedding feast explains:

Hiawatha was a man, as other men, and wooed and won sweet Laughing Water, Minnehaha, from the land of the Dacotahs. The opera opens with the festivities at their marriage, and gay are the guests as they offer their presents and receive the generous hospitality of their host.

Quip and jest pass round and Chibiabos, the singer of sweet songs, sounds the keynote of passionate love in the ears of his entranced listeners. Dance follows song. Pau-Puk-Keevis leaps and twines with the grace of a barbaric savage. Medicine Man brews a Peyote plant potion, of which the guests partake and through its magic visualize a dream ballet of childhood days. Then follows a thrilling totem dance, in which all the tribe take part and give vent to their feeling in the hiss of the serpent, the bark of the fox, the shriek of the eagle and the bellow of the buffalo, according to the nature of their totem.

The marriage feast is over. Happy and joyous, the guests depart to their wigwams and alone in the moonlight are Hiawatha and Minnehaha.

Then came pages of Longfellow's narrative beginning:

> *You shall hear how Pau-Puk-Kewis*
> *How the handsome Yenadisse*
> *Danced at Hiawatha's wedding.*
> *How the gentle Chibiabos,*
> *He the sweetest of musicians*
> *Sang his songs of love and longing*
> *How Iagoo, the great boaster;*
> *He the marvelous story teller;*
> *Told his tales of strange adventure,*
> *That the feast might be more joyous,*
> *And the guests be more contented.*
> *Scrumptious was the feast Nokomis*
> *Made at Hiawatha's wedding.*

Of course, commercialism entered into the picture. The future age of persuasion could be predicted in a Henry Buck advertisement for shirts:

> *If Minnehaha had a brother,*
> *Provided by her thoughtful mother*
> *They'd name him Mickey, for no other*
> *Name would suit her little brother.*
> *The name would be very fitting–*
> *See Minnie by the water sitting,*
> *Mother at her wampum knitting.*
> *Mickey through the forest flitting*
> *Then Hiawatha, wise and knowing.*
> *As Mickeyhaha keeps on growing*
> *Insists upon the youngster going*
> *To Buck's where springtime shirts are showing.*
> *Heeding well his elder's pleas.*

See Mickey, strolling through the trees,
Outshines his friends in grace and ease,
For none has shirts as smart as these.

"Oh, well," T.C. Fairbairn replied to my mild rebuke of the brass check, "you have to remember, the production in the Exhibition Buildings was in aid of the Australian Red Cross and War Comforts Funds." Before we left, he brought out an Indian peace pipe and we smoked it in turn with his best wishes for our success in the Canada he knew well.

I fairly pushed Eileen into the train. She seemed ready to return to Edinburgh rather than sail to Canada. It was the two o'clock from Waterloo to Southampton. Rain was lashing down when we reached the port city. Passing through customs was a breeze that led to a welcome cup of tea in the departure lounge.

We quickly toured the *Oriana's* ballroom, cinema, shops, hairdresser, post office, lounges, television room, library and launderette, before the ship weighed anchor at about 6 p.m. to a rousing rendition of *A life on the ocean wave,* followed by a deluxe dinner.

The weather had brightened, but it was still windy and sloppy on deck. We were allocated our meal table and were happy that all meals were included in the price of the voyage. After dinner we enjoyed a drink and with a long day behind us, took to bed early. Our financial affairs meant we shared different cabins at different levels. That first morning, I was wakened by a cabin steward with a glass of juice and a copy of the *Oriana News*, and by my Australian cabin mate enquiring after me. We exchanged pleasantries and I joined Eileen for a brisk walk around the deck before breakfast. The sea was choppier than on the previous day. As the ship passed, Land's End waves lashed at portholes.

I was feeling the roll more than Eileen, but not sufficiently to miss dinner and cocktails with the captain. A dance that evening brought out smartly dressed ship's officers and women in ball gowns or short cocktail dresses like the one Eileen wore.

Clocks were put back another hour that night and I was looking forward to my 34th birthday next day. What a day it was! I was sick overboard 10 times and missed all meals. Eileen was fit as a fiddle. Recovery for me came the following day, and soon she and I were playing quoits and deck tennis against my Australian cabin mate and a woman he had picked up. "Good on ya, mate! I knew you'd hit the target," he snapped.

178

Eileen, not a bit bashful, was into her bikini and in the ship's pool. I was back at the Locarno in Derby remembering Ray McVay sing about an *itsy bitsy, teeny-weeny, yellow polka-dot bikini*. We disregarded a forecast in the *Oriana News* that Hurricane Camille, with winds of 200 miles an hour, was hitting the Florida coast. We were due to dock at Bermuda the next day and the sun was shining!

Mopeds, motorcycles, open roof taxis and half-size buses dominated narrow roads on Britain's first colony in the Atlantic. Shops were shut because it was Sunday. The island seemed religiously inclined, judging by the number of black and white people streaming out of churches. We off-ship tourists were bused to the Crystal Caves, to wonder at stalagmites and stalactites that our guide said were discovered by two boys searching for a lost cricket ball.

Launched back to the *Oriana*, we learned that our ship had passed between Hurricanes Camille and Debbie. Neither hurricanes nor the Bermuda Triangle dismayed us.

Invited to the Ocean Bar (starboard side) that night by television producer George Tibbles and his wife Mildred, we learned that he was responsible for the hit American television show, *My Three Sons,* starring Fred McMurray. Before we left their company, he urged me as a writer to join his studio in Los Angeles. I was tempted. Eileen talked me out of it.

The next day the *Oriana News* told us that British troops, including my old regiment, The King's Own Scottish Borderers, were patrolling Belfast, Northern Ireland, where surging Catholic and Protestant mobs were hurling stones, bricks and even grenades at each other across barricades of flaming city buses. How wonderful it was to be peacefully cutting through the waves rather than being a journalist or soldier facing such a crisis. Two days later the *Oriana* docked at Fort Everglades in Florida. We gaped at huge cars scooting up the wide road by the sea and drank our first root beer.

When we reached the Bahamas, the first place we headed for in Nassau was a colorful straw market, where Bahamian women sold handbags, mats and dolls. Shops were well stocked but merchandise expensive. We sat down on deck chairs on a hotel beach but were soon ordered off. The beach barman sought to charge us $2 each for lemonade drinks. We left the drinks with him and escaped. We instead found a public beach and Coca-Cola at 25 cents, just 200 yards away. I visited the *Nassau Tribune* office and promised them an article on tourist ship travel. Back on the *Oriana* it was my lucky evening, because I won $150 in pounds for being nearest to guessing the distance *Oriana* had travelled since Southampton.

Eileen took a photograph of me standing at the ship's wheel and I photographed her beside the ship's huge *Oriana* sign.

Our ship continued to steam through calm Caribbean waters heading for the Panama Canal. We passed Cuba on starboard and Haiti on port. The American passengers took no notice of the communist island state but were interested in Haiti's despotic ruler Papa Doc. I dressed like a pirate and watched women passengers dance the conga and the Zorba. They wore multi-colored blouses and floozy hats. Eileen prefers Scottish country dancing, so she watched too.

A leaflet entitled, *Panama Canal, Gateway for World Trade*, was handed to me. Direct on our route were the towns of Cristobal and Colon at the Caribbean end of the canal. We learned that the two names were Spanish for Christopher Columbus. No perceptible motion or disturbance of the ship was felt as it rose 85 feet. A giant water stairway known as Gatun Locks at the Caribbean end of the canal was where we accomplished this. Three consecutive lifts took us to the level of Gatun Lake.

Our 50-mile canal passage was tortuous at times, along what resembled a big ditch. We watched mechanical mules pull us with only a meter to spare on either side. Palm trees and green surroundings were inviting from a short distance in what was the rainy season. Scottish entrepreneurs once had tried to colonize what was then a pestilent land.

The Americans controlled the canal when we passed through and American medical and sanitation experts had demonstrated that they could control its yellow fever, malaria and intestinal troubles. What they could not control was the downpour that spoiled a barbecue on deck. Making up for this, was entertainment by female Panamanian dancers. Steaming past Balboa, after the dance troupe had disembarked, we entered Pacific waters and were soon in Acapulco harbor.

All around were trees and hills into which were cut hotels, houses and wharves. A launch took us to town. Acapulco hardly lived up to Frank Sinatra's perfect place for a flying honeymoon. The folks we saw seemed genuine in nature and prices were a bargain, even if dollar-chasing boys selling gold colored dolls and hats added a bit of harmless mischief. One wanted me to exchange my hat for his puppet on a string. I thought the boy would do well in London's Petticoat Lane market shouting "Mind me barra!"

Eileen was overjoyed when I purchased for her a blue and white dress using my ship's lottery winnings. I longed to see her in it and did so that evening when we did the foxtrot on the *Oriana's* dance floor.

Next morning, we packed tight with our belongings, the goods and chattel we had picked up in Acapulco. In the evening was a London-night dinner. A cardboard bowler hat and spats were handed me when A *Lovely Bunch of Coconuts* was struck up. We retired to bed early in my cabin. This was the first time in the voyage that Eileen and I had slept together!

Disembarking passengers at San Diego had an early breakfast and conversing with them we learned that we were 25 miles south of Los Angeles. A Greyhound bus, by way of Hollywood, took us to Santa Barbara bus station where my sister Isla awaited us in her big American car.

I had mailed from Bermuda, applications for editorial jobs on the *Vancouver Province* and the *Vancouver Sun*, along with my resumé under my Santa Barbara sister's address. "There's mail for you," Isla said, when we arrived at her beautiful home inside a gated compound on the edge of the Pacific Ocean.

I opened the *Vancouver Sun* letter first. "We don't hire in this way," the editor bluntly told me. The *Province's* reply was encouraging. "Come and see me when you arrive in Vancouver."

The *Province* editor's response allowed Eileen and I to enjoy our stay in Santa Barbara. She looked enchanting in her blue and white Acapulco dress, and a sun tan from two weeks at sea accentuated this. A week of healthy seaside walks with the household's two big dogs, sunbathing, swimming in the ocean and standing to attention when the American national anthem played before a televised Super Bowl football game, was our lot for two weeks.

All too soon came the day when I could tell Isla and Jerry, that in two days we would be on our way north. The trouble was that we were almost spent out except for the bus fare. A windfall came when Dr. Jerry Ecker, after giving me a post-hepatitis medical examination and indicating "A-OK," handed me $100 and, on the day of our departure, drove us to the Greyhound Bus Station. He was that kind of American guy and a friend for life.

Chapter 33
Where Would It Lead?

"So, when can you start?" The *Vancouver Province* editor asks me after a short but pointed interview. It is the Thursday after our arrival the previous day, in the rainy city on the edge of the Pacific. "Tomorrow," I thoughtlessly reply. "No, not tomorrow, Monday," he says. "Just report to Andy on the news desk late afternoon. I'll tell him you'll be there at 4:30. And get your wife out of that hotel!"

He had made no mention of any Canadian government job permit. The permit was almost as much shut out of my mind. Uppermost was that I had clinched a job in Canada and how relieved Eileen would be. I soon learn that my salary was more than I had ever earned before.

We had taken that hotel room because the price was right, due probably to the hotel's bad reputation. We knew nothing, good or bad, about Vancouver. But I had a job and we had a weekend to find lodgings or an apartment. So Eileen and I went about it the next day.

Down by Kitsilano, near English Bay, as pleasant an area of Vancouver as we could wish for, a sign told us a room was vacant. Our prospective landlady was an Italian woman named Mrs. Shirralo. She would charge only $60 a month with access to her kitchen and bathroom. In fact, access to almost the whole house including a garden where Concorde grapes grew on a grey wall. It was within walking distance of the *Province* office on Grenville Street, so we gladly moved in.

As the mist cleared, the surrounding snow-peaked mountains and a rainbow appeared, we saw just how lovely Vancouver was. I judged the rainbow a good omen. But where would it lead us? That day, it led us to a restaurant by the bay touched by incoming Pacific Ocean waves. We had cheesecake for the first time. That afternoon, I timed my walk from our new home to the *Province* office and found it took only 20 minutes. I would certainly not be late for my first shift. I also learned that the *Sun* published from half of the same building. The *Sun* and *Province* were part of Pacific Press. And now I was too. But again, I wondered where would it lead to in the long term?

I had spent successful years as a journalist in Africa and in Britain. Finding success in Canada would be difficult. So Eileen and I headed for the Vancouver library to read as many Canadian newspapers as possible. I knew there were subtle differences between Canadian and English writing styles. I summarized that I would have to spell words the Canadian way and use singulars rather than plurals for collective nouns such as team. Little did I know the extent of these differences!

Chapter 34
The Seattle Solution

Working in an unfamiliar atmosphere with socially different Canadian colleagues, left me with reason to doubt my future. Not that they were unfriendly. Just different in voice and personality. Luckily for me, they at least spoke English.

W.A.C. Bennett's Social Credit Party had increased its majority in a British Columbia general election. I knew little about Social Credit and, for that matter, the opposition parties. Yet, there I was, editing a political columnist's view of the election aftermath. That opinion piece put me secretly on the side of the opposition New Democratic Party and against the conservative column writer. I had enough experience to correct only spelling and grammatical errors and give the article the headline *Back home from home*.

"Isn't the phrase *Home away from home?*" the chief desk editor questioned me.

"The idea is that Bennett is comfortably back home, in the political home he left to campaign in the election," I said.

"Trite! Take a line out of the article instead of inventing a head. And be quick about it!"

My second attempt, *Bennett prime news again* was no prize winner. I saw my desk boss scribble something himself. He had substituted my attempt for *Premier Bennett is prime news again*. "I changed it to differentiate between premiers and prime ministers," he explained. "Premiers rule provinces. I don't like the head, but we are on deadline. Try again for the second edition."

I didn't dare whisper back that I knew premiers ruled provinces!

Troubling me at the time, was that the Newspaper Guild was threatening strike action to obtain wage increases.

I also knew that sooner or later, I would have to confess to the Canadian immigration office that I had come to Canada and taken a job without a work permit. I knew prospective immigrants were tested and judged for legal entry as landed immigrants, by the points they scored from questions asked them. Eileen and I faced up to the work permit task, not daring to even think that Canada might send us back to Scotland.

I was nervous that early Friday afternoon, sitting before the immigration officer. He was blunt about the system in first questioning Eileen. She won enough qualifying points right away for her teacher training documents and class experience. There were no points, I was told, for being a journalist. I was struck dumb. Then, to my relief, he asked: "Can you type?"

"Yes, touch type, 35 words a minute."

"There are points there."

"I write Pitman shorthand at 200 words a minute."

"Well, that gets you enough points to be accepted as a landed immigrant," he smiled. "So both of you qualify."

I breathed normally in relief.

My relief was premature.

"There is a problem," he said, his smile vanishing. "*You*!" He pointed at me. "You are working without a job permit."

Eileen later said I had turned white. I had to think fast. "You can't get a job without a work permit and you can't get a work permit without a job."

"I know," he replied. "Come out into the passageway with me."

Strong waves could be seen at a corridor window, beating in on a wet shore. I wondered if it indicated that the Canadian government would send us home on a ship the way we had come.

"I'll tell you what to do," he said. "It's the Thanksgiving long weekend coming up. Why don't you two fly down to Seattle, then come direct to my office early on Tuesday morning?"

"With new date stamps on our passports."

I would have hugged him, but he quickly turned his back on us and left. I hugged Eileen instead. I had no need to tell her why I had quickly accepted the Seattle solution.

We rushed home to phone Air Canada and book return flights leaving the next day and returning on the Monday evening, in time for the immigration office on the Tuesday and my work that evening at the *Province*. Our official entry into Canada from America was as simple or bewildering as that. We were officially landed immigrants with the next step, Canadian citizenship.

Chapter 35
Cariboo, Here We Come!

Under federal rules, achieving Canadian citizenship would take us five years. I still had seen little of Canada apart from Vancouver. Yet I was working as a journalist on a fairly big Canadian newspaper. Could it last? The answer clear to me was probably not. Snack-break conversations in the newspaper cafeteria made it plain that I had to act, because the guild was going ahead with a strike while I was still but a probationary member. This news I broke to Eileen, when she was just getting over our near deportation saved by the friendly immigration officer and a flight to Seattle.

"What will we do?" she asked lying side-by-side in bed. I had little positive to say. It was no good praying.

Like a bolt from what is called the Cariboo, I came across a small advertisement in my newspaper seeking a news editor in Williams Lake, where the weekly *Tribune* published. I brought out my portable typewriter and applied for the job. Four days later a knock at our door revealed Alan Black, co-owner of a stable of interior British Columbia weekly newspapers that included the *Tribune.* If, by chance, I appeared amazed, I disguised it as mild surprise. Newspaper owners don't often come to your doorstep soon after you apply by letter for a job. We exchanged a few words that morning, before I suggested discussing the job over lunch at a restaurant I knew by the seashore. He agreed. I liked the fellow and he appeared to like me.

I did not tell him I was just out of England, but impressed on him that the *Province's* journalists were inevitably about to strike for higher salaries and that I disagreed with their action. It was the right reaction to get the job in William's Lake. I saw how impressed he was by my working at the *Province.* He never asked how long I had been employed there.

After an enjoyable lunch and an informative talk about Williams Lake and the Cariboo country, I was told I could start as news editor there in two weeks. I strategically told him I was contracted to give a month's notice of leaving the *Province* but would ask if two weeks would suffice. Apparently, the *Tribune* publisher, Clive Stangoe, had fallen and broken his arm while roofing his house, so Black was desperate. His newspaper depended on me. The salary was much less than that of the *Province,* but the promise of more experience of Canada and a degree of job security was not to be turned down. Nor would I let Black down. Going back to a weekly newspaper, to get more acquainted with Western Canada from the bottom up, was perfect for my career.

I told Eileen that Black had shaken my hand on a deal that could really start my career as a journalist in Canada. She was glad to hear he had also said they needed teachers in Williams Lake.

Chapter 36
First Assignment

Right off the bus, 500 miles north from Vancouver, we sought out the *Williams Lake Tribune* office on the town's attractive main street. A stationery shop assistant told me the newspaper office was upstairs. "We were expecting you," she said, after I had told her my name, why I was there and introduced her to Eileen. "Nobody's in the newspaper office right now since we published today. The publisher phoned this morning to assign you to an airplane crash at the airport. He's nursing a broken arm and fractured hip, after falling from his roof when fixing it. No, not the crashed plane."

The airport crash had happened just four or so hours previously. Two people had been taken to hospital in Williams Lake. I was told the small plane had crashed in trees at the edge of the airport on taking off.

"Clive says to take a camera. There's a *Parisian* car in our back-entrance parking lot," she added, laying keys down on the counter on finding out I had arrived by bus. "Watch the ice on the roads. I understand nobody was killed in the crash, but that two were injured. The plane is a *Piper Cub*. Good story to get your name in the news next Thursday and lots of time to write it. By the way, I'm Wendy. Can I call you Bill?" she asked.

"Sure. Which way to the airport?'

"Straight up the main road about five miles. Same direction you came in the bus but past town. Don't rush off yet. Our cameras are in the darkroom upstairs. I'll quickly get you one loaded. Have you a notebook and pen?"

"Yes–and my own camera too. But let me have the newspaper camera because I'm sure mine is not loaded. And, oh, may I have a copy of today's *Tribune?"*

Wendy disappeared up the back stairs and returned with a 35mm Pentax and a back-up film.

"I can't use that film in my Hasselblad," I quickly told her. "I'll use the Pentax."

"Take this notebook," she responded. "By the way, are you Scottish? My father is from Scotland. Is Eileen going with you to the airport?"

"I'm going for lunch," Eileen replied. "I noticed a restaurant across the road. He'll do a better job on his own."

"I'm off then, before they move the plane. See you back here or in the restaurant. Maybe you can check on hotels for us."

"Wait, here's today's *Tribune* and the car keys. Good luck!"

The drive to the airport was not without incident. Cars sped past at well above maximum. I had never before driven as big a car as the Parisian I was assigned to. Maybe I'd be taking a photograph of my own crash. I trembled as a huge logging truck rumbled by too close. Then another gave me a fright as I trundled along at my usual 50 miles an hour.

The airport terminal building was predictably small, I saw after parking and entering. An official looking fellow was crossing my path so I stopped him and, smiling politely, told him I was from the *Tribune*. "I understand a Piper Cub plane has crashed."

My camera was dangling from my shoulder so I didn't have to tell him I sought a photograph.

"Nothing to smile about!" he said rather crossly. "Other side of the airport on the edge of the woods. You work for the *Tribune?*"

"Would you drive me over?" I asked after assuring him.

"No."

"One of your drivers?" I gave him credit for being some sort of a boss.

"Maybe. Stay here while I look into it."

He took all of five minutes to return and I was wondering if I were in the wrong hands. I learned later that he had phoned the *Tribune* office to check me out. "Outside is a small bus and driver. He will drive you to the crash scene. Don't hang around too long. When you return, come into my office in the far corner and I'll give you an account of what occurred and what we plan to do about it."

I was soon zipping across the tarmac with a talkative driver who gave me a sketchy outline of the crash and rescue. "The pilot didn't get his plane in the air," he said to my astonishment. "Two men were trapped inside after the crash. We rescued them bruised and shaken, but they should be alright. So, will the *Tribune* carry the story?"

"With a picture, I hope."

The crashed plane lay in snow clad trees, its nose pointing up over the trees to the blue sky. It was difficult to take a good photograph except from the tail end upward. It actually looked spectacular from my flat-on-the-snow position, so I took a quick shot as a safeguard. There were nice white clouds beyond the propeller that had to give the photo perspective. I asked the bus driver to stand nearer the plane and point at the approachable wrecked side. He agreed to pose for me. I thought that might work since, from what I understood, he had helped in the rescue. I shot more of him.

"The difficulty was in quickly breaking into the cabin," he confided to my surprise. "I smashed my way in from one side with my bus hammer. It's not really my job. It was the only way to get the two guys out."

"Is the hammer still in the bus?" I asked.

It was just the photograph I needed. He swung his hammer at the wrecked side of the Piper, without of course hitting it. I was getting cooperation from a man proud of what he had accomplished. It was clear to me it would be in the airport manager's interest to be as forthcoming.

"How badly hurt were they?" I asked.

"Not life-threatening. They were conscious and able to help us. We had to cut some branches."

Soon there was nothing else to do at the crash site, except get the bus driver's name and telephone number down in my notebook. I thanked him for his help before we drove back to the airport building and the manager's office. He gave me the names of the injured flyers and more details of the rescue.

"It's only the second crash at this airport in my time here. The last one was three years ago. The story was in the *Tribune*. Yes, I'd say about three years."

I told him I had arrived in Williams Lake that day and that it was my first story for the *Tribune*.

"Well, I'm glad to have helped," he said, rising and offering me his hand. "Here's my business card, so you can phone if you need more information. You'll find Williams Lake a great town, especially nice on the lake in the summer. The Williams Lake Stampede is thought to be the best rodeo west of Calgary."

"I'm sure you're right," I replied, thinking it was my first day on the job and much had already happened to me in this part of Canada they called the Cariboo.

Chapter 37
Ruthless Competition

My plane-crash story led the front page. Other stories came from an ice hockey match between local rivals Quesnel and Williams Lake. The following week, a Williams Lake School Board meeting gave me a lead story about a planned new college in Kamloops, 200 kilometers south, and a Williams Lake campus. Seemed like prospective Williams Lake students favored going to college in more exciting Vancouver. "Students fleeing the coop," was my front-page lead headline in the *Tribune*, quoting the prospective principal.

Other stories came from handouts and press releases, and I was pleased that a freelance contributed a youth column. I had never forgotten my experience as Kim, youth columnist for the *Blyth News*. Worldly, wise and salty on Cariboo affairs, was Liberal MP Paul St. Pierre's political column. He was member for the immense Coast Chilcotin-Cariboo riding, and popularly known as the author of books recounting adventures and quirks of life in the Cariboo. One of his novellas, *The Breaking of Smith's Quarter Horse,* was being adapted into a film starring Glenn Ford. Also chosen for the movie was Chief Dan George, a former residential schoolboy, now in his sixties, who had played character Ol'Antoine in the CBC-TV adaptation of St. Pierre's novel, *Cariboo Cowboy.*

One unwelcome outcome came when Chief Dan arrived in Williams Lake to acclimatize himself. He was refused entry into a public bar because he was an Indian. At that time, Indians by law were not allowed in pubs, at least not in British Columbia. Even this future Officer of the Order of Canada was barred at the pub door.

There were seven of us on the *Tribune's* full-time staff of sports writer, news editor, typesetter, business manager, publisher and shop assistants.

Nancy wrote a woman's column under her own name. I was quick to realize the *Tribune* had a winner in her. Her stories were not normally for the front page, but they had a wide following. They let readers know that the bride wore a simply-styled gown of white *peau de soie* with a bodice of Chantilly lace, a floor-length skirt with white Shasta mums forming the backdrop. Those gems of sophistication to me posed questions of where a divorced woman, who sang Western songs as she worked, had learned her craft and why she was stuck in Williams Lake.

Back from a visit home to Vancouver, was our sports reporter. Bert was quick to read my stand-in coverage of the hockey match between the Quesnel Kangaroos and the Williams Lake Stampeders, and quick to advise that I let him read any of my sports stories before they were printed. He was critical of my abhorrence of blood on the ice. "Normal hockey for a derby like that," he maintained. "And don't ever call it *ice* hockey again!"

I silently resented the inference that I was chicken when it came to tough sport.

Together, we put out a reasonably good newspaper that week without the publisher's presence.

We were in the newspaper office early the Friday morning after publication, giving us time to banter on about what I inwardly thought was nothing intelligent coming from a junior.

"Do the Scots skate?" he asked me with a withering smile.

"Well, not like you Canadians!"

"The reason I ask is that *Tribune* and other media staff will be playing an RCMP team in the annual charities hockey game next weekend. Can you handle that?"

I silently clasped my hands together and stared him down for ten seconds. "I can report it."

"C'mon. It's for charity. You're the *Tribune's* news editor. Take the chance to introduce yourself in the best way, on the ice. The Mountie place is a prime news source. Get them on your side. Scramble around in your kilt," he said with a crafty smile. "I'll put you down for our team with only 10 minutes on the ice in first and second periods. How's that?"

"That sounds more like a bowler trying to rule me out at cricket," I said to puzzle him. "Ever played cricket?"

He grimaced.

I boorishly added: "I don't have skates or a helmet."

"Buy or borrow skates. We don't wear helmets."

The conversation ended when the publisher walked in with his arm in a sling.

Stangoe was a surly man and I had not warmed up to him, nor had he to me. I had been hoping his arm and hip injuries would have kept him off work for a few weeks longer. The accident, no doubt, would account for what I thought was his long face. "Let's talk in my office," he directed me. With the door closed, I slid onto a chair.

"So, you're a Scot."

"I am."

"What brought you to Canada?"

"I stuck a needle in a globe."

Stangoe groaned. He may have felt pain from his injured arm. My answer did not help.

"I had to get away from Scotland," I went on. "Canada was not my first choice, but here I am at your service."

"Well, you twice got the paper out."

"I appreciated the editorials you wrote. And your wife's feature was a gem."

"How long were you on the *Province?*"

That was the thousand-dollar question that I resented.

"Look here," I challenged him taking the bit solidly between the teeth. "I've had experience on town and city weekly and daily newspapers in Scotland, England and even Africa as well as Canada. My newspaper, before coming to Canada, was *The Scotsman* in Edinburgh. I also worked on *The Sheffield Telegraph.* It was the best provincial daily newspaper in England while I was one of its copy editors. We broke a story of police violence, but the paper did more than that each day it published. Before the *Telegraph,* I was a reporter on the *Derby Evening Telegraph,* also in England, and still earlier, on a Northern England twice-weekly newspaper called the *Blyth News.* We had no press agency copy. We filled 12 broadsheet pages twice a week. I have the experience for the job, if that's what you're asking."

"You don't have to make a speech. This isn't an inquisition."

"I hope not."

I foolishly felt I had him on the run, not having to tell him I had started as a printer's devil sweeping the *Jedburgh Gazette* office floors straight from high school or was virtually just off the boat in Canada.

"I'm asking because I have a challenging assignment for you," he went on. "There are rumors of bad treatment of Indian kids at the St. Joseph Indian Residential School here. Bishop Hubert O'Connor is principal. Here's a file on the school, going back to 1923 that you should read. You won't cover this in a week or even two weeks. On top of your routine news reporting, photography, editing and page layout, I want you to research this as a feature story. Allegations surrounding Indian children taken from their parents to residential schools are legendary. Fact is, that at least one kid who escaped to go home, died in the bush. This demands the fresh mind you have. My concern is that we don't get sued. O'Connor is popular in town."

I had no idea there was an Indian residential school in Williams Lake. The reality of residential schools across Canada was new to me, apart from a movie I had once seen.

"Rumors sometimes lead to truth," I observed.

"Okay. But beware! I'd write an editorial on these rumors, but that would draw attention to just what you say or detract from it. We're invited to cover the school's Christmas party, so make a start there. Take photos and write a short piece on the party, then interview the bishop for a feature."

He threw a flat palm in the air as if to dismiss me. "Great Scot!" he grimaced in pain.

Thoughts flew through my mind as he answered his ringing phone. I didn't know whether to leave or listen in. I wondered if he was insulting me by giving me an assignment, then telling me how to cover it to support an editorial he didn't have the guts to write. "I'll certainly cover the Christmas party," I affirmed when he laid down the phone.

"That's dandy," he replied, staring down at his desk figuring out what else to say. "By the way, I liked your airplane crash story and picture. You were thrown into the deep end. Keep up the good work, because a rival newspaper is starting in Williams Lake. The prospective publisher just phoned impudent enough to welcome me back. How he knew he would find me here is beyond me. It will mean competition because he has a printing press. As you know, we have to send our printing requirement to our sister newspaper office in Quesnel, each Thursday morning. Our rival aims to publish one day before us, on Wednesdays. No doubt, he plans to steal our thunder."

"Well, that means we won't miss anything exclusive they may have."

He considered my words for a moment, then enquired if I had found accommodation other than at the Travel Lodge.

"If not," he said, "there's a Maisie Konke, who lives not far from the airport road. She's a lively Londoner by birth, and has an empty ground floor apartment with a terrific view of the Stampede grounds and much of the town. You'll be able to cover the Stampede

194

from your window. You may have met her husband Felix, the chairman of the school board meeting you covered. He owns the Maple Leaf hotel and beer parlor in town. He's German-born with ambitions for a seat in provincial government. He used to be a professional wrestler. Maisie once hit his opponent with her shoe. People say Felix's biggest challenge is wrestling with the English language."

I said I would give Maisie and Felix a visit that evening and rose to leave.

"So that's settled," I said to my crew, after closing the door. "Let's get on with putting out the paper."

I thought what a vastly different world from Edinburgh or Vancouver I was in.

The Christmas party at St. Joseph's residential school was enjoyable. Father Lobsinger, was new as principal and he told me only good things. He stressed that seven of his Indian children were to visit Europe. Like many others, I was inexperienced on residential school affairs and had no idea, that the behavior of their priests was digging a gulf of serious dispute between Canadian governments and indigenous natives. So I was not the best journalist for this assignment.

Eileen and I attended a more suitable for me Legion Burns Supper and enjoyed the haggis! A couple of whiskies helped me photograph a young Canadian highland dancer with kilt flying above her knees. The trouble was that her highland dance teacher wrote a letter to the editor, saying my picture insulted the kilt. Even my publisher did not accept that view, although we published the Scottish lady's lively letter.

All the while, Eileen was teaching a special class of Indian children at Williams Lake Elementary School but finding that her students were routinely absent with the excuse that they had gone fishing.

Chapter 38
Grisly Encounter

The weeks flew busily by at my desk and on the street, as the competition tried in vain to close us down. The *Williams Lake News* really was dull opposition for the *Tribune* and it missed some of our stories. I could hardly miss any article it printed, although I had only one Wednesday afternoon and one busy hour on deadline the next morning to make sure of this.

The *News*, no doubt, thought they had us beaten one time, when the Indian community decided to declare operational a newly built Open House with a meeting of Indian chiefs, right on our Thursday morning deadline. Obviously, the *News* team thought they were bound to have an exclusive story the following Wednesday. To beat them, it simply came down to writing what I already knew from a handout on the Open House; pasting the story on the otherwise completed page one, leaving white space for two paragraphs to lead the story then, by attending the Thursday morning Open House; make sure it *had* opened and pasting in two lead sentences, wrapping up story and paper before deadline.

My publisher observed with baited breath, my holding up the front page slightly past our deadline. It came down to filling that small white introductory space above the text, below the already pasted headline. I bolted from the event 10 minutes after the Open House was declared open and from my shorthand notes, quoted to the typesetter what the youthful and newly elected Indian chief had said. "We've scooped them," I told the boss. "This won't be their exclusive news. Take it to Quesnel!"

"I want to talk to you now," the publisher said from behind me. "I delayed this until we got the paper on its way."

I thought he was seeking to compliment me. But no! It was the previous week's newspaper he held up when we reached his office.

He pointed to a front-page headline: *Williams Lake man fights off grisly bear* that I had written.

Then he held out his Canadian dictionary. "Look it up!"

"Look up what?" I asked.

"Hell, *grisly,* you nincompoop."

Next, he told me to read out the meaning.

"Frightful, grim, gruesome. The scary words sounded to me like a bear." I wondered what he was getting at.

"Now look up GRIZZLY with two zeds."

I glanced down the dictionary page.

"A large ferocious bear of western North America."

"Yes! A double 'ZZ' grizzly bear."

I didn't know what to say.

"You handled that Open House story well, I have to admit," he said. "But don't try that too often. What would you have done if they had delayed or postponed the opening? We might have been left with no lead story. How do you propose to correct this grisly spelling of yours?"

"By admitting an unfortunate error."

"We have three letters to the editor pointing out the error. One reader asks if we're really western North Americans at the *Tribune.* I delayed publishing them to give you a chance to put in your apology admitting your grisly error. Pray there will be a cracking good letter to the editor that steals the headline on the letters, or you'll have to think up a grisly headline."

Saying it was just a spelling error dug me in deeper.

"You mean here, in the heart of British Columbia, we can't spell grizzly."

I changed the subject: "What do you think of my international news column, to counter the dearth of foreign news due to the Vancouver newspaper strike?" I had been providing foreign news by culling from the CBC's Radio Canada International everything from Vietnam War protests through Richard Nixon's run for the U.S. presidency, to the Soviet Union's invasion of Czechoslovakia.

He lowered his arm on the table and drew himself to his full height. "I never sanctioned it. You snuck it in when I was off work. Great Scot!" He spat out his last two words in what to me was a sort of racist way. "End it next edition. Get the hell out of my office before I lose my temper!"

I had the last word in telling him I had intended ending it, since the second strike at Pacific Press was over.

His words and red face were such that I left his office thinking of resigning. Over lunch, I asked Eileen by what miracle Clive had attracted his lovely wife Irene. I knew some of the history of their relationship and I stewed over it.

Clive and she had bought the *Williams Lake Tribune* in 1950. Articles in the files showed they had spent their first six years living above the print shop, freezing in winter, roasting in summer, raising two children to the thump, thump, thump of an old Country Brower Press and a Linotype held together with bailing wire and chewing gum. I laughed to find it even recorded that the newspaper had twice goofed on daylight saving time, and there he was insulting me over a spelling error.

Irene wrote features and a column and was still doing so though working as a secretary at Columneetza High School, and I knew Clive was jealous of her friendship with the English teacher who actually was Irish. She had also written a book, *Cariboo-Chilcotin Pioneer People and Places*, and I knew her as a thoroughly nice lady, though she seldom came into the newspaper office.

An early *Tribune* story of hers was a gem, headed:

Cariboo Logic

Rancher Mickey Martin, a rodeo regular, had spent a long, hot, dusty day down at the rodeo grounds. He decided a nice cold beer would wash the dust out of his system. Mounted on his stallion, he rode uptown. Now this horse was to Mickey, what a fancy motor car was to a town fellow and he hated to be separated from the sight of this fine animal that he had imported from Alberta. Prize Appaloosa stallions were not common in the Cariboo at that time in history.

With this in mind, you can almost guess that, yes, Mickey and horse entered the Maple Leaf beer parlor together. As wild and as western as things were reported to be in those days, most people did not come in the beer parlor mounted on an Appaloosa stallion. Needless to say, the proprietor did not welcome this intrusion into his establishment and asked Mickey to take his horse back out to the hitching rail. Mickey was quite certain in his own mind that the horse should be welcome to stay and quite a discussion ensued.

The owner of the Maple Leaf at the time of the incident was a man called Benny Abbott. Benny was a well-known citizen of Williams Lake and he was often instrumental in the organization and the running of the Williams Lake Stampede. Mickey was often a pickup man for the rodeo and as well, he was a regular customer of Benny's when he was in town on business. Most likely he had stayed in the hotel on several occasions. The fact that he was well known to Benny made it so Benny wished to handle the incident with as little disturbance as possible and with no hard feelings. The ensuing discussion had several go-rounds with Benny and Mickey arguing back and forth over the fact of whether the horse should stay or go. Mickey just refused to believe that his horse was not thirsty for a beer also.

At the end of each round it was still stalemate. Now Benny was racking his brains for a way to solve this dispute without making an enemy out of his friend. As a barman, he was well experienced in persuading people to leave his establishment, but his experience with horseflesh in the bar was far more limited. He retreated for a few moments, thought, and came up with a course of action that might mean a solution to his problem.

He marched back over to Mickey and his Appaloosa stallion, which went by the name of "Nemo," and he said to Mickey, "Mickey, would you happen to know how old that horse is?"

Mickey replied: "Of course, I do! Nemo is a five-year-old stallion, why do you want to know?"

Benny replied, "Mickey, do you realize that your horse is not of legal drinking age. He is, in fact, far too young to be served alcohol in a beer parlor. He is a minor in the eyes of the law. The horse will have to leave the premises."

The upshot of it all, was that while Mickey had not been persuaded by a dozen of fairly logical reasons to remove the horse, when confronted with the law of the land, Mickey saw that he had no choice but to take his stallion outside to the hitching rail. All the logic had made no impression on Mickey, but he was a law-abiding citizen and the horse was simply not old enough for a beer.

I was later assured that versions of Irene's story had circulated for years, but so what!

My wife, Eileen, spoke of the work Stangoe had put into the newspaper in the early days. She gave him the benefit of the doubt and dismissed the idea of my resigning and her leaving her teaching job until we were ourselves ready to move. So I stayed on. Anyway, I suspected Stangoe was negotiating to sell his share of the paper to Alan Black.

That night, Eileen and I were at home just before dinner when a knock came to the door. An Indian boy with a big brown paper parcel asked Eileen, who was his teacher: "Want any Chilcotin turkey?"

What he was trying to sell her was salmon he had caught in the Fraser River. Indians selling salmon were breaking the law and I had been warned to watch out for them. I told Eileen that it was salmon and not turkey that she had purchased and it could bring her up in court for aiding and abetting.

"Well let's have it for dinner," she said. "That way the evidence disappears and saves both the Indian boy and me."

Chapter 39
The Mounties Get Their Man!

My only run-in with the Royal Canadian Mounted Police came on the ice rink. The *Tribune* sports editor had put me down in the media team to play the annual community fundraising hockey match against the Mounties. There was no way out. My size of skates was in a shop window for $40. I purchased them along with a hockey helmet and for practice, Eileen and I went skating.

On the morning of the match, Bert suggested I play in my kilt. I judged that might be a passport to just puttering around trying to touch the puck. It might even thrill the spectators. It would be clear to them that a fellow in what they might call a skirt was unlikely to be a good hockey player. I told a less-assured Eileen that it was a kilt worth wearing. After all, Scots played field hockey wearing kilts. Eileen said those were Scottish schoolgirls.

I had skated a bit, years back, trying to pick up a girl at the Richmond Ice Rink in London, England, when working on *The Sun*, but nothing like the way Canadian hockey players maneuver on the ice. My movements were directly forward. Swaying side to side backward was way out of my depth. Even my turns were in a circle around ice rink boards. I usually stopped myself from falling by grasping anything or anyone I could. The fact was, I had never before in my life held an ice hockey stick.

The puck dropped at 2 p.m. I have to admit I hardly saw it in the ten or so minutes I puttered around in circles. I was an attraction though. "Pull up your kilt," one wiseacre shouted, as I veered 10 yards behind the puck in the wrong direction. That set things going. When I slid on my bum on the ice, there came the shout, "Kiltie, kiltie cauld bum!"

When the Mounties scored their first goal, was I glad play stopped for a moment. On the restart, they rushed around our net as if they had devils inside them. I was at the other end of the rink. To me the game was holy bedlam. Sheer hooliganism!

I actually saw the black streak come from a distance to cross in front, near my stick, when a shoulder caught me, whirling me round, my high-in-the air stick coming down with a glancing blow on a Mountie's head. I was punished with a two-minute penalty. It was great to be seated in the box where I could wave to my wife. The crowd handclapped my return to the ice when the Mounties scored their second goal.

I heard Stangoe roar out "Great Scot!" He had seen and heard something that I could hardly imagine. The deafening howl sent me down on my bum again. The noise was that of a police siren. I was plucked from the ice, kilt and skates in the air, and thrust in the back of a van, watched by a disbelieving silenced crowd. The Mounties had their man!

Five minutes later at the station, I was charged with obstructing traffic on the ice. The Red Serge and their motto had throughout history attracted authors and filmmakers to create a vivid image of a fearless security force. With Nelson Eddy in mind, I judged their motto not very practical in a world where criminals sometimes had as many resources as police.

I was detained for two hours in the *hoosegow* after the hockey game ended with a 5-1 victory for the RCMP. Eileen bailed me out by contributing to their welfare fund. "The media lost when they lost you," she was kind enough to say about that bad old hockey game. I staggered home with a swollen knee, cursing my sports editor who had set me up and, no doubt, would write unfavorably about my downfall.

Chapter 40
Forest Fire

What made me first think that being stuck on a weekly paper in Williams Lake was keeping me out of real Canadian journalism, was a cross-Canada passage from one of MP Paul St. Pierre's weekly columns published in the *Tribune*. He quoted the Co-operative Commonwealth Federation party's Angus McInnis saying: "In British Columbia politics is a recreation, on the Prairies it's a protest, in Ontario it's a business, in Quebec it's a religion, in the Maritimes it's a disease."

The words made me aware that I still knew only a little of Canada. The East was the hub and it was a world away. The thoughts were at the back of my mind when walking the rounds looking for local news. I was struck to see a thick cloud of smoke billowing across the horizon that, back on the phone in the office, I traced to a forest fire in the Big Creek area, wherever that was.

"It's a big fire and the hazard unusually high. It's a result of lightning storms and winds of up to 55 miles an hour that fanned old fires and started new ones. El Niño has something to do with it. There are fires in many parts of the province and this one is the biggest," I was officially told.

That pall of smoke in the distance could clinch the El Niño story we were missing. I knew the story depended on my being on the scene of that dread of the timber country. Being there with a loaded camera!

I arrived at the fire camp at lunchtime after a three-hour drive. Huge steaks were being barbecued for professional and volunteer firefighters who had put in a morning's work. I was served, too, beside a grizzled Indian fellow who introduced himself as Casimir Charlie. He said he was 83 and a veteran volunteer of forest fires. The pay? "We earn $1.75 an hour," he replied. "The food is good."

I interviewed firefighters who had been picked up on town streets and press-ganged into service.

I drew my Hasselblad from its case, photographed Casimir Charlie and firefighters who had been press-ganged into service. That done, I made for the edge of the fire. Gaunt blackened stumps dotted the area. A few steps in, a firefighter saw me focus my camera under a sky darkened by smoke. Red-hot ash, hot dust and his shout alerted me to danger. I clicked my camera several times, then wondered which way to turn to avoid being the tragic newsboy who never got back.

"That way," the ashen-faced firefighter raised a pointed finger. "Out, now!" I reacted quickly, and on my request, he escorted me.

"I'm from the *Williams Lake Tribune,"* I explained. "How bad is the fire?"

"Haven't a clue. They say firefighters are coming from Vancouver, so it must be bad. Is there any food left at base camp?"

I had all I needed for my story. Since it was only two days to publication and because I believed I had ruined my camera, I left the scene to return to William's Lake.

The fire story led that week's newspaper and I thought in vain that my photographs might have impressed Clive Stangoe. Soon it was back to seeking news from undertakers and caretakers, digging up news from the Legion about its darts tournament and from the police about crime, with no acknowledgement from him of my fire scoop.

At a Rotary lunch, I sang in unison Canada's new national anthem, *O Canada,* and a contact gave me the idea of writing a story about a Williams Lake school principal, who still played *The Maple Leaf Forever* before her pupils.

Eileen and I joined the Legion. She as the wife of a former infantry corporal. At Friday evening dances, we stomped about like I was more a cowboy and she my highland lassie. Winning against veterans on the pool table was profitable. I soon found out that almost anyone could join the William Lake Branch of the Legion if they paraded in front of the president, and it became a great place to pick up news stories

One morning in June, I was a journalist virtually just off the boat from England with pencil and notebook, unexpectedly facing Canadian Prime Minister Pierre Trudeau. Only one question came to my mind: "Is it true you are a playboy?"

If look and action killed, it would have been my first and last day facing Trudeau. He swung round on one foot and strode off.

I was left cold, because he had been a champion of mine since becoming prime minister a year before. I had wanted him to deny what some Western Canadians were saying about his way of life, before and after he become prime minister. I wanted to hear him pledge a just society leaving no room for play.

I saw Trudeau join federal MP Paul St. Pierre nearby and probably remark something like: "Tabac! Tell that barbarian from Scotland I am not a playboy."

St. Pierre came over to put a hand on my shoulder and bring me back from nightmare to reality. "Trudeau is *not* a playboy. He is the hard-working prime minister of your country."

The front page of my newspaper that week of 1970, led with the banner headline: *"Trudeau not a playboy, says Paul St. Pierre."*

The prime minister had come to William's Lake at the invitation of St. Pierre to attend the Stampede. By chance, unknown to him, I bought him a beer the very next day. He had climbed down from sitting on the rodeo arena fence that hot summer's day and was at the center of a crowd answering questions. Perspiration was running down his face. I sensed he needed to wash heat and rodeo dust from his system. So, I quickly bought a glass of beer at the tent and, unable to move forward in the throng, thrust the glass of beer forward saying it was for the prime minister. Hand by hand it reached him. He downed it almost immediately. That went into my story too.

Photographing the Stampede Queen was easy, but interviewing her, not so easy. She said her name was Dee Watt. I made the mistake of thinking she had given me her first initial as D. I kept asking her what D stood for. Her cowboy friend nailed me for pestering his girl.

I also photographed Glenn Ford and my landlord Felix Konke together. Ford had been invited to ride sidekick on a stagecoach at the Stampede and Konke was on the Williams Lake Stampede committee.

When the *Tribune's* rival *Williams Lake News* folded, Stangoe purchased its printing press and gained the *Tribune* newspaper ascendancy in the Cariboo. A letter to the *Tribune* from the jobless former *News* editor, bitterly condemned me as good only with a pair of scissors. Stango wondered why I opted to publish it.

"It doesn't bother me," I told him.

What did bother me was when my *Candid Column* fell apart in urging the school board not to expel Columneetza High School student Jim Elleray, after he was caught with marijuana. Stangoe, in an editorial in the same edition, sought expulsion. He immediately curtailed my column. The teachers generally were neutral or supported me, but the school board supported Stangoe. The school's cheeky *Ten Penny Freedom* student newspaper supported my stand, but then its editor was the accused drug dealer.

The stage was set for the next preparation for my run-to-the-top in Canadian journalism. Someone out there appreciated my work in Williams Lake. I was offered the post of journalism instructor at Cariboo College in Kamloops.

The Mainline-Cariboo Branch of the British Columbia School Trustees Association had been working on college development for 10 years and I had been reporting their work. A plebiscite to determine the wishes of the people had passed in all six districts including Williams Lake, by a convincing majority of votes. On January 1, 1971, the appointment of Jack Harris as principal was confirmed and I knew I had impressed him with my school board coverage.

For its first two years, starting in September 1971, the college would be located in a building on the Kamloops Indian Residential School site, then, if approved by the provincial education minister, in a multi-million-dollar campus above the city. I also gave thanks to the Glaswegian dean of career studies, Tom Ferguson, for helping me rise from weekly newspaper journalism to journalism instruction.

After a year and a half, it was time to bid farewell to Clive Stangoe, who had never trusted my liberal journalism as news editor, even though we had knocked out the opposition and kept our readers well informed, not only on community news but, for a while, on foreign news and interested some of them in my *Candid Column*. I sensibly saw that embracing academia would sharpen my general knowledge and qualifications for my anticipated run east, where the big Canadian newspapers were published.

The question that lay in the back of my mind, was not whether I could teach journalism but whether journalism could be taught at all.

Chapter 41
To Strive Ahead

My hometown newspaper in Scotland, that I used to deliver, announced my appointment: *Mr. Bill Fairbairn, whose aunt, Agnes Fairbairn, resides at 10 Ettrick Terrace, has been appointed instructor of up-and-coming reporters at Cariboo College, Kamloops, British Columbia.*

Born in Hawick, he left The Scotsman *for Canada in 1970, and after a year and a half as news editor of the* Williams Lake Tribune *and a spell as sub-editor on* The Province, *Vancouver, took on the pioneering task of teaching journalism in British Columbia.*

Mr. Fairbairn, nephew of well-known Borders journalist Tom Fairbairn, started his career with the Jedburgh Gazette *and has since worked as a journalist in England, France and Africa.*

Aunt Agnes had managed to mix the facts but the report was generally okay.

Now I was faced with the daunting task of living up to it. After all, as they say, life throws things at you and you just have to handle them as best you can. Thankfully, I had Eileen to advise me on teaching techniques.

I prepared by contacting the National Council for the Training of Journalists in London, England, asking them to forward, at my expense, their lecture notes. They responded before my first class started with a full set of talks on everything from general reporting to essential law for journalists. I edited their talks by changing British spelling to Canadian spelling and British newspaper law to Canadian law.

For initial classes I prepared reporting, editing, workshop and photojournalism talks, for the one-year course preparing students for employment as beginner newspaper journalists as well as being a sound approach to further journalism studies. I added Pitman shorthand for journalists as a selective subject and, to my surprise, found the class of 13 students enthusiastic.

Assisting the journalism program were economics teacher Peter Peters and English teacher Carole Cummings, each with a string of university BAs etc. behind their names in the college calendar. This calendar of teachers and courses mentioned that the college's Chinook language motto, *Quansem Ilep,* translated into To Strive Ahead. I looked forward to a hard struggle. To my delight, when I told the principal this, he reacted positively. "Get to know your students personally as well as in the classroom," he advised me. "Remember the printed word is stronger than the sword."

Classes began the morning of September 6 with the usual introductions. That dispensed with, I outlined my career as a journalist and told them what I thought it took to be a reporter. Curiosity was what I sought. The craft also called for imagination, but not the kind that altered the facts. I might have been the most popular teacher in the world that morning, when I said a first priority, in time for the official Cariboo College opening, was to start a student newspaper. That called for immediate staff editorial positions and the class would go ahead with them forthwith, although staffing the paper would not be confined to journalism students in the future.

I mentioned that an editorial I had spotted in the previous day's *Vancouver Province* had confused Zambia, in south-central Africa, with Gambia, in West Africa, in commenting on an uprising in Gambia. Equipped with copies of the editorial to read, students would each write a letter to the Province criticizing the error. The letters would be sent as a batch. If one letter were published, then its writer would be appointed student newspaper editor.

Keeping them happy, I continued talks on the student newspaper plan by asking for ideas for a title and saying a vote would decide the winner. I learned next day that English teacher Carole Cummings had heard of my student newspaper plan and had already given students a title that, to me, was a loser, but to them, a winner.

They had decided that *Interface* would be its name. My doubts were quickly quashed. The class voted unanimously for Carole's contribution to journalism. So, *Interface* it was, rather than *Wagon Wheel*. I had not known that she worshipped Marshall McLuhan, his media-is-the-message and his book *The Gutenberg Galaxy*. His ideas were bunkum to me. I quickly had to study McLuhan when, in the weeks that followed, Carole became more popular than me in her English-for-journalists class that, to me, was undiluted McLuhanism.

She termed journalism communications and introduced that name for her course. She sought an awareness of how basic communication was at the heart of people's lives. "In many ways people unknowingly play *The Game* and problems arise as a result," she baffled me by contending and she continued:

"At university in Vancouver, folk would never be sitting rapping like us. We have billboards selling tires, nylons, paint, soup, golf balls, bacon–anything. Is consumer culture what you intend to put in the college newspaper?" She planned that my journalism students would study the media itself.

I felt I had to delicately bring her down to earth by accepting that my class needed to write better English and improve their spelling. She reluctantly agreed to help out.

Yet, communications was always what she felt ought to be taught. On Open Day, Carole put on a display to illustrate how communications had changed and were still changing. I could hardly understand her illustration of strings connecting telephone, television, newspaper and magazine to a mock human being with the message *Kill King.* McLuhan, with rants at magazine advertising in his book, *The Mechanical Bride,* was her mentor.

She was later to say that she read most of *Interface* except for the sports page. Her main criticism was that the paper was not a student paper, in that it dealt with minor college items rather than current and relevant topical discussions. Crappy ads sickened her even if they financed the paper.

For her, the media really was the message. Her forthrightness was far removed from experience as a journalist.

The *Vancouver Province* printed student Jim Schoening's letter to the editor, acknowledging that similar letters were received from 12 other journalism students. So Jim became *Interface* editor. Other students were given editorial positions. Lynda Nilsson, daughter of a Cariboo rancher, became features editor. Twenty-year-old Paris-born Pat Baehl-de-Lescure, also prepared to be known as Pat Baehl, became photo editor. Alan Peterkin was sports editor, ready to cover more than hockey. My one Indian student, Phyllis Derrickson, became copy editor as well as joint features writer.

Business administration students under Peter Peters agreed to seek out advertising and look after financial matters. The commercial art class and its Manchester-born teacher Irene Hansed, who had studied at the Manchester Art and Design Institute and with whom I shared an office, would lay out advertisements and help with typographic design. The college's fine arts teacher, Bob

Campbell, would give us a title piece of art and a student he recommended would contribute cartoons. To me it was a feast of talent from heaven. Irene even produced another artist who went to work on a cartoon over the right to hitchhike by facing off Dean of Studies Don Couch, a conservative New Zealander, with Don Marshall, a radical journalism class hitchhiker.

Interface was finally launched the day before the college's official opening, with a lead story stating that the college looked ahead with spirit, right beside a photo of a human skull found by students out in the bush, and another story outlining the development of the Open University in England and asking if the system would work in Canada. It came out on deadline thanks to hard work by the students and the help of a Kamloops newspaper editor, who agreed to put his printing staff at our disposal one evening a month during semesters.

Our first editorial asked readers what they thought was meant by the newspaper's title.

"Welcome to Interface," Jim Schoening wrote before explaining: *"The name was adopted on a vote by the paper's prospective writers and staff members, who for the first time congregated a few grueling weeks ago. Since that time, we have begun to get some feel about our work, but (and this is only the first edition) the paper's atmosphere is still developing. An interface, as defined by Random House, is a surface regarded as the common boundary of two bodies or spaces such as the city and the Indian reserve."*

He ended his piece: "It is at the edge of a specific space that things happen–where the elements of one world meet, sometimes clash, interact with those of another. Such occurrences are a riot between students and police, the killing of a president or simply surf breaking on a lonely beach. Although separated from Kamloops by the Thompson River, the college is still linked closely with events in the city. So the paper hopes to be a vital link dealing flexibly with many areas of interest common to both."

I was impressed with the resolve of the editorial, although I detected a bit of the-medium-is-the-message in it. I was becoming accustomed to the newspaper's go-ahead title and beginning to enjoy Carole Cummings as an aroused critic.

I had naturally encouraged curiosity in my students but was taken aback when the editor, seeking a story among paraphernalia in the college's attic, stumbled and unintentionally thrust his leg through the feeble wooden floor into the geology classroom below. Instructor Ron Hughes and his students were thunderstruck and he reported the incident, though later he invited me to dinner at his place to make up for it. The principal and I had a hard-to-stop laugh. I accepted his warning to be careful.

While *Interface* held our attention at Cariboo College, in far-distant Ottawa, Prime Minister Pierre Trudeau was wrestling with the War Measures Act. *Interface* did not ignore the English-French separatism crisis in Quebec that was manifesting itself all over Canada in one way or another. Helped by French teacher Yves Merzison, our front-page editorial demanded in French an understanding of Quebec and the Front de Libération du Québec (FLQ). On the back page we printed an English translation.

During the crisis, soldiers were stationed at bridges in and around Kamloops. A teacher in Dawson Creek, Art Olsen, who had discussed the FLQ in his classroom, had been fired. Seven British Columbians were in custody under the act. This was in addition to the scores of mostly French-speaking intellectuals arrested in Quebec itself. We editorialized that such actions would have "a stifling effect, and if carried to their conclusion, could harm Canadian unity and freedom."

The popular student viewpoint, however, was support for Trudeau who, asked by a reporter what he would do next with the War Measures Act, had responded: "Just watch me!"

So, *Interface's* editorial ended: *"We should all try to understand the problem, and not have to rely so much on the good fortune of having a prime minister with the background of a French-Canadian father and Scottish mother. There have been too few Canadian prime ministers with this Canadian background. So do watch him!"*

The question was whether we needed a license to publish our newspaper. Geography teacher Nelson Riis, a future MP for the New Democratic Party, brought licensing up and urged me to find out. A telephone call to city council found the municipality in a state of not quite knowing since rules for a student newspaper were new to council, although the town's high school brought a paper out. The town clerk suggested that in the circumstances of the day, I should bring a copy of our newspaper into his office for his purview and a chance to discuss the matter.

My visit to the municipal offices came the next day. The clerk shook my hand readily and I explained what had happened at Cariboo College since its inauguration. He voiced an interest in the new college, but reminded me I was there to seek license, or permission, to publish a student newspaper. "Well, it's a *college* newspaper," I corrected him, passing onto his desk the hot-off-the-press copy I had with me.

His eyes were immediately riveted on the French-language editorial on the front page.

"The object of the newspaper," I said, "is to enable stories by students and teachers to appear in print. The paper gives student reporters in the journalism class more than the skill of writing, but also the feel of editing, layout and printing processes."

I shut up while he continued to puzzle over the French-language editorial. I was fairly certain he did not know French well, if at all, but clearly, he was trying to understand it.

"The English translation is on the back page," I finally said. His eyes rose to meet mine. "Of course," he remarked with a glint, as he turned the paper front down.

The headline, *Plea for understanding,* on the back-page editorial must have mollified him. By sheer good luck, an advertisement by Kamloops Member of Parliament Len Marchand, the first status Indian to be elected to the Canadian Parliament, lay right below the editorial. It urged the people of his riding to write to him if they sought an understanding of the way Canada was being run. There, too, was a quarter-page advertisement by Simpsons-Sears, the biggest fashion shop in Kamloops. Maybe it was Marchand's photograph or the shop's sexless pantsuit illustration that helped us out. The MP and the store, along with the Chinese-born Kamloops mayor, were big players in the city.

"You publish monthly, I see," the city clerk remarked. "I'll give council acknowledgment of what I've seen. So far we have no license regulation."

I approached him with a request to allow *Interface* to report council meetings. "Certainly, that might be arranged under freedom of press laws," he replied as if he had invented them. "I'll let you know. How many are you talking about?"

"About four at a time from my class, along with myself, just for the experience gained, with no heckling, but covered by the press freedom laws you mentioned."

"Any member of the public is welcome on the public benches."

"It would encourage my students to be seated with other reporters. It's in the council's interests to put them in the right place."

He pondered my point. "Then we can try that out on Friday evening, but you must leave room for city reporters. Let me have an advertisement cost sheet for your college newspaper. From what I've seen, the municipality may wish to advertise."

Chapter 42
Press Council

When the *Kamloops Daily Sentinel's* Inquiring Reporter's column asked the question, "Do you think a press council should be established in the Kamloops area?" I asked the same thing in class and my students discussed it positively.

Alderman John Grigg had stated at the first council meeting my students and I attended, that several people whose names appeared in the press were often upset over news coverage promoting a writer's personal vindictive policy. He said the press council should be designed to nail anyone who abused the freedom of the press, and that it should have enough power to demand the discharge of reporters and editors who violated public trust.

These were serious allegations and I believed he had timed his riposte to coincide with the attendance of my student journalists.

I felt it incumbent to publicly reply, since it seemed his bringing up the contentious matter in front of beginner journalists and me as too much of a coincidence. I immediately wrote a letter to the editor of the Kamloops *Sentinel,* which the editor dutifully printed, headed:

PRESS COUNCIL

Sir: I regret both Ald. Grigg and those people interviewed on the idea of a citizens press council, distorted seriously the function and organization of a press council as set up in Quebec, Britain and in various European countries.

The British Press Council comprises daily and weekly newspaper journalists, publishers and representatives of the general public as do the Quebec and Swedish press councils.

The object in a nutshell is not–as many of your interviewees believe and as Ald. Grigg apparently would encourage–to encroach on press freedom, but to preserve it.

The British Press Council is there to consider complaints about the conduct of the press. Complaints are upheld or rejected at public hearings, with newspapers reporting proceedings.

It seems clear to me that the best way of securing press freedom is by convincing the people that the press acts responsibly for the public good. And this can be done by newspapers themselves setting up a body to which they are prepared to answer for the use they make of their power to inform, instruct, influence and entertain.

Demanding the resignation of a reporter is not the function of a press council. It should be within the editor's and only the editor's powers to take such action, knowing full well that the series of checks, which all stories go through before publication, had broken down.

Kamloops should lead the way for British Columbia and Canada with the establishment of a press council.

I was encouraged to see among the interviews published was one with Woody Cross, president of Cariboo Council Student Union. He stated: *If that kind of thing was organized, the reporters would be afraid to write anything. Sometimes I think they don't write enough on some subjects. Some things which should be written aren't there.*

Another interviewee stated: *I think it is a stupid idea. If Grigg's in public office and can't take a slap in the face once in a while, he shouldn't be there. The freedoms we now enjoy are because of freedom of the press and thought. Who does he think he is?*

A week later I received a letter from Alderman Grigg saying: *I have been very impressed with your comments in the news media in regard to freedom of the press and certainly pleased with the student presentation at City Council last Tuesday evening. I would like to discuss this issue with you and experience the opportunity to exchange views. Thank you for the invitation to speak to the college students, which I would be most pleased and honored to accept.*

The result was that a week later, any formation of a press council was forgotten and I had an alderman guest speaker taking one more tough class lesson off my shoulders.

With my work taking up most of my spare time, I saw that I was ignoring my wife. I pledged that would happen no more, when to my joy she told me she was pregnant.

Chapter 43
The Indian Problem

My five years as a journalist in East and Central Africa had convinced me non-racialism was the key to the future. So I was at first disappointed to learn that journalism student Phyllis Derrickson, raised on the Westbank Indian Reserve 100 miles from Kamloops and who had already written about Indian affairs for *Interface,* did not share my view that integration was the answer to what was being referred to in Canada as the "Indian problem."

I thought about it without realizing a big story lay under my nose. After all, we were teaching on the Indian reserve, yet, only one of my 13 students was an Indian and that was a high percentage for the college as a whole. The reason was obvious. Indians did not have the money to pay for college education, though they got tax breaks and other benefits by remaining status Indians on the reserve. I was later happy to learn that after her year of journalism, Phyllis landed an office job on the other side of the cultural divide with the Kamloops school board. Meanwhile, in contrast, three college instructors, including Nelson Riis, had gone somewhat native in renting houses beside beautiful Paul Lake on the reserve.

The native position was puzzling me and I had to learn more. I knew Len Marchand, MP for Kamloops-Cariboo and the first status Indian to be elected to Canada's House of Commons, was leaning towards supporting integration as I believed Pierre Trudeau did. I phoned him and was delighted that he would give a talk to my class. By then, I was teaching nine different course subjects in journalism in areas of current affairs, law and local government, thus putting in more class hours than any other instructor. Guest lecturers were more than welcome to take the load off my shoulders and for this guest we were teaching on the edge of the reserve.

A bridge over the Thompson River divided us from Kamloops itself. On our side were picturesque hills rising to mountains. My students had detected an interface there and making the most of it in the college newspaper.

Phyllis, a shy 20-year-old, had not written much, but then her job was copy editor. She had contributed a piece saying federal government policy on Indians was integration, but whether the Indian people would go along with this was questionable. "Indians will not easily give up the lands they have felt are theirs and have been at home on for so long," she wrote. "There remains the question of aboriginal rights, treaties pertaining to fishing, hunting, trapping and property rights. Our biggest question is what the future of the Indian people would be."

I still did not know nearly enough about Canadian Indians–indeed of Canada itself–but sharing the Kamloops Indian Residential School complex, of which the college rented two large buildings, were 270 very polite Indian children and teachers. Most of the children came from outlying districts. They were enrolled in grades 1 to 12, coming to school in September and staying until the end of June, at which time they returned to their homes on the reserves. So there was ample opportunity to educate myself.

The residence, founded in 1899, was Catholic and one of a number throughout the province and country. I discovered that such schools, originally, were built because Indians were not allowed to attend white public schools. The segregated Indian children had a history of being westernized and Christianized with mother tongues forbidden at school. Some were from broken homes. About half the staff at the Kamloops residential school were Indian.

The headmaster priest, Father Noonan, who had also taught at Williams Lake, told me he hoped that in the near future an Indian would take over his position so that Indians could run things. He wondered what the future had in store for residential schools since he believed integration would proceed to a long-term logical conclusion. With that in mind, I was pleased to have Marchand as a middle of the road guest lecturer and not let Phyllis have it all her own way.

I read in the college library that Marchand had been born in Vernon, British Columbia, and was a member of the Okanagan Indian Band.

His first education had been at the Okanagan Indian Day School at Six-Mile Creek, a one-room schoolhouse with 25 students, where he had completed grades one through eight. I was astounded to learn that subsequently he had been the first Status Indian to graduate from the public high school in Vernon, British Columbia. He had

217

also attended University of British Columbia and graduated with a Bachelor of Science degree in agriculture. In 1964, he had finished one more degree of Masters in Forestry at the University of Idaho. Members of the National Indian Brotherhood had encouraged him to work in Ottawa, where he became the first political assistant of aboriginal heritage in the office of a federal cabinet minister. He later worked for Arthur Laing, minister of Indian Affairs and Northern Development.

When Pierre Trudeau announced to the House of Commons that he was launching the 1968 general election, Marchand was watching from the gallery. Liberal friends began to phone him and send telegrams. They wanted somebody new and young to contest the Kamloops-Cariboo riding. They wanted, and they got, Len Marchand.

Marchand won the riding by 3,000 votes from Davie Fulton, an MP for two decades and a former Minister of Justice.

After Marchand's talk to the class, on the *Front de Liberation de Quebec* crisis and the Le Dain Commission's report on drugs and Indian Affairs, came time for questions.

"How are you treated as a parliamentarian?" Phyllis asked him.

"Well," he replied. "You might know that I took a few cheap shots from my own people which really hurt."

"What cheap shots?" she persisted.

"Cheap shots on being in favor of gun control and the abolition of capital punishment."

Marchand ducked answering a question on whether he was in favor of Indian integration with whites and the eventual abolition of reserves. "That's a touchy one," he replied, "when you consider one of my chief aims is to devise federal policies that recognize the rights of Status Indians to negotiate compensation for loss of aboriginal rights, although I do see a connection."

I put a question: "What do you think about the past history of residential schools such as the one next door?"

"You should really ask the parents of children who were taken from their homes and placed in such schools," he replied. "Such a parent was Johnny Sticks at Alkali Lake many years ago. The story handed down is that his son Duncan, who was a student at the Indian residential school near Williams Lake, had run away and was living with his parents back home. He is said to have been aged only seven but had made it the 40 miles home. He disappeared from the school a second time, along with eight other boys. The eight were caught but Duncan disappeared in the woods. A local rancher found his

218

body. Why did that boy die? There are other stories of boys running away. Why? What was happening at the Williams Lake residential school all those years ago? You'd like to know, probably as much as I would, since you worked on the *Williams Lake Tribune.*"

I sat there astounded, realizing this was possibly the ground-breaking story I had missed in Williams Lake. I had no hindsight into the future national scandal and inquiry emanating from residential schools. A future investigation would result in the establishment of a Truth and Reconciliation Commission that would report the residential school system having removed Indian language and culture by forcibly taking Indian children from their parents. Few others at that time had much knowledge on Indians or sought it. Whites were on a long, steep learning curve.

I ignored the challenge in Marchand's remarks on Williams Lake and simply asked what important work he intended to do in Ottawa. He said he would urge recognition of Indian despair. He would try to foster hope in a proud people who had lost belief in themselves. "My people must begin to understand that they can become whatever they wish and aspire to become whatever they are capable of becoming."

I wrapped it up by thanking Marchand and inviting him to join students for lunch at the college cafeteria.

We published extracts from his talk and featured beside them a draft copy of *A Declaration of The First Nations,* obtained, surprisingly, from the Kamloops Indian Residential School library. It declared:

We, the Original Peoples of this Land know the Creator put us here.

The Creator gave us Laws that govern our relationships to live in harmony with nature and mankind.

The Laws of the Creator defined our rights and responsibilities.

The Creator gave us our spiritual beliefs, our Languages, our culture and a place on Mother Earth that provided us with all our needs.

We have maintained our freedom, our Languages and our traditions from time immemorial.

We continue to exercise the rights and fulfil the responsibilities and obligations given to us by the Creator for the Land upon which we were placed.

The Creator has given us the right to govern ourselves and the right to self-determination.

The rights and responsibilities given to us by the Creator cannot be altered or taken away by any other nation.

These main rights, referred to by the joint council of the National Indian Brotherhood, were treaty rights recognized by the Crown and Indians in the Royal Proclamation of October 7, 1763. The Declaration stated that any changes required the consent of the two parties to the treaties. Those were Indian governments representing Indian Nations, and the Crown represented by the British Government. The Canadian Government was a third party and could not initiate change.

Chapter 44
Ma Murray

I had learned through experience that fiery newspaper editors are often fearsome creatures. Margaret "Ma" Murray, I soon realized after encountering her, was not quite as fiery in old age as in her heyday when she wrote hard-hitting editorials for her weekly Bridge River-Lillooet News in the sagebrush country of Lillooet, a two-hour car ride from Kamloops.

When I took my class of journalism students to Lillooet specifically to meet her, she turned out to be a charming, alert lady of 86, still unique in Canadian journalism folklore.

Not knowing this, we crept warily up the stairs to Ma's apartment above the printing office in the town's main street. I had read in *McLean's* magazine that she was "the salty editor who couldn't spell worth a damn and wouldn't know a split infinitive from fractured French."

Typically, Ma was writing one of those editorials she was noted for. But she took time off to show us around a newspaper plant almost as old in years as herself, explaining that the equipment was just for show since her paper was now printed by the "damned offset process that had eliminated all the hot typesetting."

A once proud Miehle flatbed printing press with attachable folder, chases, shooting sticks, planer, wire brush and quoins, equipment that previously had helped produce the printed newspaper for years, stood silent. Ma's price for the machine, its ink ducts dry on the eve of her retirement, $2 plus tax.

"I bought it for $14,000," she recalled wistfully with a laugh at the cash difference. A grimy open space next to a heavy steel-roller proof press was ominously empty. Ma's Linotype had once stood there. Now it had gone to a journalism school in Vancouver for a song.

Delving into a dusty font of 24-point Old Ionic type, Ma picked up a setting stick and set up the words, Cariboo College, by hand, saying it was not so long ago that every metal letter and text space was painstakingly put together that way. "Like soldiers standing to attention," I suggested.

"In those days," she said, her still clear eyes fixed somewhere beyond me, "it was a treat to set up a headline instead of hand setting lines and lines of text type." Then had come the Typograph machine and after that the Linotype. "Today, a composing machine resembles a typewriter and headlines are set photographically, then page pasted on top of articles. *The Lillooet News* is now printed offset at Williams Lake along with two other weekly out-of-town newspapers. We can't afford an offset press of our own. If I was a little younger maybe…"

I could see our intense interest in all things associated with herself and her operation was weakening her will to explain, so I gave her a break by picking up her setting stick and putting together the words Ma Murray with lead spacing between it and her Cariboo College line of type. I explained that I had started my career as the printer's devil setting up type.

"You don't look like a devil to me," she laughed.

I suggested to my most critical classroom student that she set a line of type and, for once, was one up on when she said she would not know where to find the letters.

Of course, we sought photographs and after snapping a few inside the office, I noticed from the printing office window a *For Sale* sign for a house opposite. Whispering to wide-eyed students to keep her not too strenuously occupied, I dashed across the road and removed the sign from its upright position in the lawn. Ma was sitting with backlight coming from the window when I got back. Gently placing the sign in her arms, I stepped back and clicked my camera. My students were astounded. Ma hardly showed surprise. It was the perfect picture and not just for *Interface.* As I explained to my students, I had realized that Ma Murray was selling herself not, just her newspaper, and that this was a story and picture for the Vancouver press as well as maybe out east. With a little cajoling, Ma promised me another interview at the weekend as we were leaving. I returned to get Ma's full story.

My article in *Interface* recalled Ma was born in Windy Ridge, Kansas, August 3, 1887, one of six in the family of an Irish-Catholic peasant who had emigrated to the U.S. in the mid-nineteenth century. Margaret Murray first worked as a housemaid and later as a clerk in a Kansas City saddle shop.

While shipping saddle harnesses to Alberta, she played what began as a practical joke. Into the packages she tucked notes describing herself as a decent, hard-working girl, anxious to marry. She received dozens of replies, including at least one that sounded interesting. So she travelled north to appraise her mail-order suitors.

On the way, she stopped off in Vancouver and met and married an Ontario-born newspaperman, George Mathieson Murray.

George had political ambitions and his chance came in 1928 when he was sent on a trade mission to the Orient. There he saw 450 million customers in China, 100 million in Japan, and countless others in the Pacific Rim. He returned to Vancouver to write a series of 50 articles and would return to China to remember twice as much, provided Margaret went with him.

The Murrays returned to China in July 1937, but were bombed out of Shanghai ten days after landing and evacuated to Malaya before returning to Canada. The experience left a bad taste in Ma's mouth, not only for communism but also for socialism, although her paper had supported the New Democratic Party candidate in the 1972 provincial election.

In 1933, when George Murray decided to go full-time into politics, he went up-country to fight as a Liberal in the provincial riding of Lillooet. He won the seat and with Margaret, launched the *Lillooet News.* George held the seat until 1941, when he lost to the depression-spawned CCF (Cooperative Commonwealth Federation), itself kept out of power by a coalition of Liberals and Conservatives.

Ma rebelled at what she saw as a betrayal by the two main parties and got herself nominated as Social Credit candidate for the Peace River riding. There she combined politics with the job of running the *Alaska Highway News,* while her son, Don, ran the Lillooet newspaper. Her staunchly Liberal family were appalled. When she announced her Socred candidacy, Don announced that his mother had nothing to do with running the Lillooet paper.

Ma ran a lame third in the election that ended her career in politics and her flirtation with Socred. In later years, she regularly drew an editorial bead on long-time Social Credit Premier W.A.C (Wacky) Bennett, calling him a gangster and a crook at different times.

Ma herself describes the years from 1933 to 1937: "It was a fairyland of adventure in the lean and hungry thirties, with scarcely enough cash to buy gas for the seven-passenger old Willys-Knight, which also served as an office, bedroom, larder and campaign headquarters. Why, the wheels were turning on cloud nine!

"The world was ours. It was full of goodies and it was an open field for anyone who thought they had something to give, and the inventiveness to try and work for it. The price of gold was raised from $20 to $35, a depression had been on the country for five years, the boom had finally cinched, the country was full of gold and it was take it or leave it.

"Once loaded and ready for the campaign, I recall we passed a hundred or more small outfits mining the bars of the Fraser River. The riding was a big one and the wolf still at B.C. doors. To us, however, every prospect pleased, and the only gamble was the franchise of the majority. To make a clean start, this scribe, before nomination, had all her upper teeth pulled, but suffered only a temporary plate to offset the worry of such an undertaking."

Ma's story became weirder as she continued unabated enthralling me.

"The car carried a removable full-length sign, *Murray's Campaign Headquarters,* and a trunk between the jump seats carried the cooking utensils and clothing. A distiller in Maple sent us two cases of snakebite cure medicine for entertaining unwilling voters. We slept in the car, cooked by the roadside and tried to win the hearts of the voters for six weeks. We could never forget, it was Lillooet constituency that gave George the nomination and the chance to save the country. British Columbia was broke, the Union government had relinquished after five years. A good friend lent us $50 and we scrounged enough butter and egg money to make it $100. We kept within our campaign costs."

Turning over back issues of her Lillooet newspaper, as I sat taking down shorthand notes, she said the paper had now been sold to her printer. She came to the 1937 editions and read out: "The Bridge River mining potential is equally as affluent as the famed Cariboo and there is plenty of work. The bread lines have faded away."

"But World War II and its ramifications were threatening," I pointed out.

"Here, today," she went on after a pause, "I'm crowding 86. This scribe has lived and survived two complete wars of aggression and we know the third war is killing off the people from the people's own stupidity, greed or apathy and ignorance. Genuine faith and the help of a higher power that prevailed despite the suffering, won the first war. The second war was won by faith and know-how, but this third war is destroying the democratic way of life and the Christian religion. In this fast fading 20th century, the status quo is lashing the steed that carries us to destruction."

I had hardly asked a question, when Ma ended her discourse with the optimistic note that she intended to continue an editor-emeritus type relationship with her former newspaper, that for years had promised "a chuckle every week and a belly laugh a month, or money back. They can laugh at me this time if they want."

"I can understand that," I remarked with a chuckle. "Even if editor-emeritus means the fast way out."

She also said she was writing a book on sex.

I was tempted, but I didn't dare laugh.

Ma then brought me a cup of tea and a scone, and in a way, I reciprocated by inviting her to travel to Cariboo College to give a talk to what I hoped would be to the whole college population.

"I would be delighted," she said. "It's much more beneficial to talk to the younger generation, because I feel that adults are so caught up in doing their own thing that one just cannot get through to them. I will tell the students to have charity in their hearts."

Near the end of the school year, I had been delighted that an article I had contributed to the British National Union of Journalists newspaper, *Journalist,* was used in full and unedited, with a photograph of my students studying *Interface,* and I showed it to Ma along with the photograph I had taken of her. The article appeared in the November 1971 issue under the headline:

Cariboo Comes On

Nine juniors have just graduated from Cariboo College's one-year pilot course for young reporters at Kamloops in the interior of British Columbia.

Though courts, councils, accidents, fires have much in common the world over to the experienced news reporter, instead of rugger the juniors covered rodeo and instead of soccer it was mainly ice hockey.

Former Sun *man Bill Fairbairn left* The Scotsman *for Canada in 1969 and after a spell on* The Province, *Vancouver, and a year as news editor on the* Williams Lake Tribune, *took on the pioneering task of teaching journalism in the British Columbia interior.*

He says the course itself does much to invalidate the old complaint, mainly by experienced newsroom trained journalists, that journalism training lacks practical content. In fact, one complaint by students is that there is too much practical work and not enough theory.

Besides classes in English and with options in sociology and economics, the juniors cover a wide range of stories including interviews with local and national figures and even the local branch of consumer's action.

There is a fairly cosmopolitan population in Kamloops (meaning meeting of the waters), so one minute they may be interviewing the China-born mayor and next the Indian federal MP.

On as many assignments as possible, the course instructor goes too. At tutorials later, the juniors' stories are compared for accuracy with notes taken by the lecturer and occasionally tape recorders.

They also produce their own newspaper, Interface, *a lively tabloid which enables their stories to appear in print and also gives the reporters the feel of sub-editing as well as make-up and the various printing processes.*

A recent issue led on the college's pending move to a new $5 million building at Kamloops, and gave student, teaching faculty and administration viewpoints fair hearings.

Inside Interface, *usually, are articles by everyone from the college principal to the janitor.*

The young reporters, though occasionally accused of forming a community within a community (usually in defense of press freedom), in fact take a lively interest in college affairs. Editor of Interface, *Jim Schoening, 20, is also secretary of the student union for Cariboo College.*

The students also take a lively interest in current and local topics. The cold war, drugs, racism, pollution, closed college council meetings (now open to the press!) also were discussed, occasionally bilingually, in Interface *columns.*

Sport has a vital place too. But usually rodeo, ice hockey or Canadian football take top headline.

Photo editor of Interface *is Pat Baehl-de-Lescure, Paris-born and also prepared to be known simply as Pat Baehl. To Pat, a picture is worth a thousand words.*

"Which thousand?" immediately asks Linda Nilson, daughter of a Cariboo rancher and the newspaper's features editor. And Linda can relate, without hesitation, the shortcomings of many a photograph that has no story.

Bill Fairbairn, who started his career on the Jedburgh Gazette *and has since worked as a journalist in Africa and France, as well as London and Edinburgh, sums up the achievements of the course in this way:*

"We are pioneers here in the interior of British Columbia. It is fitting that we should be working in this growing town of Kamloops.

"The climate of opinion here suits controversy, even confrontation, as newcomers vie with the established life of old settlers and as the Indian people flex their muscles towards meaningful freedom."

Ma was impressed when she read the article. "The picture you took of me was enterprising too."

How glad I was that I had taken my camera into a photographic shop in Vancouver before my visit to Lillooet and had it cleaned of forest fire dust.

I had, at the same time, to prove that my shorthand for journalists had stood up to the long interview.

Meanwhile, as nature would have it, I had become the father of a baby girl.

Eileen and I named her Judith.

When I told Ma, she asked: "How come you did this without reading my book on sex?"

Chapter 45
On the Run to the Top

I had known for some time that the son of the Kamloops weekly newspaper publisher had sought the position of journalism instructor at Cariboo College when I was appointed.

I suspected the better-connected Mel Rothenburg still had an eye on my job. So, after my second year of teaching, I decided a tentatively offered position on the *Montreal Star* was my better future. I had picked up on Indian studies, improved my French at evening classes and learned a great deal about western Canada and, from a distance, something of Quebec. I likely would have a teaching testimonial to add to my résumé. I suspected the *Star* would treat fairly my application for a copy editor's job at a time of crisis in that province, and to some extent nationally in Canada.

In any case, Cariboo College was being moved from the reserve to a new million-dollar location up the hill in Kamloops, and its administrators keen to teach more television and less print journalism.

Like clockwork, a positive reply came back from Arthur Wood, managing editor in Montreal. He sent me the official written application form for employment, asking for personal details, education details and former employment. He later telephoned me offering a job as night desk editor after two months on day shift. The salary would be $225 a week and a night differential of $15. Following a year on the night desk, there would be an opportunity to move either to the day desk or to reporting. He felt my western experience would be a welcome addition on the newspaper.

I immediately wrote back saying I was obliged to give a month's notice toward the end of the summer semester when my year finished. He phoned to say the job was mine. Journalism jobs were not so difficult to land in the 1970s.

The college principal had recommended me for any work in journalism and I told him I thought Rothenburg would satisfactorily fill the vacancy at the college. So, Eileen and I bid farewell to students, friends and teaching colleagues. We looked forward to seeing more of Canada from an eastbound train, during a journey that would take us three nights in a sleeper compartment with our baby daughter Judith. Ron, the carpentry instructor, had put together four plywood boxes for our belongings.

Rolling off that Sunday night from the Kamloops railway station in the autumn of 1973, awakened memories of all I had attempted in the West in preparation for my fate in the East. Our train seats folded into beds, so we knew we would sleep well. A baby carriage was brought into our roomette that suited Judith. Meals were included in the ticket price. A waiter in the dining car demonstrated how to pour coffee on a moving train without spilling it. We were soon unaware of the rattle of the train. Bingo games were entertainment each of the three nights.

The train trundled to Edmonton, where a friend, who had moved to Alberta's capital city, met us with a box of Laura Secord chocolates during a stopover. We had travelled from mountains under huge skies, through flat prairie and native territories. On line were Winnipeg's rail yards, giving us the chance to discover Canada's long train history, back to Prime Minister John A. MacDonald, and this city once known as the Chicago of the north. The line took us through the Canadian Shield, skirting lakes, then on to Union Station, Toronto, and finally, Bonaventure in Montreal.

We found short-term lodging downtown and I was emotionally roused on learning it was next door to an Adam and Eve dating service. One morning, after taking photographs while Eileen was shopping for a baby stroller and a home for us, I was looking at a poster outside our lodgings advertising the dating agency, when a soft voice asked if I was seeking a date.

I turned to find a slim, dark-haired woman of an uncertain age eyeing me. "Maybe," I curiously replied to her.

"I take it you are available and not connected with this dating agency," she went on. "How about tonight?"

"How much?" I flippantly asked.

"Take me for dinner and no charge. Or I will take you. I have a business proposition to put to you. I would not work at a place like this."

"I think you're just lonely."

"Let us make a date then. Shall I wait for you here at seven? I am not picking you up. It is strictly business of a decent sort."

229

"Make it 6:30. I'd be glad of company tonight since my wife will be busy until about 8 p.m."

To my surprise the lady accepted this. Her pick-up of me made me wonder if I had come from the Wild West to Wild Montreal.

"*En fait!* I am glad you are married. *A bientôt!*" She left me riveted to the spot, thinking the dating agency had mysteriously affected my whole being for better or worse.

I had lots of time on my hands, so I was free to take more pictures before calling on Art Wood at *The Montreal Star*. The French being spoken in Montreal was a far cry from that taught at Cariboo College. I hardly understood what people were saying. I blamed Yves Merzison for teaching me Parisian instead of Quebec French.

The underground rail city below vied with what was above. Most trains headed for the Montreal suburbs, but one I saw was going as far as New York and another to Vancouver, on the track on which Eileen and I had come to Montreal. Customers ate, drank and sought treasures in corridor cafés and boutiques. I gathered that in the winter one could walk for miles in warm air. One woman was casually strolling around with her dog. The underground trains ran on rubber wheels and an old man, seated next to me on a bench, said if one listened hard enough for a train's approach, a *do, re, me, fa, so, la, ti, do* musical scale would echo in one's ears. I heard some of the notes. I stowed in mind a future feature article on the magical sounds and sights of the Montreal Metro. Mayor Jean Drapeau's municipal government was currently expanding the train lines, so that might tie in.

The imposing cathedral outside the Queen Elizabeth Hotel caught my attention for photographs and I took a few more shots inside, despite not knowing whether it was allowed.

The *Montreal Star's* offices on St. James Street were imposing. Not knowing that staff entered on the parking or other side of the building, I used the shop side. They motioned me upstairs to the fifth floor, saying Arthur Wood was in his office. I had been with the managing editor only a few minutes when he indicated I should have phoned him before coming. He had another important appointment. Thrusting a copy of that day's *Star* in my hand, he directed me to the St. James Street pub where I would find the assistant editor, Max, and chief copy editor, Walter. They would brief me on when to start work. Maybe buy me a pint of beer. He did not even tell me their full names. It was as simple as that.

Wood was a tallish square-built man who might, in his youth, have done well on the British rugby or football fields, and his confidence in me was heartwarming.

I strolled around the newspaper office, with its huge copy-editing desk in one quiet corner and reporters working at their own smaller desks throughout the floor. I noticed a good number of small offices with names on them that I guessed were for special editors. Two photographers walked past me and disappeared down a corridor I assumed led to the darkrooms. An older reporter rose from clicking his typewriter to introduce himself, wondering who I was and why I was there. On telling him my business, he said I was joining a pretty good newspaper, wished me good luck and offered help if needed. He said reporting and editing was done on the floor we were on. Advertising was controlled one floor above, as well as in the front St. James Street shop. The rotary press was in the basement and could be viewed through back-street windows. There was a staff restaurant too.

I asked him if my half-baked French would be a handicap, and he replied that Quebec was a French-speaking province and that I would be advised to improve my French. "More than half the city's news conferences are in French," he added. "Yes, you'll be handicapped, but you're not the only one."

I told him I would be working on the desk and he said that was the easy way in. "Take French lessons or find a French-speaking boarding room on St. Catherine's," he advised.

I strolled along St. James Street thinking an interview in a pub for a newspaper job was like something out of a movie, that usually ended with the newcomer successful but half under the table. How would I identify, among boozers and smokers, the editors I sought? How would I fit into the picture? How would I get clear before the mugs of beer lined up in a threatening way?

The first task was easy and the second and third I managed. I simply asked the barman where Max and Walter were, and he pointed to a bunch of my future colleagues sitting and standing in conversation at the other end of the bar. At a gesture from Max, a fellow had made room and I was seated between him and the remarkable Walter Christopherson, with a half pint of Molson's in front of me and other English-speaking and French-speaking *Star* staffers continuing to chat about the chance of the Habs making the hockey playoffs. Mayor Jean Drapeau and the Olympic Games coming to Montreal in 1976 was another topic. Those present had

231

finished their day's work making way for night staff. Most would have one or two drinks before commuting home for dinner.

"So, you're Bill Fairbairn. Art told us he had hired you. You come from teaching journalism out West," Walter commented, before sarcastically adding: "I've heard of that being done."

"With no apology, I set up the journalism program at Cariboo College in Kamloops. I have experience, not just in British Columbia, but in Britain and Africa, both as a reporter and on the desk."

"I hear you were on *The Sun* in London and *The Scotsman* in Edinburgh," Max, an expatriate born in the English Midlands, said.

"I'm impressed," Walter critically said, glass up with a down-the-hatch cheers. "Impressed also with *Cariboo* College. Three very different entities *The Scotsman,* the *Sun* and *Cariboo* College."

"You're right. *The Scotsman* office was like a morgue where I, as foreign news desk copy editor, rarely saw the real editor. In contrast, the *Sun* floor was like a circus with big shots like Hugh Cudlipp, from its stable companion, the Daily *Mirror*, visiting to advise on news judgments."

I had no idea if they knew that Cudlipp, chairman of the International Publishing Corporation, had launched *The Sun* as successor to *The Daily Herald.* Or knew that he had quietly ordained that *The Sun* would not encroach on *Mirror* circulation. "You see," I repeated. "We were duty bound to increase our circulation to a million readers, but not at the expense of *The Mirror."*

Max quoted Cudlipp's publish-and-be-damned notion of good journalism. Things were going well. But two beers were my limit and I determined I would leave while ahead.

"Our competition here in Montreal is *The Gazette*, and it's getting tougher as English speakers leave Quebec and French takes over. We're competing for a smaller number of readers each week. With your experience, you should do well on the desk under Walter," Max said. "Did Art tell you when to start? If not, then Monday morning."

Walter nodded: "Be there at seven in the morning, prepared to do final inside page editing after the overnight shift knocks off. Max does the front page. The first edition goes to press around noon and the city edition three hours later to catch evening commuters. Reporters and photographers, meantime, are covering assignments for the night-shift news editor. Hard breaking news or anything the *Gazette* has missed, we use in the day's paper."

"Okay, right, I'll see you at seven," I said looking each man left and right in the eye. "Cheers!" The word came out of me as I slugged back a half of beer like the professional drinker I was not. "I'll see you on Monday. Got a date at six-thirty."

I left the pub thinking I had probably surprised them, but I was happy to have escaped relatively sober. My previous hepatitis had kept me on the wagon for ages and transgressing medical advice bothered me. I had my dinner date and it was almost six. I was sure Eileen would be preoccupied finding us a baby stroller and rented home. There was no need for alarm over a business proposition this pick-up artist had in mind.

Chapter 46
Oolala!

"Sorry I'm late," I said, approaching my waiting date on the sidewalk. "Would you mind if I go upstairs to my room to wash my face and clean my teeth?"

"Fine. See you in 10 minutes."

I analyzed the situation as I tidied up and rid myself of the beer smell. What could this tantalizing woman be up to? Well, men picked up women, so why not the other way around? I could hardly say she was beautiful, but certainly slim and athletic. First thing I did on rejoining her was to find out her name and try to uncover her game.

Micheline responded in like fashion, so I told her who I was "I'm new to Montreal, so please, it's your choice of where we eat and it's my treat not yours."

"I thought we might go to St. Hubert. The chicken is always good. It's not at all noisy. Service is excellent. We can discuss business there."

"St. Hubert? Isn't that a town some distance away?"

"It's a restaurant up the street. I should know."

A bevy of young women awaited us at the reception desk of the yellow towered place. One of them conducted us to a table.

"*Oui monsieur. Oui madame,*" were responses as we ordered our meals. The polite French words were music to my ears.

I quoted from the menu and Micheline added a few words about regular rather than creamy coleslaw that helped make my order understood. The waitress laughed. I wondered why.

"I'm impressed," I confided, when the chicken and baked potato arrived with dip.

"We dated without entering the dating place," she laughed. "Bon appétite!"

I could hardly take my eyes off her. "And what a way for me to improve my French," I complimented her. Sir Walter Scott's admonishment from my childhood, *Oh! what a tangled web we weave,* flashed through my mind. What would be the result if Eileen were to wander into the restaurant!

"Mais, oui!" she said bringing my thoughts back to her and French lessons.

I told her of my rail trip from Kamloops and the start the following Monday of my new job on *The Montreal Star.* "Do you work by any chance?" I asked her.

"I work here."

"You work here?"

"Yes. I'm a waitress. You are a journalist. Is there a problem?"

I was staring hard at her so it was little wonder she had questioned me in that way.

Surprises had come at me from all directions in the few hours I had known her. "Not at all," I said. *"Pas de tout,"* I added to impress her.

We sat silently eating for a good few minutes, my mind in a maelstrom around the French language and my new friend. "I'm surprised you brought me here," I ventured. "The waiters and waitresses may wonder."

"Wonder what?"

"My wonder is that you have a place for me in your *business* world."

Silence was golden for a moment. She seemed to be charging up. "I'll tell you what I want you to do."

The waitress interrupted us in French, inquiring about dessert. "The raspberry mousse is *delicieux,"* Micheline said. "We can share using two spoons."

I nodded and the order was taken with an *"ah-oui"* from the waitress.

"So, what do you do to keep trim?" I asked to break a silence.

"Trim?"

"To keep so fit and slim."

"I am a ballet dancer."

"Well, I can't help you much there. I dance like a frog. I've never tried ballet. But I once wrote a youth column in England. One young woman had criticized me for not covering ballet and covering only the sport of young men. To put things right, I reported on a ballet school probably like yours. There were about 15 women in the class. The one young male ballet dancer saved me from being the only male present. I wrote about him in my column. It did not help me win over the female ballet dancers."

"You may win me over as a good photographer."

I had been wondering when she was going to tell me what I had to do. Helping her as a dancer had seemed incredible, but I could take photographs. "So?"

"Before we met, I noticed you had a camera and watched you take photographs inside the cathedral. I need photographs of my dance routine, to take to an audition with a company doing a modern ballet version of the American musical, *Thoroughly Modern Millie*. I can't afford a professional photographer. I'll give you French lessons if you take the pictures I need. I can rent my school ballet room for half an hour. You will probably need lights. I can rent those too. Will you do it?"

"*Now* you put me in the picture, if you'll pardon the pun..."

"The pun? What is this pun?"

"A pun is...well, it's hard to explain. It's a pun when you use a word that describes two meanings. Taking pictures and being in the picture so to speak."

"*Un jeu de mots?*"

"Exactly!"

"I can teach you conversational French."

"*Mon problème est que je parle français comme un parisien.*"
"*Un quoi?*"

"My college French teacher came to Canada from Paris."

"*Oolala!* I understand," Micheline laughed. "You must practice the French spoken in Montreal. You should probably enroll at language school."

"I've been too long at college. Did I not tell you my previous job was teaching journalism?"

"I don't really know much about you."

"I taught journalism at a British Columbia college for two years."

"More important now is whether you will take photographs for my audition."

"*Mais, oui!*" I shook her hand and held it for a moment longer than necessary.

"*Alors, c'est ca!*"

"What's the deadline?" I asked, realizing that French lessons with this lively woman in return for photographs that I would enjoy taking, looked like the real deal.

"Deadline?"

"When is the audition?"

"I have to hand in the photographs the weekend after this weekend. I can buy a *pellicule* for you. Black and white photographs are requested. I'll write down the name and address of the school. Come at nine o'clock on Monday night. I'll wait for you in the school auditorium. Don't forget your camera. If you come at nine in the evening, the room will be free. You will have three days to have the photographs processed. I will right now write down the address of the school. There is a Metro station nearby."

"Eh, voila! But tell me. What is a *pellicule*?"

"I forget the English word. You will need one to take photographs."

"Oh, a film! I'll see to that."

Onto our table was served raspberry *mousse*.

I passed Micheline a spoon for her to taste, before me, the dessert placed on our table. The waitress smiled asking if there was anything else we required. I left a decent tip before helping Micheline on with her coat.

I would have to be careful to make sure Eileen understood it was only business. Things had been unusual in Williams Lake. Montreal was out of hand.

Chapter 47
Doubles or Quits?

A sharp metal spike for discarded stories, two sharpened oversize pencils, a brush, a paste pot and a blue and white copy of the Canadian Press stylebook lay before me on the editing desk. There was also that morning's rival *Gazette* to scan.

Walter Christopher sat directly opposite me, acting like a copy taster, reading and shuffling long and short story sheets straight from the wire. A brash copy boy placed more stories in his tray with the quip that I was the news.

Walter had arrived half an hour before desk editors to separate fresh and stale incoming news. One or two of the stories he passed back to Max and other senior editors who were responsible for the front page. By just past seven o'clock, six other copy editors had filled places at the desk. "You're new," said the fellow next to me. "I'm Joe and you are?"

"Bill."

"What brings you to Montreal?"

"First the *Star*, then to gain experience of Quebec and eastern Canada."

"Is that a Scottish accent?"

"Aye."

Having organized copy and scrolled with a steel rule on a page layout sheet, Walter interrupted our conversation by passing us wired stories to edit with his code of type size, column width and length of text marked on them. He sent a bunch of stories to another copy editor along with a blank layout sheet and photos, and his whole overnight tray went to another man who I assumed would taste it.

News agencies were sending in a torrent of wire copy from all over the world, almost as events happened. Notably, it came from Reuters in Britain, Associated Press in the United States and from

Canadian Press staff reporters and stringers from coast to coast. Most of it would be filtered out and spiked.

There was an animated discussion going on among senior editorial writers and a reporter about the *Gazette's* lead story, reporting that the chairman of the Protestant School Board of Greater Montreal had told a news conference he would march on the Quebec legislative assembly, protesting a decision to take immigrants out of the Protestant school system and into the Catholic system.

"He never said it!" I heard an editor yell out from his office five minutes later, after his phone call exonerated the reporter from missing the story.

My first report to edit was a Reuter piece about some Australian fellow, who had lost his Montreal born wife to a snake bite while they were hiking the outback. The copy was crisp and brief. A head came easy to me, although I had only 11 letters to a line to work into single column. What I had to do was write a two-line head and, to my joy, confirm only the text spelling and capital letters. One of my favorite Scottish songs swept through my mind. On a piece of copy paper, I wrote the code for two lines of 24-point italic type in a single column and below it, the head:

He'll surely
find another

As I paper-clipped the head to the story to toss back into Walter's in-tray, I wondered if my headline was too detached for his approval. My words had not nailed down the snake. But this was not *The Vancouver Province.* This was a more imaginative newspaper. I had read the *Gazette's* head that morning on almost the same story: *Snakebite kills Montrealer.* I had taken the story a step further and fast. *Vive la différence!* I thought to myself, while hoping it worked with Walter.

Walter eyed my headline and edited story for a moment, then nodded his head at me. He scored out something then passed it to the backbench. He had put that snakebite story up for judgment by the page one editors. I felt a surge of the confidence I had lacked since arriving in the office half an hour earlier. Walter tossed another article to edit, one that almost went into one of the cups of coffee he had treated the desk to. I thanked my lucky stars it was not me, on seeing Joe struggle on a reporter's typewriter to rewrite a story and put a headline on it.

The morning's work passed quickly with stories and headlines until noon, when the first edition of the paper was ready for the rotary press. First copies of that day's *Star* were distributed before we reopened stories and pages for the city edition. There was no important breaking news, so we were soon finished.

"Well, that's it. Coming for a beer?" Walter asked me. "We usually go to the bar across the road. I'll have a word with Max to see if he's coming. I don't see any special edition."

"Be careful," Joe whispered as Walter turned his back on us. "He'll drink you under the table. Make an excuse and don't be sucked in like I was. He invites every new deskman for a beer that turns into a dozen."

Five of us filed down the escalator to cross the road to the bar and the readied barman served up promptly. I was glad to find out that the beer was weak and in half pints. The next came before I had finished the first. Soon, three beers were standing like foot soldiers before me as I sipped my second beer. It seemed to me that our work shift was over because I could not see anyone edit a paper half drunk. That is, not until I had experienced more of Walter Christopherson. He was downing beers as if he had come back from a trek through the Sahara, like the WWII soldiers in the movie *Ice Cold in Alex.* What was I to do?

"Anyone for a game of pool?" I asked hopefully, thinking it would get me far enough from the bar to pour some of the beer down the washroom sink.

"Yes," volunteered a bystander, whom I could identify only as just a fellow in the pub. "I'll play you."

"I'm Paul," he introduced himself. "I heard someone call you Bill. Well, what's the stakes, Bill? How about $3 a game doubling up."

It occurred to me that this indicated he thought my wallet was up for grabs. Maybe I had stepped out of the frying pan, into the fire. Maybe this was a local hustler! Though I had played American pool, I was British, and much more a three-ball billiard player. Fact was, that I had been chosen to play in the British Boys Billiards Championship in London back in 1950 when I was 15. "Well, I'm new to the game here, so maybe you'll explain the finer rules," I suggested.

He seemed a bit taken aback but explained, what he called, house rules, after I had carted two beers off to the washroom and offered him the third.

"I guess you know players must pot the numbered balls, 1 to 9 in order, down to the pink to win the game. You can pocket the pink by using another ball to win. You have to hit a cushion with your cue ball when playing a shot other than potting and you have to call the pockets you intend to sink the balls in. To hook an opponent your cue ball must touch a cushion. A foul stroke means your opponent can place his cue ball anywhere on the table to shoot. Now are we going to play or not? If so what's the stakes?"

"I'll play you for $3-a-game and the table," I offered him, having thought over his rules as those I knew.

"Then it's doubles or quits for five games?"

It took me some time to figure that out. "That would mean the last game will be for $48," I said, choosing a cue from the rack.

"And quitting means quitting *now* or paying the price."

"Who breaks?"

"We'll lag for it."

I knew what lag meant, but hardly knew the weight of the green baize that might have helped me control my cue ball.

He broke the balls in all directions while I was chalking my cue. Two went into pockets and the white ball settled in the middle of the table. I did not have a shot. He sank all the balls and I forked out $3.

"Your break this time."

I tried to copy his cannonball at the assembled balls, but my white was the only ball that entered a pocket.

Again, he pocketed every one of the balls hanging over the pockets on my foul. I forked out $6 this time and tried to calm my nerves with a tiny sip of beer.

Walter strolled over to the washroom and returned, while Paul was settling in to break for the third game. Walter whispered that I was being hustled. "I know what I'm doing," I whispered back. "I don't think this Paul Newman has it in him. I've obliged to be in it to the end anyway."

"Don't say I didn't warn you."

It looked like a mugging when Paul won the third game, but the rub for him was that he took the game only after I had narrowly failed to pot the black and had set up black and pink for him, when clearly, I was on the way to victory.

Walter again whispered that I was being hustled. "Get out after five. I know this fellow. He can play."

It was my turn to break in the fourth game and I was mastering the table. This time lady luck was with me, as the black ball flew into a side pocket and left the balls scattered with an easy shot to pot the yellow. My white ball came to rest at the far end of the table. The blue ball was just beyond center table and the pink over a corner pocket. I had played the in-off billiard shot a thousand times. I was pretty sure that by striking the blue half-ball into the left top pocket, my white ball would carry at an angle to push into the other pocket the right-hand hanging pink. "I nominate blue in the left corner pocket and pink in the right," I indicated with a sweep of my cue.

It worked like the routine shot it was, although for a split second the pink hesitated in its drop and the white following through stopped precariously on the edge of the pocket. "He *nominates* balls," Walter shouted as I picked up $24. "He doesn't call shots, he nominates them two at a time!"

I imagined that my shot had distracted my opponent, when his break in the closing fifth game failed to sink a ball. So I put on the pressure by hooking him. He attempted a hit off two cushions but messed it up. That did him in. He sat down to meet his fate. To me the pockets were like volcano craters. I potted all the balls, collected $48, and thanked him for the games.

Paul looked at me: "You said you didn't know the game."

"I told you it *wasn't* my game."

"So what *is* your game? Larceny?"

Chapter 48
Le Grand Dénouement

Eileen had found us a nice temporary rented home with a garden in Montreal's smallest suburb of Roxboro. It was a commuter train ride away from downtown and there was a Legion where I could have a game of snooker.

On my night off work, I went by surface train, then underground from Roxboro to North Montreal, in fact, from the English to the French side. The school was bright with lights and there, at the reception desk, was Micheline. "*Bon nuit*," I said with a smile. My smile was not returned. "*C'est à dire, bonsoir. Repétez après moi! Bonsoir.*"

"I'll show you the auditorium and the lights I set up. Then I'll change into my ballet costume and tutu," she said briskly. "The lights are school property."

I wondered what a tutu was as I followed her.

A chandelier in the ceiling gave shadowy light to the auditorium. The floodlight in the center of the room was plugged by a long electric cord. Micheline disappeared through a corner door. I switched the lights on and off and moved them from left to right. I was primed for action with camera round my neck.

She returned filling my senses with her presence in a flimsy ballet dress, dark hair pulled straight back in a bun and rigorously telling me she needed action photos. "In that case, do a few poses before I shoot."

Every movement she made accentuated my discovery of her elegant body.

"Are you acquainted with the floodlights?"

"Maybe."

Suddenly there came, as she was to describe it, *le grand dénouement.*

The ballad, *Dance Ballerina Dance,* was whirling round my head when I swung round to more accurately focus light on her tiptoe whirl. Instead of nailing a photo, I tripped over the electric cord and sent floodlight equipment crashing to the floor with a smack, crunch and even sparks.

Micheline hit the roof and I felt I was up there, too, in the half darkness. She twice screamed. I was paralyzed. I came to with Micheline clinging to my shoulder. A janitor rushed into the hall. *"Qu'est que c'est?"* he demanded of me.

Micheline still had her arms on me and I was in disbelief saying, "I knocked the lights over."

The janitor strode to a switch in the wall that I was unaware of. Lights flooded the auditorium. He strode over to Micheline and put an arm around her shoulder. "What did he do to you?"

I heard her explain through tears that I had accidently knocked the floodlight to the ground. I added that I was about to take photographs of Micheline when I tripped over the electric cord. I offered to help him clear up the mess.

"You messed up!" Micheline reprimanded me although we were apart by then. *"C'etait le grand denouement!"*

"Yes, but, I'll hire a professional to take your audition pictures. I'll attend to it tomorrow." I immediately had in mind Brian Williams, a *Montreal Star* photographer and friend. "I'll pay the school for this debacle. Please forgive me."

"I'll clean up," the janitor said. "That was real bad luck."

I was back at school next day with my check book.

Except for photographs taken by Williams, that was the last I saw of Micheline.

Chapter 49
Bill 22 Hits Anglos

Micheline had gone out of my life as she was bound to, given my luck with women. Brian Williams had taken photos good enough to gain her a place in the chorus of *Thoroughly Modern Millie,* and I had convinced the entertainment editor to review the production in the *Star.* Life sometimes throws interesting people like Micheline at you and you just have to do the best you can with them. Lady luck had betrayed me. I consoled myself with thoughts of a better things ahead with Eileen.

After my year on nightshift, our marriage was not perfect, although by then we had a baby boy to add to the daughter in our family and Eileen apprehensively was pregnant again.

I approached the *Star's* managing editor asking for a daytime reporter's job and reminding him he had promised me that. He received me graciously and said that positive words from Walter and the news editor had convinced him to do so. He went into detail: "I want you to write mainly elementary and university education stories, but not high school. Your experience as teacher and journalist should help you. As you know, our provincial government's Bill 22 is threatening English education with tests for admission at the elementary level. You'll have to keep on top of this."

I knew what he was talking about from stories I had edited on provincial Premier Robert Bourassa's new law to safeguard French in Quebec. Bill 22 was, in a way, revolutionary, in that it all but proclaimed French to be the future official language of Quebec through the education system.

I was personally involved because, at age four, my daughter Judith was due to start school. I had thought of sending her to *classes d'accueil*–introductory French classes for immigrant children–since we were still landed immigrants and eligible. From my own knowledge, I knew that under the rules I could send her to a French language school for two years then, when she was age six, transfer her to the English Protestant school system since she had English-speaking parents who, by then, would likely be Canadian citizens. Eileen was also keen on Judith learning French so, in the words of a French school board official, we "crossed the Rubicon." Little did he know that our motive two years hence was to switch her from French to English school.

Judith's classroom at Monseigneur Valois Elementary School in Roxboro, was like a tiny United Nations with 22 children from a half-dozen countries. A school bus picked her up at nine in the morning. Off she would go with a pillow in her rucksack for a sleep break at noon. She would return by bus at 3:30. Teacher Mme LeBleu was like a mother to her pupils, and the Italian principal, Jean Bonetto, was courteous to all. The school had to deal not just with French and English kids, but also the mother tongues of immigrant children flying into Quebec from many countries, with little option but to go to French-language schools.

English speakers in areas of west Montreal and Italian-Canadians in St. Léonard were threatening to dump the Liberal government over Bill 22. The Italians said they had the support of Greek and Portuguese communities and enough influence to make a significant difference in election outcomes in 10 ridings. They scheduled a meeting at Notre Dame de Pompeii church, where they slammed Education Minister François Cloutier. They knew the advantages for their children speaking English in North America. After a month of campaigning, against a law that would move any child who did not have a firm grasp of English into French-language schools, they established the *Consiglio Educativo Italo-Canadese,* which set up private schools in church basements to prepare immigrant children for English-language tests.

I reported one Italian-Canadian mother saying that, in a test, her five-year-old had failed to identify a lemon in English. "How could she know the name when I never use fresh lemons in my kitchen? I only use lemon juice!"

Teachers, politicians, school boards and mothers screamed for weeks at each other and this former newsboy was supposed to analyze the hullabaloo for *The Montreal Star* editorial writers, as well as write reports of school board meetings and teacher union press conferences.

I made the acquaintance of René Lévesque, who led the Mouvement Souveraineté-Association, at a news conference in Montreal. Reporters were vying with each other with their questions. They spoke French fast and I had a hard time understanding. Lévesque's equally rapid replies were, for me, even more difficult to follow since he was smoking at the same time. The questioning went on unabated for an hour. Sometimes he was answering two reporters at the same time. My notebook was almost empty except for a bit of doodling. And still the reporters chattered on with Lévesque, talking reams of detail to promise Quebeckers sovereignty association with Canada.

I concluded that his idea of separatism was more restrained than that of his firebrand rival, Ralliement National leader Pierre Bourgault, whose comments I had reported the week before.

I filed uneasily from the conference room, dreading that the fully bilingual opposition *Gazette* reporter would scoop me the next day.

I saw Lévesque go to the adjoining bar with two friends, so I sidled up saying I was from the *Star* and sought a few words alone in English about what had transpired. He smiled in his inimical way and led me to a quiet corner table. I brought out my notebook and pencil and simply asked what had been going on at the news conference. He brought out a cigarette, saying slowly in perfect English: "For my part, creating a more transparent and democratic government than that of Premier Robert Bourassa's Liberals."

"What did you tell the news conference you intended to do?"

"More transparent and democratic government, as I said, progressive social measures, such as free public day care, and a boost to the economy by supporting small and medium-sized companies."

"Sovereignty association also came up."

"Yes, but that's on the back burner."

"Can you win the election?"

"I told reporters that 43 per cent of Quebeckers support my party. I do not count on an easy win. The results of the last two elections prevent this. On the advice of my council, I plan to run in the working class riding of Taillon on the South Shore. Excuse me now. My friends beckon me back to the bar. I agree we Quebecois talk too much. You really have it all in a nutshell. Good luck, Scottie!"

Lévesque spoke as good English as his French, as far as I could hear, and being a journalist himself, had summarized the news conference well. He had even spotted my Scottish accent. I went back to the office and wrote my report in an hour, rather than the three hours it might have otherwise taken. Although the *Montreal*

Gazette, as I had predicted, had a better story the next day, my account in the *Star* was fine in the circumstances.

Life for me was not all thorny French language news conferences and school boards. The Olympic Games were coming to Montreal and I thought how wonderful that was, after a winter of hockey and a summer and fall of Canadian football and baseball.

The games were a hive of controversy, as Montreal Mayor Jean Drapeau gambled millions of dollars that he would get the Olympic Stadium finished, then had to appeal to provincial Premier Bourassa to help him out. Bourassa went to his aid and the stadium was built in time. Before the Olympics, I was assigned a news conference called by former Prime Minister John Diefenbaker.

I asked Diefenbaker if he believed Rhodesian athletes should be taking part in the games. We both knew that African countries were threatening to boycott the games ostensibly, because the New Zealand rugby team was preparing to tour apartheid South Africa. The African countries knew that white Rhodesian government soldiers were fighting black African nationalist guerrillas to keep their minority white dominated country. They were aware that *apartheid,* rising out of colonialism, had kept black athletes of southern Africa out of the games for decades. Diefenbaker first pooh-poohed a question he clearly did not wish to answer.

I waited five minutes then took my chance again.

This time he came clean. "I do *not* support Rhodesian participation," he replied. "If it means the African countries boycott the games, then the Rhodesians should not be here."

My story made page one that next day and I was assigned to more Olympic coverage.

While strolling beside the Olympic Stadium, a workman pointed out to me a black figure gazing at its magnificence. Close up, I found the man, as the workman had said, was Jesse Owens, winner of four gold medals in sprint and long jump events at the 1936 Olympic Games in Berlin. "Did Adolf Hitler shake hands with you?" was my question that rainy day.

He smiled saying that was an old story he did not wish to get back into. "I'm not seeking to raise old ghosts," he said. "I'm here for the 1976 Olympic Games. So please excuse me."

Thirty African countries refused permission for their athletes to compete in the Games. It was sad for track fans like me, because at that time Tanzanian Filbert Bayi, who had defeated Kip Keino of Kenya at the African Games, was in a class with top New Zealand

and American middle-distance runners and his nation was one of the boycotting countries.

A report I did on a stock car stunt was ridiculously interesting. A performer was set to accelerate up a ramp and jump over a line of cars. I was seated in an inside gallery observing. Just as the driver started his run, a woman in front of me turned her back on the event. I was told she was his wife and hated seeing him risk injury. When the driver crashed into the last car in line, he was injured and she distraught. I interviewed the lady in question and my photographer took a picture of her.

Three days after the photograph appeared on the front page, a woman came into Art Wood's office saying the lady in the paper was not the driver's wife. "I'm his wife," she claimed, "so what are you going to do about it?"

Art called me in and we agreed that I should go to the hospital where the driver was a patient and let him tell me which of the women was his wife. The trouble was that he had not only a broken collarbone but also a broken jaw. He was lying in hospital all wired up. That man would not be speaking for at least six weeks or even months.

It turned out the woman photographed by my colleague was his common law wife and the other one he had divorced. The former wife was never seen at the office again and the worrying incident thankfully was forgotten.

I was happy to land an assignment in Nova Scotia, to cover the Acadian blossom festival to be attended by Prime Minister Pierre Trudeau. I saw the Acadians crown two youngsters playing the roles of Evangeline and Gabriel, in tribute to Longfellow's separated lovers of Grand Pré and his story of her search for her husband after his deportation by Britain to Louisiana.

The festival went off without a hitch, beside the sea and under the apple blossom, on the 300th anniversary of Acadian settlement with vivid recall of the tragic deportations of Acadian men, despite their claim to neutrality between English and French adversaries. An ecumenical service was held in a replica of the church to which Acadian men had been summoned and guarded, before being shipped off to New England colonies, Louisiana, and a few to France and Britain.

The statue of Evangeline oversaw the festival, and I saw her appear to grow older in her long search as I slowly circled it.

I wrote a memo in my notebook that if Longfellow's bust in Grand Pré National Historic Park had had eyes, he would have seen the Acadians write a new chapter for *A Tale of Acadia.* Longfellow would have seen fourth generation descendants of returned Acadians still proclaim their neutrality.

In Yarmouth, I heard Acadian teachers and parents demand French-language texts for math and science instead of English texts. Paul Gaudet, a director of the Nova Scotia Acadian Federation, said the reality of the Acadian school was being questioned.

My intention was to get my stories out fast to my newspaper.

"It's no use," was the heartbreak telephoned answer from the newspaper office in Montreal. "We're on strike. I'd enjoy a Nova Scotia holiday if I were you!"

Chapter 50
Radio Canada International

I had picketed outside *The Montreal Star* on guild pay for three weeks and helped bring out a strike newspaper. Neither management nor staff was blinking. My savings were drifting down and I was not the only one. Michael Ballantine, one of the *Star's* editorial writers, had broken ranks by going to the Canadian Broadcasting Corporation to ask for a job. Instead of walking the street with a placard like me he was writing for *Radio Canada International (RCI)*. What was stopping me from trying the same thing?

So off I went to the 15-storey CBC building and was told to return the next morning for an interview with Monsieur Bernard Daudier. I trusted the interview would be in English, but I had enough faith to believe I could answer a few questions in French. The meeting went well. Next day, I received a letter dated February 18, 1977, from Marie Jose Laverdure, *superviseur de l'Emploi et de la Selection*, asking me to present myself with her letter *au bureau de la Securité* (B1) between 9:00 and 11:00 to obtain my identity card. I, too, had broken strike ranks.

I started work the following Monday in the RCI newsroom on the 12th floor. Opposite me on the desk was Ballantine. Our job was to type out short bulletins of news in English from wire copy chosen by the line-up editor.

RCI history told me Leonard Brockington had proposed the international service to the government back in 1937. A task force in 1973 reformulated its operation and a booklet outlined its intention.

"Radio Canada International is directed by the CBC to provide a program service designed to attract an international audience, with the purpose of further developing international awareness of Canada and the Canadian identity, by distributing, through short-wave and other means, programs which reflect the realities and quality of

Canadian life and culture, Canada's national interests and policies, and the spectrum of Canadian viewpoints on national and international affairs."

The booklet claimed RCI did not spend much money. Its operating budget was about 1.5 per cent of the total CBC financial tab. "What did the country get for its money?" the booklet rhetorically asked. "About 10,000,000 short-wave listeners a week, at a weekly cost per listener of 1.2 cents!"

Our competitors were the Overseas Service of the British Broadcasting Corporation, the Voice of America and Radio France. In 1976, RCI was broadcasting in French, English and nine other languages, based mainly on translations from English and French bulletins. I was writing those bulletins morning, afternoon or evening, five days a week, and also putting together a news program to Mexico.

RCI was also responsible for a CBC network of English programs for military stations operated by the Canadian National Defence Department. News bulletins and programs were broadcast to the Inuit in the north. Employees were warned against undertaking specific campaigns of any kind that might originate in events coming from their original home countries.

The instructions laid down: "It's important, even when reporting the bad news, about dissidents in Russia or repression in South Africa for example, or violation of civil rights in Cuba or Chile, or, (perhaps in our own small way) in Canada, not to do so in a tone of invective insulting a whole listening population. That tone is offensive and self-defeating, wherever directed. Honesty and objectivity, and what one might call Canadian cool, should be not only RCI's method, but also its principal product. The trick is to be a good journalist and prove accusers wrong."

I particularly liked the last sentence when studying the booklet and listening to the British Broadcasting Corporation's short-wave news service. I knew my bulletin writing the next morning would often be based on the same news, so listening in to rival newscasts always gave me a good start.

Michael Ballantine's long experience writing editorials served him badly in writing objective news bulletins. We were both at first on probation and whereas I was taken on full time, he was not. He subsequently took a job with *Readers Digest,* where he was more at home. So I was happy for him. I was pleased with myself too. Not only was the pay better, but I was meeting radio and television journalists and newscasters every shift, and this former newsboy enjoyed lunch with up-and-coming television anchors Lloyd Robertson and Peter Mansbridge. One morning, I said hello to Ernie Combes (better known to TV children as *Mr. Dress Up).*

I knew that René Lévesque had worked as a journalist at *Radio Canada International,* and reached the pinnacle of his broadcasting career with Radio-Canada in a live half-hour news magazine called *Point de Mire* on the air at 11:15 p.m. An old- timer on the French side of RCI told me, Radio Canada had not expected his intellectual program to be popular with the general public in giving it this time slot. However, Lévesque believed Quebeckers were more than ready to look beyond their provincial concerns. He had international experience during the Korean War and he wanted to be the man who would bring that experience home to Quebeckers. "Every week," my colleague said, "*Point de Mire* focused on different world news stories."

While having lunch in the CBC restaurant, I cast my mind back to the classic confrontation that occurred between Lévesque and Pierre Trudeau in the canteen where I was sitting.

Trudeau had come to find out if Lévesque would contribute to his *Québec Libre* newspaper. They had spoken courteously for a while, until Trudeau said he knew Lévesque could broadcast. "But can you write?" he asked.

I was told Lévesque took umbrage at Trudeau's question and air of superiority, and immediately rose and left. The two giants of Quebec and Canadian politics rarely saw eye to eye in the following two decades, when the future of Canada was at stake in referendums.

Of course, I got too big for my breeches at RCI. I wondered that since I had made it to CBC radio, might I not do the same by breaking into television.

I knew that after eight or so years in Canada, I retained the dialect I had acquired on the banks and braes o' bonnie Scotland. I deemed my accent less pronounced than the thick Glasgow brogue of Jack Webster, a contemporary successful Vancouver television and radio personality, so that encouraged me. But I had to admit that when I played back outgoing messages on my telephone answering machine, I could detect a Scottish dialect. I was not certain whether this was an asset or a liability. I leaned optimistically toward the former.

I had been brought up in a Scottish town where women working in hosiery mills gossiped loudly over noisy machines, as they wove or dyed jumpers and twin sets. The town's dialect was formed in these mills. The men played or watched rugby on Saturdays and few used "please" and "thank you" in clubrooms and pubs, where their accent also gained ground. Hawick talk was reckoned broader than that of Glasgow, though less broad than that across the English border in Newcastle.

When people heard me speak and said, "Oh, you're Scottish, aren't you?" I would reply, "No, I'm Canadian." Not wanting to admit they had made an error, they usually tried to reach an ethnic balance and say, "Well, you're Scottish Canadian."

The CBC television job interviewer immediately detected my dialect. He even considered himself witty enough to mimic me. And that had happened to me before! This time I took offence. I reacted by saying I was clearly wasting his time and mine and cleared out of his office to go back to my safer radio job.

My years of work as a journalist in Africa caught up with me, when I was putting together the day's last international newscast late on a Sunday night. In a wired agency report of new Rhodesian martial law measures, the rebel prime minister Ian Smith termed President Julius Nyerere of Tanzania a black warmongering racist. I chose not to let Smith get away with what I considered a slanderous attack. I checked our reference book on Africa. It supported my up-close experience belief that Nyerere was a politician of "intelligence, principle and modesty, who was turning Tanzania into a stable country." I added that to the news bulletin quoting it as the belief of most Africa experts.

Next day my supervisor, Dave Struthers, collared me saying he had listened to the previous evening's broadcast and wondered why I had added praise of Nyerere to the wire story he had in his hand. I had difficulty explaining, except to say that I knew that Nyerere was not racist or a warmonger, so I had sought balance.

A written memo came from Struthers saying my years in Africa had influenced my credibility as a non-partisan journalist. If it was balance I had sought in the Rhodesia report, why could I not have simply spiked it rather than add adjectival words of praise for Nyerere?

I thought his memo a bit off mark and immediately wrote this reply:

The paragraph on Dr. Nyerere, which you refer to in your memo, was inserted in the interest of a fair and balanced report as I tried to say in reply to your spoken criticism.

I thoroughly agree with you about the limited use of adjectives in radio news writing. And, except in very limited circumstances, I rarely use them. The question: "Is this a quote from the wire service?" The answer: "No, it's from our reference book on Africa here in the CBC newsroom. It never occurred to me to eliminate Smith's scurrilous words."

Finally, since I have had far more first-hand experience in our European and North American target areas, than the five years I spent as a journalist in Africa, I do not consider myself more involved in African events than in events elsewhere. I assure you of my honest attempt to preserve our service and reason for employment.

My reply went to Struthers with a copy to the boss, Bernard Daudier. I never heard another word about my alleged partisan transgression.

Next day there was a debate on South Africa around the news desk and, to my surprise, my senior colleagues did not know that black people were disenfranchised in *apartheid* South Africa. The line-up editor finally phoned the South African Embassy and, luckily for me, the respondent admitted it was true that blacks were not allowed to vote in that country's elections. Coming out on top did not increase my popularity.

I heard no more of those affairs as the Rhodesian dispute continued to make warfare and headlines. Smith's unilateral declaration of independence (UDI) from British control was still popular in right-wing circles, and Margaret Thatcher's vouching for the 1978-79 coalition names of Ian Smith and Bishop Abel Muzorewa as leaders of a country named Rhodesia-Zimbabwe, simply added to confusion.

A truly independent Zimbabwe, after bloody warfare had won liberation, came about in April 1980, under nationalist firebrand Robert Mugabe. Mugabe's presidential leadership started well, then went downhill until Zimbabwe faced ruin, mainly, in my opinion, from trade and travel sanctions imposed by Britain and also implemented by America and Canada, on grounds he had faked an election victory after murdering rebel tribal opponents. Worth noting is that in Zimbabwe's early years, Canadian Prime Minister Brian Mulroney called Mugabe the darling of the Commonwealth.

Chapter 51
Thatcher the Vote Snatcher

When the *Ottawa Journal* advertised for a copy editor, I applied and was interviewed by its editor Sandy Gardiner. He was a Scot like me and was impressed by my having worked for *The Sun* in London. He hired me as photo editor, although *The Journal* had no photographers on staff. It used two contracted Canadian Press photographers. Both were professionals and one, Robert Cooper, later became official photographer to Prime Minister Pierre Trudeau.

Mike Ridewood, the other photographer, and I went out to shoot ice sculpting at Ottawa's Winterlude Carnival. I had never before seen ice made into physical figures of grace. My experience covered snow for snowmen. The photos of the sculptures were okay for inside pages and I knew the *Citizen* would be doing the same layout, so we needed something unique. I spotted a children's ice slide. "That's the photo," I burst out. "I'll slide down with my notebook and pencil in the air and you can shoot me halfway. I'll do so a few times to get the best shot."

Journalism has its ups and downs as Bill Fairbairn
discovered covering the 1980 Winterlude in Ottawa.
PHOTO: MIKE RIDEWOOD

That shot of me, *The Journal's* new photo editor, went on the front page the next day and temporarily boosted my image. Even Gardiner, a hard man to impress, clapped me on the back.

Then came my backward slide, when it was announced that the Chinese speed skating team were to race in an evening encounter with Canadians in Ottawa's east end Balena Park, where there was a 400-metre-round speed skating circuit. The evening weather was ominous and cloudy. To my dismay, when my photographer and I arrived for the assignment, the park was almost shrouded in obscurity. Skaters flashed by at high speed like ghostly shadows, one after the other. Photography was impossible. I tried to set up a posed shot in their caravan base, but it was useless.

The next day, the *Citizen* came out with a photo spread of sheer physical beauty. It had been taken at a practice in the afternoon when conditions were perfect. I was devastated, but Sandy Gardiner's fury drove me over the top. "What the hell were you thinking about?" he asked next day, with the *Citizen* scoop before us on his desk. "Don't you know it gets dark at night?"

"I was assigned to it in the diary as an evening event. I had no idea there was an afternoon practice."

Gardiner, on the spot, transferred me from being photo editor to the news desk.

Challenging was the task of mastering the computer technique that *Journal* desk editors used to edit stories and write headlines. I was given three days of instruction by a capable young woman, who was also busy keeping other desk editors right.

I told her I had come up the hard way from hot metal, but she didn't know what I was talking about and ignored my plea for priority help. Now, green letters on the computer screen were hypnotizing me. The challenge, around changing type-sizes, faces and measures, until length of text and headline were reached on the computer screen without losing the story, was formidable to this then-computer-rookie. After three days of instruction, I was placed on the day-shift desk.

That first week, the British people re-elected Margaret Thatcher as their prime minister. This was our main lead story on the front page and a headline was required. Word went around the desk asking for suggestions. I put forward *Thatcher the vote snatcher*, without saying it was inspired by her cutting off milk to schoolchildren when she was education minister and being called *Thatcher the milk snatcher*. I was sure my headline would not be used because I knew the *Journal* was a conservative newspaper.

"Well, it was only a suggestion," I said, thinking they were letting a good head slip by.

One morning I was asked to clean the duplicating machine used for photo proofs and fix what had broken down. Not long after that, I was put on the nightshift desk.

I had some good productive nights when given foreign pages to lay out with my own selected stories. I was out of my depth on my next landing on the finance pages.

I was filling finance with dull copy and lousy photographs of bankers running the country, when a big shot from head office in Winnipeg walked into the office. After peering around over copy editors' shoulders, he arrived behind me. Let me make it clear. I knew the price of gold that day had gone up to over $1,000 an ounce. The price had been $999 the previous day, so I thought little of it.

"You're not leading page one on the price of gold!" the big shot exploded on the news desk slot editor, after putting a heavy hand on my shoulder.

Turning again on the desk, he shouted out that gold should be the front-page story. "This clot has it under a single-column head buried on the finance page!"

It seemed I was back as the printer's devil, blamed for everything, though I guess he had a point.

Sandy Gardiner finally disliked me intensely, when he read my requested report on the newspaper's photographic operation, although I was no longer photo editor. I could do no less than urge the newspaper to set up its own darkroom and hire at least two photographers. After all, my first much smaller weekly newspaper, *The Jedburgh Gazette,* had a darkroom. He told me it was the last thing he wanted to hear. Also at proven risk, I urged immediate settlement of an ongoing printers' strike, to rid the office of pickets outside the entrance to the newspaper office that I used each night.

Not least in the list of my *faux pas,* was the night I was struggling at the 6 a.m. deadline, to get my final foreign page layout finished and downstairs to the composing room. A meeting on reorganization of editorial staff had been called, with its venue a restaurant across the street from the newspaper office. Sandy Gardiner was to address the meeting. I had been told nothing official, only on the side by a colleague. I was ten minutes late getting to the meeting, though in time for a coffee and the close of Gardiner's talk. I saw then that Gardiner had no place for me in his *Ottawa Journal* staff. A week later, I was given a month's notice. I was glad to be out of the strike-hit *Journal* salt mine. Firing me preceded by four months, the demise of the *Journal* in 1980 after 95 years of publication.

Chapter 52
My Joust with Ravens

I pestered the CBC for my old job back that winter of 1979, until, I think, management broke down in anguish.

Eileen, more worried than me, had taken a job with Shoppers Drug Mart to help make ends meet.

"No, I could not get back with the international service because casuals at the service were awaiting full-time positions. A four-month contract job was vacant at CBC Yellowknife and could I reply within a week?"

I brought out my atlas and located Yellowknife, way up there just below the Arctic Circle. It was do or die. I accepted the offer, bought a parka, leather mittens, winter boots and searched out my toque. Next step was to pick up air tickets at the CBC office and kiss Eileen and the children goodbye.

I was off again, though this time in an aircraft. The flight to Yellowknife seemed par for the course to me, by then feeling like a vagabond newsboy. I was promised an apartment at CBC expense, and envisaged skiing and conversations with Dené trappers and gold prospectors.

The apartment was there for me all right, but, not long after I had been shown in, I realized it was nearly as cold inside as outside, and it was -30 Celsius outside. The previous tenant had left the kitchen window open and frost had frozen it open.

When I went shopping for milk and bread, I discovered that my four-month stay in Yellowknife might bankrupt my wife and I, since food prices were so high and I had no cow to milk. To send more of my earnings home to Eileen, I determined to bake my own bread.

The smell of bread baking in the oven filled my small kitchen. The warmth of the oven was overcoming the cold. Suddenly, barking ravens attacked with beaks well inside the open window. I realized I had read somewhere that Yellowknife had the largest concentration of ravens in the world. I dashed out to find the caretaker. He laughed when I told him the problem and answered, "Well, yes, I should have seen to that window. Did these thieving ravens get at you?"

"I'm raving mad," I replied. "Do the job now and there's a loaf of baked bread for you!"

He went upstairs to my apartment, shooed the birds away with a broom, clamped down the window with a mallet and accepted my bribe.

Work at the CBC started at 6 a.m. the next day. I trudged over to the office after listening to the early morning newscast, feeling cold and realizing my parka was not built for Yellowknife. I edited news bulletins from the wire and cut tapes from local correspondents. The line-up editor was a New Zealander, and two nights later in his kitchen, I helped him carve up a bison he had shot. I had gone from the Wild West of the Cariboo in British Columbia, through the French-English language quagmire in Quebec, to a hunt for cheap food in the North West Territories.

Thankfully, the CBC loaned me a real warm parka that I used for my daily circular walk over crisp snow and ice on Great Slave Lake. The walk took me to the just-opened Prince of Wales Heritage Centre, over to the warmth of the Chateau Nova Hotel for coffee, and up the main street to the Wildlife Café for gossip and lunch. I almost lived on borsch from the town's Ukrainian restaurant. I would often carry it home to my apartment and enjoy it with my home-made bread.

One morning, the station manager came up to my desk. It was January 22, 1980, and quoting Robbie Burns's line, *A man's a man for a that,* he named me to address the haggis at the Yellowknife Burns Supper the following Friday. "The man assigned to the haggis is stuck in Tuk," he explained. "He'll never make it back here this weekend. As a Scot can you do the address for him?"

"I don't have my kilt."

"We'll get you a kilt."

The borrowed kilt tartan was a Mackenzie. I was addressing the haggis that Friday night because I was Scottish. I wondered what Robbie Burns would have thought. Anyway, at least it was not my first Burns supper, although the others had been as a reporter.

"The Selkirk Grace," I announced to a gracious crowd through a handheld speaker, before telling them I had been born 10 miles from Selkirk in the Scottish Borders.

I spoke up in this time in the right dialect:

Some ha'e meat and canna eat
And some ha'e none that want it.
But we ha'e meat and we can eat
So let the Lord be thank-et.

I stabbed down into the haggis and felt the silver dirk go through the tray into the wooden table below. I later learned I should have deftly slit the haggis ready for serving.

My plight retrieving the dirk drew a few laughs, but by my side was a trusty kilted aide who, like a Highland retainer, lifted tray, haggis and dirk, and smiling broadly marched it off to the serving table.

I was seated at the top table beside a Scots-born lady well into her eighties. When a young woman acknowledging the *Address to the Lassies* started her speech by saying, "TGIF," (thank God it's Friday), my table companion blanched and turning to me said the lady was a tramp. I nodded agreement not knowing what either one was talking about.

The evening progressed with Eightsome Reels and Gay Gordons and more toasts to Robbie Burns. I galloped The Dashing White Sergeant to the distress of my table companion who preferred a stately St Bernard's Waltz, and who later introduced me to Yellowknife's Scottish Country Dance Society for lessons from who else but a Mountie.

For days on end, my early morning work continued routinely at the CBC, followed by a late afternoon walk, dinner at the Wildcat Café, and a movie in the one cinema in town or, occasionally, a party with heavy drinking. I once partied with a couple of home-baked loafs and a bread knife, and recall the food being gobbled up in half an hour by Yellowknife's stalwart men.

Then came the 1980 Canadian general election, with Pierre Trudeau sliding down Great Slave Lake's ice in a snowmobile and giving a speech in the Heritage Centre. On election night, to my disappointment, I was the gofer, ferreting around the edges of election coverage. Trudeau's Liberals beat Joe Clark's Conservatives that time and I won the office pool for being closest in predicting seats won by each party.

After four months, my northern misadventure ended and I was back home in Ottawa with Eileen without a job.

On the brighter side, the National Educational Company of Zambia in Lusaka, a publishing company of the Kenneth Kaunda Foundation, had published my first of four books, *Run for Freedom.*

Chapter 53
The Falklands Fiasco

My thoughts for a job turned to the Montreal *Gazette,* which had an English language monopoly in the city after the demise of the *Star* as a result of another strike. The *Gazette* had moved into the old *Star* building and I felt there was a good chance I would get work there.

The usual editing test, that I had experienced a half-dozen times, was administered on interview, and soon I had moved onto my old newspaper floor as a desk editor. A few of my former *Star* colleagues were there, but others had fallen by the wayside due to computer technology they could not master.

I was not the stranger I had been when I first joined the *Vancouver Province* 10 years previous. The difficulty was commuting each weekend to and from Ottawa, where Eileen and I had purchased a house. The mundane challenges were to find lodgings in Montreal and a weekly return rail pass between Montreal and Ottawa. I considered moving in with a French-speaking family to improve my French, and hindsight tells me I should have done so. I chose instead Westmount, the heart of English-speaking Montreal, perceived in some circles, though not by me, as a thorn in the heart of French rise to power.

My landlady, Mrs. Dolan, was in her eighties and could trace her family background back 100 years in Quebec. Over her nutritious lunches, she taught me a lot from the wisdom she had acquired by way of Jesuit influences when she was a young woman.

Her late husband had been a debt collector and she had in her library a 20-set volume, *The Great Events by Famous Historians,* only 100 of which the National Alumni had published in 1905, and which, I learned, her husband had inherited in lieu of cash from a failed entrepreneur. The first book was well read by me during the four years I stayed with her. My landlady handed me the collection as a farewell gift.

My most memorable evening on the *Gazette* came on Friday, April 2, 1982. All the desk staff, except a sports copy editor monitoring the result of a late-night overtime hockey game, had left me alone on the news desk around midnight to deal with any breaking story. After all, it was the weekend. A news item on the wire at 12:15 a.m. alerted me. Margaret Thatcher had launched warships heading for the Falklands. The dull lead story on our front page was about the addition of another CBC television channel. I relegated it down page and led on the Falklands. I had no knowledge of an inside page editorial ridiculing the chance Britain would go to war with Argentina and, if I remember correctly, headed *The Falklands Fiasco.*

I went to bed at 1 a.m. that morning, praying the latest Falklands news bulletin was accurate. Awakening at 6 a.m. to the radio, I was vindicated. The 74-day war was on. I thought my *Gazette* work that night worth a medal, but it was never acknowledged. I never learned who had written the editorial.

My four years on the *Gazette* were highlighted when the union won a 42-per-cent compounded wage increase over three years. It would eventually put the *Gazette* into second place for the highest journalism salaries in North America. To my knowledge only the *Washington Post* paid more.

My move back home to Ottawa came when *Legion Magazine,* located in the nation's capital, advertised for an assistant editor. I figured my two years of British national service as an infantry corporal and Legion membership in Williams Lake might clinch my application.

It was a wet day in March when I showed up at the magazine office, then on Kent Street. I had a date with editor and general manager Jane Dewer and assistant editor Mac Johnston. As soon as I took off my raincoat in the outer office to await my interview, I discovered I had forgotten to put on my suit jacket presumably lying on my couch at home.

Jane smilingly brushed aside my apologies and went ahead with the usual questions to which I gave the usual answers. Mac, who had been sitting silently to the side, asked why, a man with my newspaper experience, had not applied for a job on *The Ottawa Citizen.*

Jane pooh-poohed his question. Yet I had to answer. I told him I wanted something different from the day-to-day deadlines and headlines of a daily newspaper and sought to use my military as well as journalism experience for *Legion Magazine.* I added that the magazine would give me more time to edit efficiently and write better. From Jane's expression I had it right. I left with four typewritten trial stories to edit, headline and return.

One was a financial story about the chances of the Canadian dollar rising or falling. I sent that one back edited and topped with *Mirror, Mirror, on the Wall, Will the Dollar Rise or Fall?* I wondered if my head contained too many words to impress Jane and Mac. Yet, I considered it read well and covered the indecision in the article.

A *Legion Magazine* welcome-aboard letter arrived a week later, confirming details of the job even down to the working hours of 8:30 a.m. to 4:30 p.m., the hour's break for lunch and a shorter working day by half an hour in the summer. That sounded ideal to me. There was a six-month probationary period that bothered me a bit but did not stop me catching the train to Ottawa to start work on March 10, 1984. This former paperboy could hardly believe how time had flown since his arrival by train in Montreal some 11 years previous, ready to change the world through spectacular yet responsible journalism. Older and wiser, I considered it now unlikely this would happen.

My first chance of a feature story in *Legion Magazine* came unexpectedly. I was summoned for jury duty. I hinted at the possibility when I revealed to Mac that I was listed as a potential juror. Mac said the chances of being chosen were slim because journalists were not usually chosen. The likelihood of jury duty had come in the form of a questionnaire sent by the sheriff's office. I was one of a list of people drawn from the electoral rolls. Later came a registered letter from the sheriff placing me on a jury panel of 150 people from the trial district. That's the time to be excused if one has good reason.

My mail carrier confidentially told me I was on jury duty before I had even opened the envelope. He was close. I was prospective juror No. 48.

Two weeks later, I took my place in county court along with 119 other prospective jurors for final selection of 12. Another 30 had been summoned to Supreme Court. Rumor had it that we were being chosen to sit in judgment of Armenians accused of wounding a Turkish diplomat in Ottawa.

"You know what that means if it's true," said prospective juror No.118, a Carleton University professor of Bangladeshi origin. "It means a long trial."

266

I wondered how that might affect my new job on *Legion Magazine*.

The court clerk shushed us. Chatter ended. It was no Armenian who appeared in the dock to plead not guilty to aggravated assault. It was a well-dressed young man with immaculate shoulder-length hair and a soft Canadian voice.

"Oyez, oyez! All persons having anything to do before Her Majesty's judge at this general session of the peace for the judicial district of Ottawa-Carleton, draw near and give your attendance and you shall be heard. God Save The Queen!" cried out the clerk.

Judge Edward Houston addressed us: "The object is that the accused will get a fair trial and the Crown a fair hearing. You must declare if you know anything about the trial. You must understand English. You must be able to hear the evidence and decide what evidence to believe. Those who are stood aside by the Crown or challenged by the defense counsel, should not take offence. Jury selection is not a precise science. One of the best counsels in Canadian history, J.J. Robinette, once said his method of selecting a jury was by the way their shoes were shined."

I glanced down at my shoes and at those of my fellow prospective jurors.

Judge Houston handed us over to the court clerk. What followed reminded me of a game of bingo.

Cards with our numbers were drawn randomly from a wicker basket. We had to line up in front of the jury box so that the accused could see each one of us and the prospective juror see the accused.

"Accused look at the juror, juror look at the accused," intoned the clerk.

At this vital stage, Crown attorney or defense counsel could challenge and exclude a juror without explanation. I was later told they relied on courtroom instinct combined with knowledge of the case and the issues likely to arise. The accused looked dispassionate, but his counsel made rapid decisions in challenging jurors. Only four were picked from the first batch of 20. Journalist or not, I was fairly quickly chosen to serve.

Before the jury had been completed, the judge was consulting the clerk on whether the defense counsel had used up his 12 permitted challenges.

We who had been chosen had by then sworn on the Bible or solemnly affirmed, that we would "truly try and true deliverance make, between our sovereign lady the Queen and the accused at the bar, who we shall have in charge and true verdict give, according to the evidence."

Judge Houston opened the trial, warning us not to discuss the case outside the jury room. "Yours is a sacred duty to be performed without fear or favor. If anyone approaches you, you must tell him or her to go away or, if they persist, report them to an officer. There are many busybodies wondering how or why you came to your decision. Disregard any courtroom drama you may have seen on television. Follow the law as I tell it to you."

One jurist stood up to say she had once lived next door to a person with the same name as the stabbed man. "What if it turned out to be the same person?" she asked the judge.

"Find out the past addresses of the victim," the judge asked the court clerk. But the witness had already left for lunch.

"Well, find out before the case proceeds," the judge said tersely, aware that a replacement jurist would be hard to find because they had also gone for lunch.

At 2:30 p.m., having been assured that the two with same name were not the same person, the judge finally got the trial under way.

The case began with a statement by a walrus-mustached attorney on what the Crown intended to prove. He elicited from witnesses their stories on a fight outside the Carleton University pub a year previous.

The defense counsel, bearded with reddish-brown hair, cross-examined aggressively.

"How cute they both were," one woman on the jury remarked to me with a twinkle.

A buck knife, ripped jacket and photographs of beaten up faces and scars were shown to us and marked as exhibits.

The court reporter had sat knitting a quilt during jury selection. Now she was recording every word by talking into what looked like a World War I gas mask. How vital her work turned out to be.

Defense counsel was tearing into a witness he clearly regarded as hostile, when the judge broke the tension. He judged it time for tea. We were marched to the jury room by the court constable, served and locked up.

Fay, Jim, Bob, Mary, Jeanette, Tom, Dee, May, Marian, Jerry, Eleanor and I got to know each other for the first time. In no way did we resemble John Bunyan's jury of Mr. Blind-man, Mr. No-good, Mr. Malice, Mr. Love-lust, Mr. Live-loose, Mr. Heady, Mr. High-mind, Mr. Enmity, Mr. Lyar, Mr. Cruelty, Mr. Hate-light and Mr. Implacable bent on one verdict alone.

The jury room was a downer but not without reason. It resembled a large jail cell, windowless with grey walls, two toilets and bells to summon advice or indicate a verdict. We were sealed from homing pigeon, flashing light and semaphore. Notices warned, "Any juror who discloses any proceedings of the jury when it is absent from the courtroom, is guilty of an offence punishable by summary conviction."

The case in open court continued with differing accounts of the brawl. Memories were hazy. The stories reminded me of a dull rugby game, written in glowing terms in the paper the next day. Had the writer been to the same game? This time there appeared to have been five games.

There followed a *voir dire*–a trial within a trial–in which the judge had us locked up while he listened to evidence that might not be admissible.

It gave us a chance to exchange views on the demeanor of the witnesses and break the tension with a joke about the Newfie who addressed a judge as "Me Old Trout!"

Having decided the evidence–a four-letter slur word used by a witness about the accused, the morning of the fight–was admissible, the judge adjourned the case until the next morning. We were shepherded into pouring rain and warned that our lips should remain sealed.

The jury woman who had found the court lawyers cute, confided: "I was so nervous when called up, my legs were ready to give way."

"I nearly cracked up," said a second.

"I forgot my specs and could not see the accused when the clerk told me to look at him. What if he had turned out to be my next-door neighbor?"

A fourth juror said she had tried to get off by reason of vacations but dropped the idea when the sheriff's office started asking her questions about dates and bookings.

All four, in subsequent days, proved to be serious-minded jurists probing for the truth.

I told them I had approached the sheriff asking if I could be excluded because I had started a new job.

Courtroom drama reached a peak the next day, when the accused testified in his own defense.

The sixth version of the brawl livened up proceedings.

Five other young men had charged at his friend and him like a herd of buffalo.

The description subsequently became a herd of elephants when repeated derisively by the prosecution. The defense reasserted they were buffalo. The judge seemed as amused as some of my fellow jurists.

Both sides summarized, the trial was adjourned to the following morning and we put on our raincoats.

Next morning, the judge instructed us on points of law and summarized the evidence. A blood-tipped knife was recovered from the scene of the brawl. Had the Crown proved who had wielded it, or if any other weapon had been used? The blood on the knife was not the same type as that of the victim. The accused said he had cut his finger and the blood on his knife was his own. The judge repeated the tenet that for a conviction the case against the accused had to be proved beyond reasonable doubt.

The court constable was then sworn to keep us locked up until we reached a verdict and this time led us to a different jury room– older and spacious with windows we could open. "In the old days," he explained, "with farmers and workers serving on juries, fresh air was needed."

Our first task–at a late stage I thought–was to choose a jury leader.

With the traditional title "foreman" in disrepute and foreperson sounding not quite right, reformists had come up with the word "president" for the job. Some old hands still preferred "foreman" or "forelady." The woman we elected was wearing dungarees and really looked the part. It took us only an hour to agree there was reasonable doubt from the evidence.

When our jury leader stood up and announced "Not guilty," all further references became foreperson.

Outside the courtroom, the sun broke through and three of us halted at the edge of the curb on seeing a red light. Who caught up to us but the acquitted young man and his mother, father and sister?

We turned and shook hands with the grateful defendant.

"Don't go celebrating in a certain pub tonight," a jury colleague advised the acquitted man, giving me a Hollywood-style kick in the tail for my first feature story in *Legion Magazine*.

Chapter 54
At Last the Love of My Life

I met Janina Nickus on the rowing machines at the Ottawa Athletic Club. I had noticed her as she filed into the club in front of me. I particularly noted her slim body, face oval as a rugby ball and her high shoulders.

After changing and entering the gym, I sat down at the rowing machine next to her and made light conversation as we pulled the operating chain handles in unison. She spoke about her home up north in Sudbury and said she worked at the international tax office, then located across the road from the club.

I was smitten!

The club was holding a dance the following weekend, so I asked her to partner me. Smilingly, she turned me down saying she did not know me well enough and moved on to other exercise machines. I was down but not out. The next day, it occurred to me that maybe she would be back at the club straight from work at the same time. So off I went at 5:30 p.m.

There she was, looking more beautiful than ever. I went across to her and confessed I was there to again ask her to go out with me. "Well, maybe," she said as she stretched the arms I wished I were inside.

This time we exchanged first names, and I told Janina I was nobody special but had worked as a journalist for a good number of years and now was with an Ottawa magazine. I guessed journalism, to her, felt more exciting than the tax department of Revenue Canada.

I asked her a second time. "Yes," she replied. "I'll go to the dance with you."

I went a notch further: "After our work-out, we could find out more about one another over dinner at St. Hubert. The restaurant, two turns up St. Laurent Boulevard, has a French touch." I knew what next to say. "It serves a chocolate mousse *delicieux.*"

That won her over, and after showering and changing, we met in the parking lot. The idea was that she would follow my car in her car. After one turn, she was still in sight behind me, but on the second turn, her car disappeared. I cursed my luck. She had gone straight on. Was she gone forever? I had no street address and did not even know her surname. What could I do but return to the OAC parking lot hoping she would do the same thing.

Like magic, Janina Nickus was there standing by her car, waiting for *my* return. The word telepathy came to my mind. We had to be for each other!

We went to the dance that weekend and gently rocked–she was as bad a dancer as me–to a Chris de Burgh recording singing his song, *The Lady in Red*. Janina was dressed in red and soon we were cheek to cheek and was I in love!

Little did I know that we were being watched from the balcony by Neil, my youngest son. On spotting him, I waved and he joined us. I introduced him to Janina. That way, she learned that I was separated and the father of not only Neil, but Keith and Judith too.

Three days later, a letter in the mail invited me to a spaghetti dinner at her place. We sat by the fireside and I kissed her. I boasted that Scotsmen were the most romantic lovers in the world. She took me down a peg by saying she had thought I was English. We spent New Year's Eve together, when she unexpectedly turned up at my door in Ottawa, after driving all the way from her home in Sudbury, to be with me.

Janina had joined Revenue Canada in Sudbury, as a casual after studies at Laurentian University. She had transferred to the Ottawa Tax Centre five years later. My assignments for *Legion Magazine* were not sensational stories, but they impressed her. I proposed to her in France while covering for my magazine a WWII anniversary of the battle of Vimy Ridge. Just like that, we were engaged.

Janina had met challenges in her employment. "When I started at the tax center," she said, "there were no electronic returns, no computers, and after I arrived in Ottawa, only one phone line for the public to use with regard to non-resident issues. One gentleman actually flew in from England to have his tax problems solved. Now there are teams of people to answer calls from Canadians living abroad. I actually have a client who lives on boat at sea and challenges our ruling that he has to pay Canadian taxes."

I couldn't believe how much we had in common when she moved in with me. As a result of her sedentary work, she enjoyed sport of every kind, so we skied, played tennis, enjoyed aqua fitness, occasionally golfed, swam, hiked, hunted moose with a camera, and made love. She even went with me to rugby games, and she watched me win the National Press Club's annual snooker tournament.

We drove to Sudbury in her small car for me to meet her parents.

Marga was German-born and had immigrated to Canada after a rough time as a child in Essen, during World War II. She was fond of opera, books, and movies. I enjoyed her cabbage rolls and insights into wartime Germany.

Nick was Lithuanian and had taken his four daughters ice fishing when they were young. He would preserve cabbage for sauerkraut and tell tales of days back home in World War II, when he was a farmhand caught between, first, the German advance through his country to the gates of Moscow, then, the German retreat from Russians all the way back to Berlin. He had worked, first, in Canada as a lumberjack, and later, for Inco nickel mine in Sudbury. I understood only half of what he said and no doubt he had difficulty with my accent. I judged there must have been the attraction of opposites at work in his marriage to Marga.

They had both come separately to Canada by sea and met at a wedding in North Bay.

Janina introduced me to her three younger sisters, Audrey, Donna, and Teresa, and they, no doubt, wondered intently about this older man their sister was associating with.

Janina was Catholic and I, nominally, Protestant, but that mattered little. The retired Chaplain General of the Canadian Military Forces, the Rev. David Estey, whom I had met during an anniversary Remembrance assignment in Europe, was on church furlough. He came back to marry us in Orleans United Church on July 24, 1993. We held a reception in the Legion hall in Orleans and, driving Janina's car, decorated by my artistic brother-in-law Morgan, who was married to my half-sister Rhona, honeymooned in Nova Scotia. From then on, we were inseparable night and day.

Chapter 55
Cimitero de Geurra Canadese

I had been told, on joining *Legion Magazine*, that its assignments were a passport to seeing Canada. In fact, they were much more. They were an introduction to Canadian veterans and government remembrance events around the world, and Janina sometimes accompanied me.

Legion Magazine assigned me, at short notice, to go with selected veterans and other writers to cover the WWII war anniversary, "Canada Remembers Italy."

The article I wrote tells of my most memorable of many assignments for *Legion Magazine.*

Canada Remembers Italy

Conversations on the Veterans Affairs Canada pilgrimage buses are peppered with reminiscences, as 55 campaigners return to WW II battlegrounds from Sicily to northern Italy and to war cemeteries where more than 5,900 comrades are buried.

Former infantrymen question Lauréat Laberge when he tells them he was with them at the front, without carrying a gun. He explains he was a stretcher-bearer with the Royal 22nd Regiment. His defense was a prominent red cross.

"Yes, it was dangerous," says Laberge, 72, of Ste-Foy, Quebec. "You never knew what the other fellow might do, but I don't believe I was ever targeted with a rifle."

Other veterans on the Canada Remembers pilgrimage, had no such protection when they fought for 20 months from 1943-45. Those among the 163,000 Allied soldiers, on nearly 3,000 ships and landing craft that invaded Sicily's beaches July 10-11, 1943, recall light resistance from Italian coastal troops around Pachino. Today there's a marble monument to the 1st Division, proclaiming "They came in the name of freedom."

Italians were soon surrendering, but Germans at Leonforte, Nissoria, and Agira gave Canadians a blooding to remember. "The Italians had old Mussolini to contend with, and he was a real tyrant. They were on the German side but had no choice," observed Jack Jolleys, representing the Legion.

Nicknamed the *Red Patch Devils* by the Germans, because of their red shoulder patches, the Canadians fought against an enemy well established in key vantage points atop mountains and well-fixed hill positions. German commander-in-chief General Albert Kesselring said at the time: "It is the Fuhrer's explicit order and also my belief, that we must bleed the enemy to exhaustion by hard fighting."

Fight the Canadians the Germans did!

Estimates vary on how many of the 93,000 Canadians who served in Italy became casualties but, in some battles, nearly half were killed or wounded. Malaria and jaundice also attacked Canadians as they climbed, marched, and fought through summer dust and biting insects around Mount Etna. Mules burdened with mortars, guns, ammunition, and supplies, accompanied the troops as they trekked up rugged hills.

At Agira Canadian War Cemetery, Mayor Gaetano Giunta and other Sicilians reaffirm links forged long ago with Canadians. It took five days of hard fighting to seize the medieval town in that year of 1943. How did the Canadians take it?

"They did it the way porcupines make love–with great difficulty," says Stanley Mullins of Manitoulin Island, Ontario, then a platoon commander with the Irish Regiment of Canada. Veterans say the 490 graves tell the story. Among them, are 57 from the Seaforth Highlanders of Canada, 47 from the Loyal Edmonton Regiment, and 38 Van Doos. This war cemetery is the only World War II cemetery that is exclusively Canadian. Buried side by side, are the then commanding officer of the Royal Canadian Regiment, Lieutenant-Colonel Ralph Crowe, and second-in-command Major Billy Pope.

Standing grave-side, Francesca Ferugia of Agira says, "I honor the dead, because they did so much to defend us."

A pincer movement by General Bernard Montgomery's 8th Army–to which the Canadians belonged–and the 7th Army of General George Patton, ensured quick victory in Sicily. This strategy prompted Benito Mussolini's overthrow. But most of the German army escaped to the Italian mainland. It was German panzers that awaited pursuing Allied infantry and tanks.

Instead of flying with the veterans, I travel by truck the wartime route of the 1st Canadian Division. Driver Claude Caron and I carry Canadian wreaths and flags from Sicily across the Strait of Messina, through WWII landmarks of Taranto and Bari, to near Foggia, where vital airfields were seized from the Germans. We skirt battle-famed Campobasso to rendezvous with the main party who had flown from Sicily to Rome, then bused to Ortona.

Field battles and house-to-house fighting marked the epic struggle for Ortona. The Canadians endured 11 German counter-attacks. Winter had come and a gully blocked the way. "Right there, in this gully, were probably the toughest battles," says William Graydon of the Hastings and Prince Edward Regiment, who fought his first battle at Ortona.

The Canadian Corps chose a site near the Moro River for a cemetery. As well as 1,375 Canadians, 167 Britons, 43 New Zealanders, 16 South Africans, five Indians, four Australians, and two Yugoslavs lie there. "Every infantry component lost half its strength," Lawrence MacAulay, then Canadian Secretary of State for Veteran Affairs, notes.

In cemeteries of Montecchio and Gradara, rest Canadians who fought to break the Gothic Line–one of Hitler's lines of defense in northern Italy. Tears flow from Stacy Gloster's eyes, when she and fellow youth representatives Chantal Maynard, Ian MacIntyre, and Stephane Turgeon, find a 16-year-old Canadian soldier's grave.

Coriano Ridge War Cemetery is also a fitting stop. The ridge was the key to the capture of Rimini along the Adriatic coast. Coriano was in ruins with 75 per cent of its buildings damaged when the Allied forces entered. "By Rimini, we began to realize we were knocking down everything but the German troops," says one Canadian veteran.

Attractive Coriano Mayor Ivonne Crescentini ensures the veterans that Italians do not intend to forget the past or the 497 Canadians buried in the Coriano graveyard. "We want to set up in Europe, a world of peace, where Nazism and Fascism will not find roots again," she says.

From Rimini the road led to Ravenna, the ancient capital of the Roman Empire liberated by the Canadian Corps in December 1944. There, exuberant Italians watch MacAulay place a wreath beside a monument to Italian partisans. "They were tough buggers, often packing sawed off shotguns," comments Chuck Watson, an artillery sergeant in WW II, who hails from Saskatoon. "It was men like them who strung up Mussolini."

Women of the Comitato Antifascista, serve cool drinks and cookies. Veterans hand out small Canadian flags to schoolchildren. One older Italian woman places a wreath after the dignitaries have gone. She was 21 when she hid in a stable during the bombardment. She returned home to find a Canadian soldier slumped dead over her desk. He had been writing a letter home when a grenade killed him. "I wanted to kiss him," she says.

At Ravenna town hall, the Canadian veterans hear Mayor Pier Paola D'Attore discount fear of a rise of fascism in Italy, despite the election of the right-wing government of Silvio Berlusconi.

At Cesena War Cemetery–a half-hour drive from Ravenna– Ernest (Smokey) Smith pauses at the grave of Major Bobby Clark, his first officer. The cemetery is near the Savio River where Smith helped hold a bridgehead to win the Victoria Cross. Alert as ever at 80, he refuses to pose with a broomstick to demonstrate for photographers how he knocked out a tank with a PIAT, a shoulder-fired weapon. "Show me the gun–I don't play games!"

We travel from Ravenna to Rome, to honor Canadians buried at the Rome War Cemetery.

I'm shopping for a dress for Janina and had spotted a beautiful off-shoulder orange creation, when Smokey Smith's wife, Esther, taps me on the shoulder and says I can't buy that dress for my wife. She chooses a rather more conservative one that I buy to my later regret when I show it to Janina. I decide not to award Esther the Victoria Cross for her dress choice. Clearly, I had failed to tell the well-intentioned lady that my wife was much younger than me!

At Anzio, another famous battleground, the First Special Service Force, an elite Canadian-American combat unit, lined the Mussolini Canal for 98 days until the Allies broke out of the beachhead to lead a pincer squeeze on Rome. Veteran Jim Summersides of Welland, Ontario, remembers the canal well. "There was no place on that beach-head Jerry couldn't reach with his artillery."

Polish veterans almost steal the show at Cassino War Cemetery. More than 2,000, mainly members of the Polish Combatants' Association, have come from Poland, Britain, Canada, and the United States, to a British-organized ceremony. The Duke of Kent, president of the Commonwealth War Graves Commission, places a simple wreath at the Cross of Sacrifice overlooking 4,200 graves. MacAulay follows suit with a Canadian wreath for the 855 Canadian graves. The Poles place a huge wreath–it was them who captured Monte Cassino.

They also captured what remained of the Benedictine monastery perched atop the mountain. The abbey–established in 529 A.D.–was destroyed three times over the centuries. Each time it was rebuilt with greater majesty. American bombers flattened it again in February 1944, by request of New Zealand's Lieutenant-General Bernard Freyberg. His troops had tried in vain to rout Germans defending their mountain observation posts.

Many people died in the bombing, but a handful of monks who survived, swore the Germans–though on the mountain–were not in the abbey. One story claims German paratroops dropped in after the bombing and used the ruins as gun posts to check the Allied attack for three months. The Poles finally captured the monastery and 50 years later, are trying to figure out how. "I look up (at the abbey) and I still don't know," says Wladyslaw Szwender of Edmonton, who fought with the Second Polish Corps.

Stanislaw Toporowski of Ottawa, representing the Polish Combatants Association of Canada, knows at what cost. The wartime lieutenant says 860 Polish soldiers died and 2,822 were wounded. "Right here at Monte Cassino was the breakthrough. The road to Rome opened here–and we did it," says Toporowski. Rome, which had been declared an open city to save it from destruction, fell June 4, 1944.

"You think you're tough, but you see the graves and find you're pretty soft," comments Stan Archer, 78, of Auckland, who was traveling with a group of New Zealand Cassino veterans.

The Italy campaigners were given the nickname *D-Day Dodgers*. It was said that Lady Nancy Astor, the first female member of the British Parliament, bestowed the name on the Italy campaigners, implying that they had deliberately avoided the real war in Northwest Europe while living it up in Italy. The troops responded with their *D-Day Dodgers* song. To the tune of *Lili Marlene*, the full version chronicles a life of luxury they never led:

We're the D-Day Dodgers
Always on the vino, always on the spree.
Eighth Army scroungers and their tanks
We live in Rome among the Yanks.
We are the D-Day Dodgers. Over here in Italy.
We landed at Salerno, a holiday with pay.
Gerry brought the band down to cheer us on our way
Showed us sights and gave us tea,
We all sang songs, the beer was free

We are the D-Day Dodgers, way out in Italy.

The last verse, to be sung with vino on lips and tears in eyes, went:

So listen all you people, over land and foam
Even though we've parted, our hearts are close to home
When we return we hope you'll say
"You did your little bit, though far away
All of the D-Day Dodgers, way out there in Italy."

"We should have spanked that lady's backside," grins Robbie Robertson, once a machine-gunner with the Saskatoon Light Infantry, adding, "Or set her to work doing our laundry. Did she know who won?"

"The agony of the Italian campaign, is that history will always treat it as a side-show," adds veteran war correspondent Doug How.

"Italy campaigners held down more than 20 of the best German divisions," estimates Major General Pat Bogert, who commanded the 2nd Infantry Brigade of 1st Canadian Division in WW II.

The finale to the Cassino commemoratives, is an international military parade with bands marching below the restored monastery. Britain's Green Jacket riflemen parade with German paratroops. Canada's flag party stands out among battle-dressed infantry of many nations. The commands of Chief Petty Officer Chris Dykman of Ottawa, resound through the stadium. The troops are inspected by Italian President Oscar Luigi Scalfaro, and the white-haired president eulogizes peace.

The word "peace," to my delight, ended my article.

I thought how lucky I had been, a decade after the defeat–some say liberation–of Italy, to have peacefully served my two compulsory years of British military service.

The highlight of the Italian trip was a phone call from Janina at midnight, when I was almost asleep in my hotel bed in Rome. I told her like any serving veteran, that I would be home soon and that I loved her to bits.

Chapter 56
The Voice of Veterans

Fifteen years after writing my first feature story for *Legion Magazine,* I was writing my last. It was the year 2000 and I was retiring, after 50 years of journalism since my start as printer's devil and rugby writer in Scotland, but ready for more years ahead in Canadian community newspaper journalism.

Royal Canadian Legion leadership was passing to military veterans of a different day and age. I had learned much from older veterans. Youthful veterans were taking over. Yet the old voices were not stilled that millennium year.

"He who is greatest among us serves."

I used this quote as a lead for my last feature story.

Speaking was Legion provincial command president, Lieutenant-Colonel Ralph H. Webb, mayor of Winnipeg and one of several speakers at the Manitoba Legion Command Convention in Winnipeg, January 21-22, 1927. Webb, a World War I hero, had played an important role in the creation of the Legion in 1925.

The September 2000 magazine I was writing for, was the 75th anniversary special entitled, *Legion through the years.* I incorporated all I knew about journalism and the Legion.

This once Scottish newsboy, today writes, photographs, and delivers *The Riverview Park Review* in Ottawa, and serves on the management board. What goes around comes around. I'm the newsboy again, distributing a newspaper after 74 years.

During seven decades of newspaper work, I had dreamed of being *the* editor. When *Riverview Park Review* editor Carole Moult appointed me *editor emeritus*, that dream came true in spades.

"Wakey!" I'm roused by Janina, home from the tax office. She's already counting those hot-off-the-press newspapers we deliver as newsboy and newsgirl.

"I was just snoozing!" I contend, wondering if I can handle the snow and ice outside.

"Then, Mr. Snoozeboy, you deliver one side of the street, I'll take the other. After that, we'll tackle aqua fitness at the Ottawa Athletic Club and I'll treat you to dinner at St. Hubert!"

This Time as Epilogue

When they who have striven and suffered to teach and ennoble the race

Shall march at the front of the column, each one in his God-given place

As they pass through the gates of The City with proud and victorious tread

The editor, printer and newsboy will travel not far from the head

-Will Carleton

Final Note

Why did Bill Fairbairn write his memoir? When drawn into the discussion, he acknowledged that the popular 1934 novel, *Goodbye, Mr. Chips* by James Hilton, influenced his decision to write his fifth book.

Substitute the 83-year-old classics teacher, Charles Edward Chipping, who saw the passing of monumental world events, and compare his musings with the reflections of an 82-year-old journalist of the old school giving sober thought to a bygone newspaper world.

Mr. Chips recalls his 58 years spent at the same well-respected boy's school, while Bill Fairbairn brings the world of print journalism from his perspective of having worked for 15 different newspapers, CBC international radio, Legion Magazine, and as journalism instructor on a Canadian Indian reserve.

This book provides an insight into what actually happened around those newshounds of the old school, pounding Underwood typewriter keys with scant knowledge of the technical revolution ahead - *Carole Moult, editor, Riverview Park Review, Ottawa.*

www.ingramcontent.com/pod-product-compliance
Lightning Source LLC
Chambersburg PA
CBHW051945090426
42741CB00008B/1272